ERNEST HEMINGWAY

ERNEST HEMINGWAY: MACHISMO AND MASOCHISM

Richard Fantina

ERNEST HEMINGWAY

First published in 2005 by
PALGRAVE MACMILLAN™
175 Fifth Avenue, New York, N.Y. 10010 and
Houndmills, Basingstoke, Hampshire, England RG21 6XS
Companies and representatives throughout the world.

PALGRAVE MACMILLAN is the global academic imprint of the
Palgrave Macmillan division of St. Martin's Press, LLC and
of Palgrave Macmillan Ltd. Macmillan® is a registered trademark
in the United States, United Kingdom and other countries.
Palgrave is a registered trademark in the European
Union and other countries.

ISBN 1–4039–6907–8

Library of Congress Cataloging-in-Publication Data

Fantina, Richard.
    Ernest Hemingway: machismo and masochism / by Richard Fantina.
        p. cm.
    Includes bibliographical references and index.
    ISBN 1–4039–6907–8 (alk. paper)
        1. Hemingway, Ernest, 1899–1961—Criticism and interpretation.
    2. Hemingway, Ernest, 1899–1961—Knowledge—Psychology.
    3. Hemingway, Ernest, 1899–1961—Psychology. 4. Masculinity in
    literature. 5. Masochism in literature. 6. Machismo in literature.
    7. Sex role in literature. I. Title.

PS3515.E37Z5885 2004
813'.52—dc22   2005043182

A catalogue record for this book is available from the British Library.

Design by Newgen Imaging Systems (P) Ltd., Chennai, India.

First edition: September 2005

10 9 8 7 6 5 4 3 2 1

Printed in the United States of America.

Contents

ACKNOWLEDGMENTS

A debt of gratitude is owed to many who enabled me to complete this book. I would first like to thank my friends and former colleagues at Florida International University, in particular Bruce Harvey who directed a very early version of this work when it was in its thesis phase. His continued support and encouragement since that time has been more than I could have hoped for. I would like to thank Mary Free for what can only be described as brilliant suggestions and astute editing on a very rough first draft of this study several years ago. Richard Sugg, who also read the early version, offered useful comments at the time and valuable advice since then. Special thanks are due to Tometro Hopkins for her support through many years. Thanks to Kathleen McCormack who collaborated with me on a presentation at the Hemingway International Conference in Key West in 2004. Special thanks to Kimberly Harrison and to Jean Muteba Rahier with whom I worked on a daily basis. Special thanks go to an emeritus member of the FIU faculty, Adele Newson-Horst, now at the University of Wisconsin, who reintroduced me to Hemingway's work quite a few years ago. I would also like to acknowledge my appreciation to my new colleagues at the University of Miami, especially to John Paul Russo and Kathryn Freeman who have been especially supportive of my work.

Special thanks are due to Debra Moddelmog who read the manuscript prior to publication and was generous and supportive in her remarks. Thanks to Amy Vondrak and who reviewed the manuscript and offered detailed and constructive comments. Thanks to Susan Beegel of *The Hemingway Review* for her brilliant editing of an excerpt from this manuscript. I also wish to express my appreciation to The Hemingway Society and to the Northeast Modern Language Association (NEMLA) for their awards of, respectively, a Smith-Reynolds Founders Fellowship and a Summer Research Fellowship in 2003 that enabled me to view the Hemingway collections at the John F. Kennedy Library in Boston and the Scribners archive at the Firestone Library in Princeton. Thanks to James Roth at the JFK Library for his help in viewing the collection.

Very special thanks go to Carl P. Eby who has generously supported this project for nearly three years and who reviewed the manuscript prior to publication. Although we disagree on some of our interpretations, Carl has been my earliest and strongest supporter in Hemingway circles and it is not too much to say that I owe the completion of this book to his encouragement. He has unselfishly given his time to answer in detail even my most insignificant questions on Hemingway and on literature in general. Carl's advocacy of new ideas in Hemingway studies serves as an inspiration to all developing scholars in the field.

Thanks to my editor at Palgrave Macmillan, Farideh Koohi-Kamali, and to her assistant, Lynn Vande Stouwe, and to production editor, Yasmin Mathew for their courtesy and professionalism in guiding the manuscript through to completion. Thanks to Newgen Imaging for their excellent production work. Special thanks to Dr. Ferdie Pacheco (and to Luisita) for kind permission to reproduce the beautiful portrait of Hemingway. And a final note of thanks goes to Paul Kachur, both for his long friendship and for his technical expertise in helping me prepare the manuscript for publication.

INTRODUCTION

Ernest Hemingway, long regarded as the personification of All-American dominant male values, reveals a contradiction in his portrayal of the ideal woman. Far from upholding the image of the macho warrior, he often suggests a profoundly submissive and passive side to his sexuality both in his work and in what can be read between the lines of his biography. The ideal Hemingway woman—as revealed in *The Sun Also Rises* (1926), *A Farewell to Arms* (1929), *Across the River and Into the Trees* (1950), and other texts—demonstrates power and a will to dominate. This becomes particularly apparent in the posthumous *The Garden of Eden* (1986), in which Hemingway celebrates a woman who manipulates and controls the sexual relationship with her husband. The dominance of Catherine Bourne in that novel has led some scholars to reappraise the foundations of Hemingway's machismo, which coexists with an alternative, masochistic sexuality. The mythical image of Hemingway as the embodiment of virility in his writings, his exploits, and his very physical presence, asserts itself as quintessentially dominant and aggressive masculinity. Only with difficulty can we visualize a man with Hemingway's imposing, hirsute, and muscular appearance, and his hard-boiled style of writing and conversation, as submissive to women. Yet his fiction unmistakably reveals this side of his sexuality.

Although many critics now readily dismiss the old Hemingway myth of machismo, few seem prepared to acknowledge the masochism that prevails in much of his work. Traditionally, when critics comment on masochism in Hemingway they generally do so metaphorically, without touching on the sexual implications, by referring to the many physical wounds his characters suffer. Yet the wounded heroes exhibit a nongenital sexuality and occasionally submit to passive sodomy. Their general physical and psychological submission to women, who alternately punish, humiliate, and nurture these suffering men, convincingly demonstrates masochism. Revisionist criticism of Hemingway that questions his status as the ultimate American macho began even before the publication of *The Garden of Eden* with Aaron Lathan's 1977 essay, "A Farewell to Machismo" and Gerry Brenner's

Concealments in Hemingway's Work (1983). Mark Spilka's *Hemingway's Quarrel with Androgyny* (1990) portrays its subject as almost a feminist. More recently Carl P. Eby unequivocally identifies *Hemingway's Fetishism* (1998), and in *Reading Desire* (1999) Debra A. Moddelmog finds "transgressive desires" in Hemingway's work.[1] As these and other authors have established, Hemingway need no longer be interpreted one-dimensionally as the prototypical he-man, but while pointing to Hemingway's "homoerotic wishes,"[2] "suppressed femininity,"[3] and "transvestic impulses,"[4] none have acknowledged his masochism.

To account for the apparent anomaly of Hemingway's masochism, biographical and psychological factors may help in providing insights. Yet Hemingway, always a resisting analysand, seems to defy psychoanalysis. The purpose in these pages is not to offer another psychoanalytical interpretation but rather to discuss Hemingway's work in the tradition of literary masochism and the critical responses to it. Psychoanalysis has a long tradition of diagnosing and trying to "cure" masochism and has been challenged increasingly since 1969 with the publication of Gilles Deleuze's defense of masochism, *Coldness and Cruelty.*[5] Deleuze's work remains important in that it places masochism within a tradition of masculinity that had been denied or disparaged by psychoanalysis. Deleuze insists on the idea of masochism as an arena in which masculinity can assert itself. The avowal of masochism as a tenable masculine position allows for new interpretations of some classic literature. In recent years masochism has come under increasing study in literary circles although Hemingway's work is seldom addressed. According to the *New York Times:* "At the Modern Language Association's annual meeting last month [December 2000], three hours were devoted to masochism."[6] Other academic conferences now routinely feature panels on literary masochism. Critics such as Kaja Silverman, Carol Siegel, and Laura Frost have demonstrated how male masochism informs the work of authors as diverse as Henry James, D.H. Lawrence, James Joyce, and others. Elements in much of Hemingway's work indicate a masochistic sensibility that coexists with his cult of masculinity. Hemingway apparently saw no contradiction in this duality but he no doubt tried to obscure his masochism because of its reputation as a repulsive perversion. As Anita Phillips points out, "[m]asochism seems to draw down an unequivocal scorn in a way that other human tendencies rarely do" (75).[7] However, despite this reputation, as an artist Hemingway expresses this alternative masculinity that on the surface seems diametrically opposed to that which he publicly embraced. Both paradigms of masculinity (and others, including gay models) now have a more recognized validity despite a century-long tyranny imposed by the legacy of the Victorians. Hemingway's embodiment of diverse models of masculinity may be *his* greatest legacy.

After more than a century of efforts by psychoanalysis to penetrate its mysteries, masochism remains a thoroughly misunderstood practice. Despite the limitations of psychoanalytic readings of masochism, because of their long-unquestioned premises and persistent influence, any discussion of the phenomena must begin there. According to Freud, certain factors "such as the castration complex and the sense of guilt" can produce "extreme cases of masochistic perversion."[8] But Freud went much further when he included masochism and other "perversions" among his "chaotic assembly" of "grotesque monstrosities" and "mad, extraordinary and horrible things," and that attitude continues in some quarters today.[9] The use of the term "perversion" fell out of favor in the decades of the 1960s and 1970s, because it implies a judgment that many hesitated to make in areas of consensual sex. Yet "perversion" is now embraced again by observers on both sides—those who find it wayward, immoral, and wrong; and also those who have appropriated the epithet to proclaim their alterity. Many of those who work within the psychiatric field have abandoned the term while others, including some defenders of masochism, insist on the viability and precision of "perversion," preferring it to the more innocuous "paraphilia." As early as 1975, psychoanalyst Robert Stoller remarked that it is "a term that is becoming passé," while arguing for its continued usage.[10] Deleuze and others, who do not seek to "cure" masochism, also use the term even while rejecting many psychoanalytical tenets. In general, I prefer to use the term "alternative sexuality" in discussing Hemingway's masochism while relying on the work of many who have no problem with "perversion."

Despite the limitations of strictly psychoanalytical approaches, it remains necessary to refer to "perversion" often. In *Sexual Dissidence*, Jonathan Dollimore "recognize[s] the inadequacies of the sexological and psychoanalytical accounts of desire generally and of perversion specifically" but proceeds to "deploy psychoanalytic categories."[11] Dollimore "concede[s] the inconsistency without regarding it as an insuperable methodological problem" (170). This study of Hemingway's alternative sexuality takes a similar approach. As Frost notes (of James Joyce but it can apply to Hemingway as well), masochism "shows erotic fantasy to be saturated with references that exceed, contradict, or do not necessarily register on psychoanalysis's scale of interpretive priorities."[12] Hemingway's work does not always lend itself well to a strictly psychoanalytical interpretation. Eby's study of Hemingway is remarkable for what it accomplishes as an exhaustive psychoanalytical case study of a fetishist and he provides countless new insights into his subject's psychosexual motivations. But the approach here seeks to move beyond psychoanalysis, to the degree that it is possible to do so, and to examine the nature of Hemingway's sexual desire and how it is often at odds with his social ideology in ways that cannot always be explained by Freudian paradigms.

The term "masochism" was coined in the late nineteenth century by Richard von Krafft-Ebing from the name of Leopold von Sacher-Masoch, whose *Venus in Furs* (1869) marks the first detailed modern literary treatment of the subject. Krafft-Ebing insists on masochism's basic "femininity," despite acknowledging that the phenomenon he describes occurs almost exclusively in men. He theorizes sadism as a pathology of normal male sexuality and considers masochism an inversion. Krafft-Ebing goes so far as to assert: "The masochist considers himself in a passive, feminine role . . . The pleasurable feeling, call it lust, resulting from this act differs per se in no wise from the feeling which women derive from the sexual act."[13] Freud continued the male identification of sadism and reinforced the idea of masochism as "characteristically female."[14] Freud describes a typical heterosexual male masochist whose fantasy "has for its content a feminine attitude without a homosexual object-choice."[15] This suggests that the masochist would likely prefer to be dominated by a woman with masculine qualities. However, the dominant woman of masochistic fantasy is almost exaggeratedly feminine in every aspect of her appearance and demeanor. Such an image cannot be easily squared with the conflation of masochism and femininity and/or homosexuality. Over the years, Freud promulgated several differing views of masochism. When their varying threads are untangled, what presents itself is a "feminine" male subject. In the case of Hemingway, this poses an obvious problem. It remains difficult to ascribe femininity to a writer who nearly defined masculinity in twentieth-century literature.

Carol Siegel argues that literary critics should work toward "[f]reeing our understanding from psychoanalytic paradigms" and that such work "means detaching masochism from femininity."[16] Siegel highlights the shortcomings of classical psychoanalysis when she asks: "what sense can it make to analyze gender relations by foreclosing the issue of the gendering of masochism as is done when we adopt Freud's vision of the male masochist as a 'feminine masochist'?" (139). As Moddelmog notes: "[I]t is actually possible for someone who *acts* heterosexual to *be* homosexual under the dictates of this discourse" (67). Psychoanalysis has perpetuated the arbitrary and denigrating identification of masochism and sodomy with homosexuality and/or female sexuality. But as Dollimore notes, "[t]he association between homosexuality and femininity is not necessarily insulting to either (263)" despite the pejorative intention of so many of these associations. The linkage of both to heterosexual male masochism can be seen as a productive (if reductive) indication that human sexuality is more diverse than psychoanalysis often tries to construct it.

Psychiatry and psychoanalysis began to come of age in the late nineteenth century and to a great degree accepted late Victorian constructions of gender. Masochism, characterized by passivity, must be feminine according to the values of that era. And as Foucault notes in the *History of Sexuality*, medical thinking in the Victorian era instituted the "psychiatrization of perverse pleasure," and male masochism fit neatly into its overall project.[17] As Sacha Nacht points out, "Masochism, while it is as old as the world, was only identified as a sexual anomaly in the nineteenth century."[18] Phillips writes:

> Early psychiatry named masochism, and this naming came about in a particularly unsympathetic, even violent way. But psychoanalysis inherited the concept, kept it alive, and tried to make it perform a minor role in the Freudian opera. When we use the term "masochism," we cannot help but be complicit with this tradition, in the same way that the term "inversion" (meaning "homosexuality") has negative connotations due to its historical currency as a perversion in normative psychoanalysis. (26)

Phillips's comment on complicity does not prevent her from using the term "masochism" for lack of a better word. But as the title of her study, *A Defense of Masochism* (1998), suggests, she is acutely concerned with reimagining the concept in terms that do not conform to the limitations of psychoanalysis. Siegel also ponders this phraseology when she wonders "if it is politically incorrect for feminists to use the psychoanalytic term *masochist* when referring to men who eroticize female dominance" (as Hemingway did). But Siegel finds that not to use the term would be utopian for it is the only term commonly understood to represent a variety of psychological states and behaviors. However, if we accept a limited Freudian view, Hemingway's masochism must be viewed as dysfunctionally male, and as unmasculine. While few would question Hemingway's claim to a robust masculinity, some may argue his masochism. Yet his work convincingly demonstrates both.

This discussion focuses attention on male heterosexual masochism as it appears in Hemingway's work, a subject hitherto neglected or misunderstood. Earlier discussions of Hemingway's men in pain often focused on the portrayal of the virtues of courage, stoicism, and sacrifice as essential elements of the "code hero" who is often a man in pain. However masochism, as it is more properly understood, should not be confined to issues of physical pain but rather should encompass the general passivity involved in the submission of the body through an act of will that may or may not include the endurance of physical pain. Nor is masochism incompatible with the "masculine" virtues that Hemingway more directly portrays.

The employment throughout this study of the term "masochism" does not correspond to the colloquial usage in which it denotes an individual's apparently compulsive or spontaneous enjoyment of any random pain or adversity. Nor does it correspond to the notion of masochism as a symptom of a person who seems consistently to make his or her own life more difficult with self-defeating behavior. In 1987, the American Psychiatric Association removed masochism from the *Diagnostic and Statistical Manual of Mental Disorders* (DSM) and substituted the phrase "self-defeating personality disorder."[19] While this concept roughly corresponds, in theory, to the "unconscious guilt" that characterizes Freud's "moral masochism" (XIX 169–170), there is no reason to believe that sexual masochists necessarily engage in self-defeating behavior. Nor is there evidence that persons who exhibit such behavior are sexual masochists. "Self-defeating personality disorder" has little relation to this discussion of heterosexual male masochism, which refers to the specific sexual desire of a man to become the passive partner in a heterosexual relationship; to submit himself sexually to, and to suffer pain and/or humiliation administered by, a woman whom he has elevated into a position of superiority and dominance.

The definition of masochism offered here differs from some commonly accepted psychoanalytical ideas of the relationship between masochism and sadism. Following Deleuze, and in agreement with much of the literature by defenders and detractors of masochism, the essence of the masochist's desire depends upon the cooperation of a sympathetic accomplice in the fulfillment of that desire. A sadistic personality must necessarily be excluded since it would have a totally different agenda and be unresponsive to the actual wishes of the masochist.[20] Heterosexual male masochism seeks to submit the male body to the female body in an often ritualized exchange of sexual power. The woman is called upon to exert both the primary will and physical aggression. Because of the negative public image, largely due to the conscious reversal of traditional gender roles of dominance and submission, many male masochists (including Hemingway) and their lovers have not often historically revealed this element of their relationships.[21]

Although little attention has been devoted to Hemingway specifically, male heterosexual masochism represents an alternative form of masculine sexuality and has been the focus of study in recent gender theory. This book seeks to contribute to this body of knowledge. Because of their complexity on many levels, this study makes no attempt to explore other aspects of Hemingway's writing but instead endeavors to isolate his masochism in several texts. Hemingway's work does not feature incidents of female domination in the sense of the woman with the whip who so intoxicated Sacher-Masoch. But despite the absence of the dominatrix, Hemingway's submissive sexuality reveals itself at times more subtly and at times more dramatically than the ritualized fantasies of *Venus in Furs*. In Hemingway's work, we can discern several, but not all, of the elements symptomatic of masochism.

This study is neither an exercise in hero-worship nor iconoclasm. It grows out of a love for Hemingway's work and an admiration for many of the personal qualities that enabled him to produce the most important American literature of the twentieth century. Even a brief glance at the voluminous criticism reveals that Hemingway can be read on more different levels and interpreted through more different lenses than any author, perhaps, since Shakespeare. While we can fault him severely at times for his failings—and they were many—it is important to remember that he was a product of his era and we cannot hold him to a higher standard than his contemporaries. And this book does not fault, but rather commends, Hemingway for his masochism, which is seen here not as a perversion but as a distinctly nonaggressive and relatively selfless expression of male sexuality. Hemingway gave voice to enduring masculine qualities throughout his life and only with hindsight can we recognize that his work sought to expand the parameters of acceptable masculine experience, in particular in the area of sexuality. With this realization we can appreciate all the more the honesty and courage he displays in his art. His embrace of masochism, even if never publicly acknowledged, should serve to validate that impulse in other men and gain the appreciation of many women readers.

This book asks those who already enjoy Hemingway to look at a side of his work that has perhaps not been examined before and to find that his sexuality enhances rather than limits our appreciation. Many of the traditional masculine virtues—courage, duty, a sense of honor, physical prowess—that Hemingway celebrates in his work have been justly recognized as superior human qualities. I do not try to make a case that Hemingway did not sincerely share those virtues, but simply that he shared others as well, such as chivalry, humility, empathy, and selflessness. This book also asks those who may have long had an aversion to Hemingway to look again at his work and try to see beyond the image that has been so successfully, and so often destructively, created around his name. A closer look at the self-effacing qualities of many Hemingway characters allows us to see the author as much greater than the larger-than-life hero, sportsman, hard-drinker, and womanizer of his legend. Many women have rediscovered Hemingway's work in recent years—especially since the publication of *The Garden of Eden* nearly two decades ago.[22] His reputation as a misogynist continues to ebb, almost in spite of himself, as his perceptive creation of compelling female characters is explored with critical values markedly different from previous generations.

This book argues, as others have, for male masochism's subversive potential. Male masochism represents a clear threat to patriarchal notions of gender relations as it goes even further than advocating equality. Part of its essence lies in its inherent belief in female superiority, at least in sexual relations. This is not to say that all men who practice masochism—Hemingway included—carry their sexuality into the social sphere. Hemingway generally subscribed to phallocentric notions of power arrangements. His work also features incidents of misogyny, homophobia, and unenlightened attitudes toward race, which many justly deplore and which will be critically examined in the following pages. But his work features just as many incidents of respect for, even awe of, women. While Hemingway could never quite integrate the implications of his sexuality with his worldview, we should not judge him too harshly for that considering the negative influences of the Victorian legacy that informed his development.

It would be gratifying to be able to claim Hemingway as a self-conscious advocate of a progressive gender politics, but the evidence does not support such a view. Despite this, we can still appreciate Hemingway's many portrayals of gender that challenge the oppressive binary of the traditionally masculine and feminine. The interpretations here of Hemingway's depictions of masochism do not reflect negatively on his character. On the contrary, these comments are intended to humanize an author so often considered almost impossibly superhuman. Reading Hemingway's masochism can help us to understand how an author, who often comes across as hard-boiled and sometimes brutal, is yet always capable of rendering fully developed and poignant characters. No serious scholar can deny Hemingway's importance in the literature of the twentieth century and this study does not dissent from that view. Rather, it invites the reader to recognize and valorize some of the qualities in Hemingway that may have been overlooked by some, both defenders and detractors.

Masochism provides an indication of the "crisis in masculinity" that characterizes literary modernism. While Hemingway's masochistic desire highlights this crisis, his ideological orientation denies it. This contradiction may help explain the appeal and influence of his work to the present day. His writings allow the enormous comfort of the vulnerability inherent in masochism while preserving and reinforcing traditionally stoic masculine values. Many men no doubt identify with both traditional masculine concepts and with masochism. It could hardly be otherwise for many since one acts as a counterbalance to the other. Hemingway, no doubt, felt this dual masculinity and many of his male admirers must feel it as well.

The thriving businesses of thousands of professional dominatrixes provide ample evidence of the wide practice of male masochism in its many forms. Krafft-Ebing noted this, well over a century ago, as he quotes one of his patients: "[T]he number of masochists, especially in big cities, seems to be quite large. The only sources of such information [are] prostitutes . . . Every experienced prostitute keeps some suitable instrument (usually a whip)" (175). With the burgeoning of the sex industry, houses of female domination have become common in Europe and North America and cater to unknown thousands of submissive men. These women remain in business because they answer a sexual need in many men who are either denied sexual domination by their female partners or, probably more likely, are afraid to ask for it. Angela Carter finds that most such commercial enterprises represent little more than "a mutually degrading pact"[23] between the dominatrix and her client, and this may be true for those furtive and closet part-time masochists and the convincing actresses they hire to enact their sexual fantasies. But many men and women, it would appear, are becoming increasingly curious about the possibilities of exchanging or at least balancing traditional gender roles. Masochism provides a significant and immediate means of doing do. Requesting domination from a loved one might be seen by many men as far too risky, that the domination once begun would take on forms other than the sexual. Many women, too, it seems, resist this type of power-exchange because it may carry risks for them as well in that it involves new responsibilities as well as new opportunities. Hemingway apparently negotiated these issues directly in his relationships with his wives (with the exception of his third, Martha Gellhorn) who were eager to fulfill his desires.

In the portrayals of gender in the works of Hemingway several patterns emerge, and basic attitudes toward women present themselves as emblematic. A consciousness, often seemingly insincere, of male social superiority dominates many of the texts, while the portrayal of individual women varies greatly. Hemingway shared chauvinistic views with most American men of his era and his characters resent certain domineering, as opposed to dominant, types of women, probably because of his ingrained hatred (that is not too strong a word) of his mother, and the threat, long perceived, of the growing importance of women in literature and in modern society in general since the emergence of the New Woman in the late Victorian era. As Siegel states it, "Victorian men saw women acquiring unprecedented access to public speech and control of cultural discourse" (12). And Charles Hatten notes that Hemingway, born late in this era, came to see women as "formidable agents of power, rather than passive objects to be pursued."[24] Hemingway became personally acquainted with the cultural threat from women, both in his early Paris years and later in the person of his third wife Martha, whose writing for a time competed directly with his own.[25] Yet Hemingway and his literary creations prove capable of a passionate attraction to women bordering on devotion and worship. This passion becomes all-consuming to the point of a desire to merge, or perhaps submerge, the male hero's identity with that of the lover. Many of Hemingway's fictional women appear as transcendentally superior to his male characters, while others are portrayed negatively or inconsequentially. Because Hemingway was not insensitive, one can discern a sense of guilt in some of his work resulting from his characters' mistreatment of women. These characterizations reflect events in the author's personal life, especially those surrounding his desertion of his first two wives, Elizabeth Hadley Richardson and Pauline Pfeiffer.

The nature of Hemingway's sexual desire forms the subject of some recent scholarship, stemming largely from Spilka's book (although Brenner had addressed many of the same issues earlier). As a Hemingway scholar since the 1950s, Spilka has consistently endorsed Hemingway's work as a masculine paradigm.[26] As notions of gender have become more fluid, Spilka resolves the contradiction between the old Hemingway and his new "androgynous" incarnation.

Spilka's work demands attention because it has become a standard revisionist text in Hemingway criticism. However, to comment on both Spilka's interpretation and the work that has followed it, and on the nature of Hemingway's sexuality, one must speculate. Though an extremely public figure Hemingway nevertheless managed to keep the details of his sexual life relatively private, his numerous self-serving boasts of imaginary conquests notwithstanding. As much as Hemingway played the macho hero and attempted to control the actions of the women in his life, some of his texts demonstrate a masochistic desire to yield to a willful, dominant woman. Evidence exists in his earliest work and culminates in the outright celebration of what Spilka calls "androgyny" in *The Garden of Eden*. The trouble with the term "androgynous," meaning "being both male and female," lies in its acceptance of essentialist and traditional gender constructions. As Moddelmog points out: "The concept of androgyny gives critics permission to avoid looking at Hemingway's explorations of sexual identity" (32). Donald Junkins calls for a more comprehensive definition of androgyny based on Jungian analysis that implies more of an "interplay" of masculine and feminine anima and animus rather than the binary oppositions that Spilka and others find in Hemingway's work. According to Junkins, "Spilka appropriates the concept of androgyny in the service of, not gender clarification, but gender stereotyping."[27] The "male" and "female" characteristics Spilka focuses on generally uphold hegemonic notions of gender. As Kenneth Lynn points out,[28] in his published work Hemingway uses the word "androgynous" just once, in a description in *Death in the Afternoon* of the paintings of El Greco.[29] It seems more appropriate to use this term as Hemingway apparently did, to describe physical rather than psychological attributes.

As Spilka and others have noted, Hemingway, born in 1899, came of age when a Victorian concept of masculinity prevailed. Widely divergent masculinities competed for hegemony at the turn of the century. This competition can be seen, reductively, as a battle between Muscular Christianity and *Tom Brown's Schooldays* on one extreme, and Walter Pater's aestheticism and *The Picture of Dorian Gray* on the other, with the former emerging triumphant, especially after the fall of Oscar Wilde. The trial and imprisonment of Wilde symbolically marks the beginning of the era of what Adrienne Rich calls "compulsory heterosexuality" in modern Western culture with the accompanying societal prohibition of all alternative sexualities, including homosexuality and masochism.[30] This prohibition coincided with the development of psychoanalysis with its preoccupation with "deviant" sexualities. As Siegel describes it

> In the homophobic late nineteenth-century, constructing a new story of love as domination of woman was made possible by the new sexology's nonsensical conflation of male homosexuality with submissively expressed male heterosexuality and its touting of female masochism as essential femininity. (16)

Spilka and others have remarked on the influence of this new dominant school of masculinity, in particular the works of Kipling, on the young Hemingway. Men of Kipling's inclination easily vanquished the remnants of the decadent movement and exerted a cultural hegemony over popular conceptions of manhood. Men as diverse as Hemingway and T.E. Lawrence subscribed to this concept, yet both exhibited a submissive, or what is often thought of as a "feminine" side to their sexual natures.

Part of the purpose of this book is to reject a simplistic conflation of submissiveness and femininity and, following some feminist and gender studies arguments, to note the passive and masochistic quality present in many men, including Hemingway. As Dollimore notes, "the erotics of active/passive should not be identified as coextensive with masculine/feminine, and should not be thought identical across the hetero/homosexual divide" (263). Commentators recognize the masochism of certain writers, in addition to Sacher-Masoch, both gay and straight, among them the aesthetes and decadents, who used artifice and a self-conscious theatricality in their work. Swinburne's homage to a "Lady of Pain" in "Dolores" and Wilde's *Salome* provide erotic examples of the despotic woman. Though Hemingway's sparse prose has few affinities with this school, a submissive quality manifests itself in different ways in his work as well.

Hemingway's letters indicate his disdain for psychoanalytical interpretations of his life and work and he correctly sees a limit to how near such interpretations can approximate the whole truth. He successfully suppressed one such study of his work in 1934 and considered an attempt to do the same in the 1950s.[31] Since his death, especially in the past two decades, many critics have freely probed Hemingway's writing from psychoanalytical and more broadly psychological perspectives. Eby's work offers intriguing hypotheses concerning Hemingway's sexuality while focusing on aspects of his fetishism, and suggests, perhaps inadvertently, masochism in the texts. Nancy R. Comley and Robert Scholes, in their compelling study, *Hemingway's Genders* (1994), also suggest areas of inquiry into Hemingway's sexual desire (60) but remain reluctant to draw any firm conclusions.[32] But to try to gain an understanding of what drove Hemingway's life and art, speculation is essential. In some cases, we have nothing else to go on. This informed guessing, particularly on the nature of Hemingway's sexual life, must remain just that, unless a new manuscript surfaces or a surviving and believable acquaintance publishes something substantial on Hemingway's relationships. The conjectures here are based on Hemingway's own words, both in written texts and conversations; on the memories of acquaintances, friends, and enemies; and on the interpretations of scholars, critics, and literary and cultural theorists. Enough emerges to lead to certain inferences about Hemingway's life and art, some perhaps controversial, that seem irrefutable based on the available evidence.

Where possible all citations from Hemingway's writings are from his works as published. Critics and scholars have pointed out that many of these were censored or otherwise altered but they received the author's approval prior to publication. The exceptions, of course, are the posthumous works including *A Moveable Feast* (1964), *Islands in the Stream* (1970), *True at First Light* (1999), and especially *The Garden of Eden*, which has produced the most controversy. In a celebrated review, Barbara Probst Solomon calls *The Garden of Eden* as published "a literary crime."[33] Comley and Scholes write that "the Scribners text of this novel does its author a disservice, and the publisher's ending is truly unfortunate" (103). Despite allegations of license bordering on fraud by Scribners, critics do not deny that the written words are indeed Hemingway's, however heavily edited. And Lynn refers to the "brilliant, drastic editing" of Tom Jenks who prepared the novel that most readers know (541). Yet even as strong a critic of Scribners and Jenks as Moddelmog concedes that "the published version contains substantial traces of the manuscript's obsession with homosexuality, although critics . . . have avoided exploring these vestiges" (67). Scribners's *The Garden of Eden* is the text that has stood since 1986 as a Hemingway novel and even this heavily edited version contains important revelations of Hemingway's attempt to come to terms with his own masculinity. That *The Garden of Eden* in its present form is not what Hemingway would have published makes it, perhaps, even more revealing of the author. Though no doubt Hemingway would have revised the manuscript in a radically different manner, he would have had to acknowledge the published version as his work. In the pages that follow, I refer to the original manuscript of *The Garden of Eden* where the Scribners edition has deleted entire sections, characters, and subplots.[34]

Moddelmog criticizes Jenks for what she considers his evisceration of *The Garden of Eden*. Despite her objections and those of other critics, the main issues relating to gender remain in the published version. As Moddelmog rightly points out, the manuscript "is sequestered on the shelves of the Hemingway Collection in the John F. Kennedy Library" and "only scholars with time, the library's approval, and financial backing for travel to Boston may read Hemingway's novel" (90). She adds that "the fact remains that it takes a Herculean effort and a sizable bankroll" to see the original work (90). I was fortunate enough to receive grants that enabled me to view these manuscripts and I comment on those sections that bear directly on Hemingway's alternative sexuality. In addition, Moddelmog notes that Toni Morrison, in *Playing in the Dark*, provides a penetrating analysis "without benefit of the full manuscript" (59–60) indicating that a fair reading of *The Garden of Eden* can be accomplished by consulting the novel as published. Though one may miss the omitted material, what appears in the published novel contains important revelations of Hemingway's alternative sexuality. Readers can hope for the day when the complete novel will be published. The unexpurgated version of *Look Homeward Angel* by Thomas Wolfe, another Scribners author, finally appeared in 2000 as *O Lost: A Story of the Buried Life*, and there is reason to hope that someday the complete *The Garden of Eden* will be made available as well.

Much of the following analysis of Hemingway and his male characters' relationships with women is based on a reading of his texts and an interpretation of the biographical details of his life. To repeat: much of the analysis involves speculation, but perhaps not nearly as much as that of some critics. The goal is to illuminate an area of life that nearly always remains hidden. Many of Hemingway's acquaintances have revealed what they know of his love life in memoirs and interviews, many brought together by Denis Brian in *The True Gen* (1988). However, despite these remembrances, questions remain and some imagining and inference based on Hemingway's writings can complement the recollections. Hemingway's work presents evidence of a masochistic preoccupation that could be used for a more extensive analysis of particular texts but this method will not be pursued here. Instead this book offers a general overview highlighting aspects of Hemingway's masochism. Comley and Scholes refer to possibly hidden sexual content in the novels and stories and suggest that "[m]any such moments in Hemingway's writing lead us to believe that the Hemingway Text often extends beyond the words on the page and requires the active participation of a reader who is not afraid to extrapolate from hints" (134). The present work is undertaken in this spirit.

Chapter 1 focuses on recent theories of literary masochism and attempts to find answers to questions posed by the contradictory findings of some scholars regarding masochism's political orientation and Hemingway's place within that spectrum of views. This chapter examines theories of masochism and places them into two gender-political categories: Progressive Masochism and Reactionary Masochism. Hemingway's work, while discussed throughout these pages, is not the chapter's central focus. Chapter 2 continues by locating Hemingway's work within the general theoretical discourse of literary masochism by alluding to examples from his texts that highlight key elements including fetishism, humiliation, suspense, the contract, and pain and violence. Chapter 3 looks at Hemingway's contradictory attraction to sodomy on the one hand and his homophobia on the other, as well as his reputation for misogyny. Chapter 4 traces biographical factors contributing to Hemingway's perception of women and includes a discussion of the sense of guilt in his work through the 1930s focusing particularly on the literary expressions that accompanied the dissolution of his first two marriages. Chapter 5 begins with a discussion of the major texts of Hemingway's early and middle periods and proceeds to focus on *The Garden of Eden* as the defining text of masochism in his work. Chapter 6 offers some comments on the conjunction between masochism and colonialism as well as Hemingway's attitudes toward race and how they may or may not relate to his masochism. Chapter 7 concludes with further comments on Hemingway's misogyny and homophobia and the attempts of recent critics to reinterpret these in light of his "androgyny." The argument reaffirms Hemingway's basic conservatism in gender identification despite his enthusiasm for an alternative sexuality.

Chapter 1

Hemingway and Theories of Masochism

Masochism and the Art of Fiction

More than most authors, Hemingway dwells at length on the process of artistic creation and few have taken the aesthetics and mechanics of fiction and the production of art in general as seriously as he did. Jake Barnes, a reporter in *The Sun Also Rises*, and David Bourne, a novelist in *The Garden of Eden*, are just two examples of Hemingway heroes who reflect on the art of writing. Robert Jordan in *For Whom the Bell Tolls* (1940) considers writing of his experiences and Thomas Hudson in *Islands in the Stream* is a successful painter. These characters, together with Hemingway's accounts of writing in *Green Hills of Africa*, *Death in the Afternoon*, and elsewhere, all point to his self-conscious identity as artist. Psychoanalysis offers some theories to account for artistic production.

Freud states that the "instincts occur in pairs of opposites, active and passive," and he names as "the most important representatives of this group the desire to cause pain (sadism) with its passive counterpart (masochism)."[1] While many advocates and defenders of masochism assert its incompatibility with sadism and deny a truly sadistic presence in its operation, psychoanalysis finds a close relationship between the two and suggests that sadism can transform itself into masochism. Accepting for the moment the position of psychoanalysis, one might point to Hemingway's fascination with blood sports—such as hunting, fishing, bullfighting, and boxing—as indications of sadism. Freud associates sadism with "looking" and with "curiosity."[2] These qualities, essential for a journalist, inform much of Hemingway's work and he did his earliest professional writing as a reporter. Writing of *The Sun Also Rises*, Thomas Strychacz comments on the importance of foreign correspondent Jake Barnes's observations, his "watching."[3] Two of Hemingway's most famous nonfiction works, *Death in the Afternoon* (1932) and *Green Hills of Africa* (1935), both involving blood sports, contain many of the elements of journalism.

In opposition to these "sadistic" characteristics, the depictions of passivity in characters like Jake Barnes in *The Sun Also Rises*, Frederic Henry in *A Farewell to Arms*, and David Bourne in *The Garden of Eden* suggest masochism. In one of Freud's many contradictory comments on masochism, he sees in it "the impulsion to artistic and theatrical display," which can account for Hemingway's gift for fiction.[4] According to Leo Bersani: "The jouissance that transforms sadism into masochism would also be an effect of such sublimated appropriations of the real as art and philosophy."[5] This analysis can account for a similar transformation in Hemingway that enabled him to produce his greatest works. If we accept Freud's idea of the "impulsion to artistic and theatrical display" and Bersani's "appropriations of the real" along with Deleuze's insistence on masochism's "aesthetic" quality (134), Hemingway's art can be seen as sublimations of his active and passive drives.

The notion that a masochistic aesthetic informs much of the world's finest artistic production has gained some acceptance in recent years especially following Bersani's comments on the process of artistic creation in *The Freudian Body* (1986) and other works.[6] Siegel and Deleuze at least partially support this view. Hemingway's work aestheticizes a new form of modernist masculinity that is by turns both traditional and stunningly new. As Hatten notes of *A Farewell to Arms*, "Hemingway's stubborn commitment to masculine codes is resolved through an aesthetization of masculine experience," while he longs for "other types of experience which a traditional masculine identity . . . precludes" (82–83). The sexual submission of women to men was a cultural given well before and beyond the 1920s, and Hemingway inverts this notion throughout much of his work in his central characters' readiness to assume positions of subservience to the women they love.

Gaylyn Studlar's *In the Realm of Pleasure* offers a compelling explanation of the masochistic approach to artistic expression, although its main emphasis falls on cinema:

> [T]he masochistic aesthetic extends beyond the purely clinical realm into the arena of language, artistic form, narrativity, and production of textual pleasure. Emerging as a distinct artistic discourse, the masochistic aesthetic structures unconscious infantile sexual conflicts, conscious

fantasies, and adult experience into a form that is not only a measure of the influence of early developmental stages but also a register of the transformative power of the creative process.[7]

While Studlar, who appears to have coined the term "masochistic aesthetic," writes of the cinematic collaboration of Josef von Sternberg and Marlene Dietrich, her insights have wider-ranging applications. Studlar disagrees with the premise of Laura Mulvey and other feminist film scholars who find that movie narratives—comprising the scenario, the direction, the camera, and the entire apparatus of cinematic expression—generally involve a sadistic sensibility and that the audience (or in the case of an author like Hemingway, the reader) vicariously takes part in the spectacle as a constituent of the controlling gaze. On the contrary, Studlar finds "that the psychic processes and pleasures engaged by the cinema more closely resemble those of masochism than the sadistic, Oedipal pleasures commonly associated in psychoanalytic film theory with visual pleasure" (6). Studlar sees the audience as passive, absorbing the action and the controlling gaze of the film, and finds "subject–spectator positions that do not adhere to models . . . based on castration fear, Oedipal desire, and a sadistic voyeurism" (6). A case could be made, and Bersani comes close to making it, that the same principle holds true for much written fiction and reader response to it. Studlar asserts that the masochistic aesthetic embodies

imaginative excess balanced against the limitations of external reality, the tragedy of an obsessional desire disavowed through irony, ritualized torture contrasted with fetishizing romanticism. [And it is] aesthetically oriented, and centered around the idealizing, mystical exaltation of love for the punishing woman. (18)

Because of the theatrical and ritualistic nature of male masochism, exhibitionism assumes a prominent place. The subject needs to display himself in an exposed or helpless position before the beloved. Many masochists report fantasies of wishing for an audience to witness their disgrace. A common masochistic fantasy envisions the despotic woman humiliating her lover in the presence of female, and occasionally male, friends and even "loaning" her slave to them. Reik notes that "the masochist needs witnesses to his pain and degradation."[8] Ironically, this very humiliation reinforces the masochist's sense of his masculine identity.

Strychacz suggests that in *The Sun Also Rises*, the bullring serves as the arena for a "ritual of manhood" and that "the presence of the audience, in particular, is crucial."[9] The audience, says Strychacz, acts as an "agent of legitimization . . . to appraise rituals of manhood and bestow praise or condemnation on the protagonist" (54). While this refers to Hemingway characters, the enactment of a similar scenario occurs in the writing and publication of his fiction. The audience, or the reading public in this case, perform "empowering acts of watching" (52). Whether the protagonist (or the author) succeeds or fails, says Strychacz, "[m]asculine display implies a loss of autonomy and authority to the audience" (52). In masochism, a similar loss of authority comprises the entire purpose. The masochist puts himself on display to symbolically lose his manhood by submitting himself completely to a dominant woman. Although Strychacz does not address masochism directly, his interpretations of Hemingway fit its aesthetic when he writes: "Performances of manhood imply a radical lack of self that must be constantly filled and refashioned" before an audience.[10] He adds that

> Hemingway returns repeatedly to the arenas where, he suggests, men act out their dramas of power and shame. Some . . . demonstrate the authority accruing to the successful self-dramatist. More often, exposure to the watching crowds brings humiliation. (76)

The nature of masochistic performance guarantees its success as it constitutes a drama of both power and shame. As Robert E. Gajdusek points out, a major theme in Hemingway's work lies in its "unremitting message to the male reader: that the individuated male consciousness must be purchased through a daring act of surrender to the feminine."[11] Only by degrading his manhood by submitting to the dominant woman, can the masochist bring about what Deleuze calls "the birth of the new man" (101). According to Phillips, Sacher-Masoch's creation of Severin in *Venus in Furs* represents a hero who "engineers his own affliction as an unorthodox manner of achieving manhood" (24). Similarly, Hemingway puts on literary displays of the suffering and humbling of his characters. By publishing his fiction, Hemingway displays himself before the audience and becomes thus "empowered." While this may seem to reverse Studlar's concept of the audience as passive, it actually involves a symbiotic reaction between author and audience. When Studlar writes of the cinema audience as passive and masochistic, this does not imply that the filmmaker, or in this case the author, is sadistic especially if we accept that sadism and masochism do not represent binary opposites. In much cinema, as in much fiction, an empathic relationship occurs between the work of art and the audience.

The ideas of Studlar and Strychacz can be applied to *The Sun Also Rises*. In that novel, Jake Barnes competes in a very public social arena for the affections of Brett Ashley. Pedro Romero, the bullfighter, need only compete in the *corrida*. Jake suffers from the continuous application and withdrawal of the attentions of the sexually liberated Brett. According to one aspect of Freud's theory of masochism, application of painful stimuli provokes sexual arousal. Brett continually raises Jake's hopes in this novel, only to dash them after periods of suspense and anticipation. Hemingway's desperate characters repeatedly and painfully submit to authorial stimulation. Such "repetition" of painful action conforms to Freud's view of masochistic pleasure (XIX 160). The act of creating a character like Catherine Bourne in *The Garden of Eden* for her husband to submit to, satisfies the more overtly sexual nature of Hemingway's masochism. In addition, this novel presents some of Hemingway's finest reflections on the art of writing fiction as he describes David Bourne's attempts to create. In discussing the masochistic aesthetic at work in the films of von Sternberg, Studlar writes: "The cold irony of the films also relates to the distance that von Sternberg maintains between his authorial presence and characters who, as he remarked on more than one occasion, represent aspects of himself" (118). This remark could be applied to much of Hemingway's work, including his creation of David in *The Garden of Eden*. Jacqueline Tavernier-Courbin succinctly summarizes what many critics have maintained: "Most, if not all, of Hemingway's fiction contains numerous autobiographical elements, and his protagonists are often conscious projections of himself."[12] Hemingway's characters represent aspects of his personality and, like von Sternberg in his films, he maintains a detachment from them. A literary relationship also suggests itself to Sacher-Masoch, "whose life and writing," according to Victor N. Smirnoff, "are more intimately interrelated than usually appears in the work of artists."[13] Many critics have noted the same autobiographical impulse in Hemingway's work and, as much as Sacher-Masoch and von Sternberg, he portrays the submission to women.

While the contention that sadism and masochism represent binary dualisms remains the subject of a continuing debate, agreement exists on the passivity of the masochistic subject. Psychoanalyst Rudolph M. Lowenstein notes that "passivity is not a result of masochism but, on the contrary, a prerequisite for it."[14] The passivity of many Hemingway characters has been widely recognized. Even his men of action, like Robert Jordan in *For Whom the Bell Tolls* and Harry Morgan in *To Have and Have Not*, are battered by forces that lie far

beyond their control. Wyndham Lewis, an early critic and acquaintance of Hemingway, remarks that Jake Barnes in *The Sun Also Rises*
and Frederic Henry in *A Farewell to Arms* represent the passive voice
"*of those to whom things are done*, in contrast to those who have exec-
utive will and intelligence."[15] Brenner concurs saying that "the heroes
in his fiction are more passive than active" and remarks on Frederic
Henry's "noncommittal blandness" (20). David Bourne surpasses
either of these characters in his passivity before his wife, Catherine,
and can only be stirred to action by her destruction of his manuscripts.
Frederic Henry does nothing really decisive until he is faced with the
prospect of a firing squad. And Jake, arguably, never moves to significant action at all. The passive nature of all these Hemingway heroes
illustrates one of the core components of masochism: the abdication
of the will before the dominant woman.

Deleuze attempts to rehabilitate the reputation of masochism by
repeatedly insisting that it is not the reverse of sadism as psychoanalysis claims. "The concurrence of sadism and masochism is fundamen-
tally one of analogy only," he asserts, "their processes and their
formation are entirely different" (46). He further states that sadism
and masochism "represent parallel worlds, each complete in itself, and
it is both unnecessary and impossible for either to enter the other's
world" (68). He and many others now reject the claims of psychoanalysis of the connection between sadism and masochism. Deleuze
remarks that

> a genuine sadist would never tolerate a masochistic victim . . . Neither
> would the masochist tolerate a truly sadistic torturer. He does of course
> need a special "nature" in the woman torturer, but he needs to mold
> this nature, to educate and persuade it in accord with his special project,
> which could never be fulfilled with a sadistic woman. . . . We tend to
> ignore this obvious difference. The woman torturer of masochism can-
> not be sadistic precisely because she is *in* the masochistic situation, she
> is an integral part of it, a realization of the masochistic fantasy. (40–41)

The "special 'nature' in the woman torturer" represents not sadism
but empathy, a quality found throughout Hemingway's work. Deleuze
reemphasizes the incompatibility of sadism and masochism when he
points out the "contrasting processes" between the two with sadism
relying on "the negative and negation" while masochism relies on
"disavowal and suspense" (34). Deleuze finds that "[s]adism is in every
sense an active negation of the mother and an exaltation of the father
who is beyond all laws" (60). Masochism disavows the father and seeks

a pre-Oedipal, oral mother, characterized by three elemental qualities Deleuze finds in nature: "cold—maternal—severe," and alternately, "icy—sentimental—cruel" (51). While Deleuze's choice of those six adjectives is patently subjective, it lends an air of nuance to the phenomenon he describes: the masochistic man's central place in a predominantly female universe from which the father has been banished.[16]

Echoing Deleuze's characterization of the oral mother, Susan Beegel notes how Hemingway in *The Old Man and the Sea* refuses to "masculinize" nature, as she writes of the fisherman Santiago that, "against his view of Mother Sea as a beautiful, kindly, and generous feminine power . . . he sets an opposing view of feminine nature as cruel and chaotic—spawning poisonous creatures, sudden storms, and hurricanes."[17] This imagining reflects what Deleuze sees as the aesthetic quality in masochism that is totally absent in sadism and he continually points to the deep flaw in Freud's conception of sadism and masochism as complementary. Deleuze believes that the linkage of sadism and masochism functions as a result of "pre-Freudian thinking which relied on hasty assimilations and faulty etiological interpretations that psychoanalysis merely helped to make more convincing, instead of questioning their reality" (133). Deleuze insists that he is "questioning the very concept of an entity known as sadomasochism" (13), which he adds, "is one of those misbegotten names, a semiological howler" (134). Siegel agrees when she writes:

> The conflation *sadomasochism* troubles me, not because it simplifies Freud's extraordinarily convoluted discussions of sadism and masochism but because it avoids extreme qualitative differences in the attitudes toward authority expressed through sadistic and masochistic pleasure, fantasy, and ritual. (31)

Because both sadism and masochism privilege pain, many commentators have found it easy to equate the two. Studlar explains the common misperception: "If qualitative differences are disregarded and only the pain/pleasure content considered, then sadism and masochism might well be regarded as complimentary" (14). But the qualitative differences stand out and cannot be ignored. Phillips remarks: "Masochists are not a complementary breed to sadists, it is just that the binary dualism is so bright and shiny, so attractively user-friendly, that it has been convenient to go along with the idea that they are" (13). She adds that "[t]he masochist is a conscious manipulator, not a victim" (19) and that "consensual sadomasochism is essentially in the service of masochism, rather than sadism" (66). And while this may often be the case, masochism requires a great deal of discretionary participation by the woman. This follows the pattern developed by Sacher-Masoch in *Venus in Furs* in which the hero, Severin, instigates his own enslavement to Wanda. A true sadist would seek his or her own pleasure by inflicting pain, regardless of the wishes of the masochist. Masochism demands a pliable and cooperative partner to assume the role of the dominant to serve its interests and also expects significant agency, which represents one of the contradictions that some critics have found. Masochism wishes both to control and be controlled. Writing from a psychoanalytical perspective, Smirnoff notes that: "Masochism is a defiance . . . In fact, the masochist knows that his position is simply the result of his own power" (69). Sadism, on the contrary, does not grant any power to its object. Smirnoff, like many outside of psychoanalysis, asserts that "there is no complementary agreement between the sadistic and the masochistic desire" (63).

Frenetic and violent sexual activity characterizes Sade's work. These qualities are absent in the writings of Sacher-Masoch. Sade's characters present relentless displays of self-conscious debauchery and have impossibly limitless energy. The emphasis lies in the quantity, diversity, and violence of the sexual encounters. In Sacher-Masoch's work, the self-consciously aesthetic quality of the experience holds far more importance. As Studlar points out, "The masochistic formal treatment of sensual movement is totally at odds with the sadistic economy of constant sexual activity" (125). The erotic scenes (they cannot be truly called "sex scenes" because no actual sex takes place) in *Venus in Furs* are controlled, prolonged, and heightened by suspense. The frequent whippings and the humiliations occur with Severin's explicit consent but Wanda controls the irregular timing and severity of his punishments. Such controlled violence and consent would be unthinkable in Sade's work which is self-consciously pornographic. Sacher-Masoch's writings are almost coy in comparison. As Deleuze states, "they always bear the stamp of decency" (26) which reflects many of Hemingway's understated love scenes. These two aesthetic approaches highlight the differences between sadism and masochism. Hemingway's aesthetic consists of highly stylized and often erotic prose, which is at the same time subtle and understated.

HEMINGWAY AND THEORIES OF PROGRESSIVE MASOCHISM

In addition to Deleuze and Studlar, several other scholars have addressed the theme of masochism in literature and find it socially progressive. Dollimore, who writes only briefly of male masochism, nevertheless suggests that "perversion" in general remains "a concept bound up with insurrection" and he seeks to "replace the pathological concept with a political one" (103). In recent years, two of the most significant cultural studies of male masochism are those by Kaja Silverman and Carol Siegel, both of whom emphasize its progressive qualities.

Silverman's ambitious work, *Male Subjectivity at the Margins* (1992), argues at length in favor of masochism's politically subversive potential. She seeks in alternative masculine sexualities "the historical moment at which the equation of the male sexual organ with the phallus could no longer be sustained."[18] She locates this moment predominantly in the post–World War II era and inquires into "the larger political implications of these 'deviant' masculinities, some of which indeed say no to power" (2). Exploring the possibilities of a "model for a radically reconstituted male subjectivity," Silverman seeks modes of countering the "dominant fiction" of "the unity of the family and the adequacy of the male subject" and believes that "[m]ale masochism represents one way of doing so" (16, 213). Silverman specifically searches for works in which the male sex organ has lost any true correlation to the phallic signifier. According to Silverman, this dislocation can occur at times when "history may manifest itself in so traumatic and unassimilable a guise that it temporarily dislocates penis from phallus, or renders null and void the other elements of the dominant fiction" (47). The belief system of modern Western civilization "depends upon the preservation of two interlocking terms: the family and the phallus" (48). Hemingway's work can be seen as subversive to both these ideas.

The nuclear family plays no major role in Hemingway's fiction. Aside from minor characters, the family remains virtually absent in *The Sun Also Rises*, *A Farewell to Arms*, *For Whom the Bell Tolls*, *Across the River and Into the Trees*, and *The Garden of Eden*. Harry Morgan in *To Have and Have Not* is a family man as is Thomas Hudson in *Islands in the Stream*, but in both those cases the family unit is destroyed by violence. In *A Farewell to Arms*, Frederic and Catherine plan to start a family but this attempt proves dramatically abortive with the stillbirth of the child and the death of the mother. Hemingway appears distinctly uncomfortable in the family setting. His hatred of his mother and his estrangement from his father, then his sister, and finally one of his own children, indicate this discomfort. Many of his major characters—Jake Barnes, Frederic Henry, Robert Jordan, Richard Cantwell—represent alienated beings divorced from any idyllic familial ties. An exception is Harry Morgan of *To Have and Have Not*, whose own nuclear family appears relatively normal, but the character himself and his wife are socially dysfunctional.

Silverman locates the "historical trauma" as the period of World War II and its aftermath. Silverman, of course, does not suggest that the erosion of the "dominant fiction" began suddenly at this time and cites earlier transgressive moments in a long chapter on T.E. Lawrence and a discussion of Henry James. However, one could argue that modern Western society's period of "historical trauma" began during World War I. The Great War saw a flowering of nontraditional expressions of a homoerotic masculinity in the poems of British soldiers such as Wilfred Owen, Rupert Brooke, and others. Greg Forter writes of this period and the response of American modernists, including Hemingway, as a "reaction to the loss of masculine authority and potency" before "the onslaught of a destructive and emasculating modernity," a reaction characterized by nostalgia for a "disappearing ideal of male autonomy."[19] Hatten suggests that *A Farewell to Arms* was written in response to "threats posed by a feminizing social world" (77) and that it reveals Hemingway's "sense of the diminished degree of male autonomy in economic and political life" (81). This was the period of the emergence of modernism and self-conscious literary pessimism and many works from this era demonstrate a disenchantment with Silverman's "dominant fiction."

Much has been written about the decline of Victorian values in the wake of World War I and the modernist response to this. This loss of faith is evident in the works of authors as diverse as James Joyce and D.H. Lawrence. Hemingway's work, despite its vastly different style and content, also shares the modernist reaction to the "historical trauma" of the Great War. Neither Joyce nor Lawrence served in the war but they could not, of course, escape its impact on Western society and the accompanying erosion of Victorian values. Of the modernists, Joyce approaches masochism most directly in the "Nighttown" passages of *Ulysses*. Joyce's familiarity with *Venus in Furs* is evident in both the mention of Sacher-Masoch's novel and in Bloom's humiliation by Bella/Bello. Bloom enacts a version of the masochistic scenario to which Joyce adds forced feminization as well as scatological and coprophilous elements.[20] In contrast to the conscious assimilation of literary masochism in *Ulysses*, Lawrence's tortured men, especially in *Women in Love* and *The Rainbow*, exist independently of such allusions. Hemingway, who saw action in Italy during the war, arguably has more at stake, risks more, in embracing masochism. Having played out what he saw as the best of what the remnants of Victorian masculinity had to offer in the form of militarism, Hemingway's disillusionment serves both to reject that, along with its chauvinistic attitude toward women, and to simultaneously seek to erect a new, individual masculine ideal based on some martial elements of the old paradigm.

Silverman feels that for the soldier, "the fiction of a phallic masculinity generally remains intact only for the duration of the war" (63). *The Sun Also Rises* can be read in light of this statement because the ex-soldier Jake sustains no support from postwar civil society and feels more than most what Silverman refers to as "the incommensurability of penis and phallus" (63) because of his genital wound. While subsequently Hemingway so often chose men in war as his heroes (*A Farewell to Arms, For Whom the Bell Tolls, Across the River*, and *Islands in the Stream*), he seems both to confirm in some and contradict in the others, the subject position we might expect from Silverman's theory. Hemingway's characters become lost when "peace breaks out," unable to negotiate the mandate of phallic authority away from a wartime setting. Harold Krebs flounders helplessly in his hometown in "Soldier's Home." Jake Barnes, traumatized by both his war injury and his inability to adjust to civilian life, joins the disillusioned postwar expatriates in Paris. And in *A Farewell to Arms*, Catherine Barkley compares Frederic Henry out of uniform to "Othello with his occupation gone."[21] One could make a case that for Hemingway, the phallic signifier "works" in the inherited masculine preserve of warfare but not in peacetime relations with women. To follow Silverman's analysis, the "historical trauma" serves to "dislocate penis from phallus" in Hemingway's dramatizations of heterosexual love. However, it fails to "render[s] null and void the other elements of the dominant fiction" (47). This divide makes Hemingway so continually enigmatic despite his plain prose and also helps to explain his appeal to a widely diverse audience.

In addition to the abrogation of family contracts, Hemingway's work, as we have seen, undermines the other essential ideological belief that comprises Silverman's "dominant fiction"—the correlation of penis to phallus. *The Sun Also Rises* has assumed such canonical status that few now marvel that the main character, Jake Barnes, lacks a full complement of male genitalia. Jake represents the embodiment of what Silverman calls "phallic divestiture" (9, 160). That an author so identified with traditional masculinity as Hemingway could render a character like Jake seems more remarkable today perhaps than when the novel first appeared in 1926. The abolition of the phallic signifier in the hero of *The Sun Also Rises* conforms to Silverman's reading of a cultural production that consciously undermines an obsolete equation of the penis and phallic power. This novel's enormous appeal to three generations of readers provides evidence of the resonance that such an emasculated character engenders. That three generations of readers can consider Jake Barnes an antihero for their times points to the negation of phallic hegemony on some significant level. In this sense, the novel does indeed call for a questioning revisitation of the concept of traditional masculinity. Hemingway implicitly condemns contemporary Western standards of manhood. But while wallowing in the depiction of wounded masculinity, Hemingway seems to project a self-conscious vision of a newly restructured male subjectivity. The new construction would elevate the more sensitive qualities of Jake Barnes and combine them with the solitary, heroic qualities that Hemingway invests in the matador Pedro Romero. This duality represents a construction that has exerted a powerful appeal to readers.

Much of Silverman's discussion centers on the positive Oedipus complex and on Freudian notions of castration. In this view, of course, the female is considered "castrated" by male perception.[22] The possession of male genitals implies a phallic authority that is biologically foreclosed to woman by her essential "lack." Silverman focuses on several American films of the 1940s to demonstrate "historical trauma," a condition, she believes, "which brings a large group of male subjects into such an intimate relation with [their own] lack that they are at least for the moment unable to sustain an imaginary relation with the phallus" (55). Accepting Silverman's vision of "historical trauma," but predating it to the post–World War I period, Jake Barnes personifies this lack. His character embodies this failure to uphold traditional masculine values in a supposedly harmonious peace time. Of the film, *Best Years of Our Lives*, one of the Hollywood productions she discusses, Silverman writes: "Far from obliging the female subject to display her lack to her sexual other, it repeatedly calls upon her to look acceptingly at *his*—to acknowledge and embrace male castration" (emphasis in original, 69). This female gaze imposes itself throughout *The Sun Also Rises* as Brett Ashley comes into intimate contact with Jake's lack.

Despite the erosion of the phallus, the resiliency of the "dominant fiction" of patriarchal values must be emphasized. Silverman accounts for this largely due to the "conservatism of the psyche—with its allegiance to the past" (48). If the effect of "historical trauma" on Hemingway led to the rupture of the penis/phallus correlation in his characters' relationships with women, a basic conservatism remains at work in his acceptance of other social implications of phallic power inherited from the past, and reflects the resilience of Silverman's "dominant fiction" in his worldview.

The genitally wounded Jake Barnes in *The Sun Also Rises* is only the most pronounced example of the negation of the phallus. Hemingway's novels and stories, of course, contain many treatments of heterosexual love. Hemingway was, after all, heterosexual, even if he cannot be considered exactly straight. While Jake remains the only major Hemingway character to actually lack a full penis, the other heroes rarely make use of that organ in lovemaking. Hemingway's narrators seldom dwell on genital penetration. Leslie Fiedler contends that Hemingway "is much addicted to describing the sex act" but the descriptions are often elliptical.[23] Writing of *The Sun Also Rises*, Brenner remarks on "Jake's inability (and Hemingway's unwillingness) to penetrate" (59). An exception to this reticence occurs in the early story, "Up in Michigan," which specifically presents penetration but remarkably from the point of view of the penetrated woman. In *For Whom the Bell Tolls*, there is little doubt that Robert Jordan penetrates Maria in the act of love in the famous scene in which the "earth move[s]," and again in chapter 37.[24] Yet some of the most prolonged discussion of penetration takes place in a passage where it never actually occurs. Maria, who has been raped by the fascists, regrets that she cannot give herself to Robert Jordan because "there is a great soreness and much pain" (368) due to the attack upon her. Robert and Maria discuss, but reject, alternatives to his penetrating her. This leads in turn to a discussion of the events leading up to the rape but stops short of the sexual assault. Robert does not insist on having sex with Maria and even declines her offer, "Is there not some other thing I can do for thee?" (369). Robert remains content to lie by Maria's side and to defer sexual gratification.

Love scenes in Hemingway usually receive scant description. Even after publishers relaxed their standards to allow for more explicit sexual content, Hemingway still shies away from the penetration of the woman by the man in the act of love. Often he uses a single word, such as "Then"[25] or "Afterwards"[26] to inform the reader that lovemaking has taken place. This reticence in the description of physical love probably owes much less to a sense of decorum than to Hemingway's reluctance to relate the nature of his own sexual experiences. Arguably, the most vivid description of penetration in Hemingway's published work occurs when Catherine Bourne sodomizes her husband in *The Garden of Eden*.

Hemingway's male characters do not seem concerned with the sexual exercise of phallic power, which marks a clear divide between his work and that of D.H. Lawrence. While both writers, each with many who claim them as the greatest author of the twentieth century, celebrate physical heterosexual love, including sodomy, they do so in dramatically different fashions.[27] Hemingway admired some of Lawrence's work, such as *Sons and Lovers* and in particular the homo-erotic "The Prussian Officer," which bears resemblance to his own "A Simple Enquiry." Siegel includes Lawrence in her study of authors who exhibit a masochistic sensibility and clearly in *Women in Love*, Rupert and Gerald find themselves overpowered sexually and psychically by Ursula and Gudrun, despite Lawrence's holding aloft the banner of a "phallic consciousness." Lawrence, perhaps more than most modernist authors, consciously celebrates male phallic power in much of his work. But Siegel, discussing the maternal references in *Sons and Lovers*, correctly sees how Lawrence occasionally undermines his own concept with his images of dominant women. Siegel adds: "These images also oppose Freudian interpretations that particular-ize the mother figure as an imago of the subject's actual mother" (93). Though Siegel does not discuss Hemingway, his fiction also works to counter the prevailing Freudian view and supports her asser-tion. Hemingway sincerely hated his own mother. Yet his male char-acters, even when exhibiting the most virile and independent qualities, consistently seek an identification with, and the protection of women.

Some of Hemingway's characters treat women in the tradition of chivalric romance, which Siegel and others see as one origin of literary masochism. The battle-scarred, dying, 50-year-old Colonel Richard Cantwell in *Across the River*, which takes place in postwar Venice, conducts a worshipful relationship with Renata who is 30 years younger than himself. The adoring pose adopted by the colonel in the presence of Renata recalls Severin's admiration of Titian's *Venus with the Mirror* who he prefers to call *Venus in Furs*. In the Hemingway novel, Colonel Cantwell displays his own admiration of Titian's pow-erful nudes when he remarks, "He painted some wonderful women."[28] Biographers note that the character of Renata in this novel found its inspiration in a relationship that developed between Hemingway and a young Italian women, Adriana Ivancich, which his wife Mary had little choice but to tolerate. Hemingway's significantly chaste affair with Adriana contained elements of a father–daughter relationship with erotic overtones, which were apparently never acted upon by mutual consent. Yet Hemingway's relationship with Adriana had masochistic overtones as well. This is suggested by Linda Wagner-Martin who, citing some of his letters to Adriana expressing his love and loneliness without her, finds "evidence of the human response to pain and to the continued power of Hemingway's sexual text, writer as earnest and dedicated lover, crushed by the disdain of his 'lady.' "[29] Much of this feeling finds its way into *Across the River*.[30]

Colonel Cantwell, an old and battle-hardened soldier with a crippled hand and numerous other wounds, idealizes Renata and the narrator invites a comparison, by denying it, of their relationship to Othello and Desdemona (211). In his final days, Cantwell reflects on his past relationships: "I have loved but three women and lost them thrice. You lose them the same way you lose a battalion; by errors of judgment; orders that are impossible to fulfill, and through impossible conditions. Also through brutality" (91). Renata has awakened his finer, submissive feelings toward women and the world at large and, as they embrace in the gondola, leaves a chastened colonel "lying under the blanket in the wind, knowing it is only what man does for woman that he retains" (143). What the colonel does for woman here is remarkable as he provides Renata with orgasms while expecting and receiving none in return.[31] He acts upon this new sense of devotion and subservience when he submissively tells Renata: "I'll take you home and you sleep good and well and tomorrow we will meet where and when you say" (149). The colonel does not demand reciprocal sexual satisfaction from Renata.

While the novel deals with two of Hemingway's major concerns, love and war, it contains few explicit descriptions of either yet both preoccupy the text. Renata visits the colonel's hotel room and "[t]hey kissed for a long time . . . in the cold open windows that were onto the Grand Canal" (105). This is followed by a Hemingway shorthand—the word "Then" followed by a comma—for lovemaking. Renata, though she clearly takes the initiative, appears to enjoy some pain herself, even while retaining control of the relationship. "Kiss me once again," she bids the colonel, "and make the buttons of your uniform hurt me but not too much" (105). Shortly after this, she "kissed him hard so that he could feel the sweet salt of the blood inside his lips. And I like that too, he thought" (106). Immediately after this, the lovers get ready for dinner. Renata says, "Now I will comb my hair and make a new mouth and you can watch me" (106). The colonel then retires to his toilet as well and surveys his face in the mirror, noting "the different welts and ridges" and "the thin, only to be observed by the initiate, lines of the excellent plastic operations after head wounds" (107). The colonel has been battered by injuries in wars and seems to fetishize his wounds. Typically, a masochist takes pleasure in admiring the wounds received at the hands of the beloved. Siegel comments in this vein when she writes: "[T]he knight who displays his love wounds like medals and kneels to receive more no longer stimulates sympathy and reader identification. Rather, in our era of the egalitarian love ethic, he is read as repellently exhibitionistic and masochistic" (140). While Cantwell's wounds were sustained in combat and not as the result of a masochistic experience, it remains significant that he examines them after a sexual encounter with Renata.

Cantwell describes Renata's voice as reminding him "of Pablo Casals playing the cello" and "it made him feel as sad as a wound does that you think you cannot bear." (108). Before she leaves his room, the colonel tells Renata, "I love you, devil," and adds, "you're my Daughter, too" (109). In at least two other novels (*Islands in the Stream* and *The Garden of Eden*) written in the 1940s and 1950s, Hemingway characters use the term, "devil," to describe the dominant women in their lives. Earlier in *Across the River*, the colonel mentally reminisces about the dead he has known, continuing a long Hemingway tradition, as he muses, "you only felt true tenderness and love for those who had been there [to war] and had received the castigation that everyone receives who goes there long enough" (71). The colonel continues his reverie: "And any son of a bitch who has been hit solidly, as every man will be if he stays, then I love him" (71). Hemingway's expression of love for men here contains more elements of camaraderie than homoeroticism but such expressions command attention because they are rare in his work. They provide an example of his empathy with wounded masculinity.

The colonel's relationship with Renata finds expression in an empathic and self-abnegating love. As in many other Hemingway works, the lovers express a wish to merge identities when Renata asks the colonel, "Couldn't I be you?" And he answers, "That's awfully complicated. We could try of course" (146). (This theme, which finds its fullest expression in *The Garden of Eden*, is discussed in chapter 2.) The colonel's identification with Renata, including an identification with her sexuality, leads him to passively react to her very being. The colonel cherishes her presence without an aggressive male desire. Far from acting dominantly in their relationship, the colonel even accepts Renata's commands. Renata asks to hear the colonel's war stories but he does not want to speak of them. She tells him, "You are going to have to tell them to me later." The colonel initially bristles at this command replying, "Did you say *have to*, Daughter?" His experience has left him unaccustomed to taking orders but he relents and then assures her, "You can use *have to* if you want, Daughter" (134). Later, in the gondola, Renata wishes to shift positions and tells the colonel,

"Change over." He replies, "Good. That is a sensible order" (142). She directs the colonel's physical movements as they jockey in the gondola. She tells him where to put his good hand and his bad hand. At one point as they lie under the blanket, the narrator informs the reader how "his ruined hand searched for the island in the great river with the high banks" (143). Renata herself refers to her sex as "the unknown country" (145). She continues to direct his movements " 'Please don't move,' the girl said, 'Then move a great amount' " (143). Renata clearly controls their sexual encounters. The traditional, aggressive, male sexual agency remains absent in *Across the River*, as the colonel responds to Renata's initiatives and commands as they make a kind of one-sided love with Renata setting the parameters.

Even when Hemingway depicts the sexual relations of an earthy couple like Harry and Marie Morgan in *To Have and Have Not*, penetration of the woman by the man is not apparent. Indeed, in this novel, we find the stump of Harry's amputated arm stand in for the penis. Jake Barnes, arguably Hemingway's most famous creation, lacks a complete complement of male genitalia and is incapable of penetration. The central conversational point of Hemingway's story, "God Rest Ye Merry Gentlemen," concerns an attempted self-castration. Even more significantly, the confused boy of the story misunderstands the meaning of castration and amputates his penis. This shocking act takes place amid the amused and detached conversations of the doctors and staff at a Kansas City hospital. The reader comes away with the impression that the spectators hardly take this event seriously, as if it is already understood that the phallus represents a vestigial part of the modern man. Though the narrator does not, of course, endorse self-mutilation, that it provides the pivot on which the story turns indicates Hemingway's consciousness of emasculation as a central pitfall of masculinity. The story, "Mr. and Mrs. Elliot," relates the events in the life of a couple who spend their wedding night in a hotel. "They were both disappointed," the narrator informs the reader in a reference to impotence, "but finally Cornelia went to sleep."[32] They endeavor to conceive a child but "Cornelia could not attempt it very often" (112). The epynonomous couple continue to "try very hard to have a baby" (113–114) but without success. Eventually, a "girl friend" moves in with them. Mr. Elliot spends more and more time alone in his room. "Mrs. Elliot and the girl friend now slept together in the big medieval bed" (114) as Mr. Elliot becomes redundant in his own marriage. These unmistakable images of male phallic erosion lead one to question Hemingway's ultimate confidence in the role he assumed in his public life.

Perhaps Hemingway's most prolonged description of the male sex organ occurs in the chapter of *A Moveable Feast* entitled "A Matter of Measurements." This bizarre passage discusses not a phallic lack but an inadequacy. Hemingway relates the story of F. Scott Fitzgerald's anxiety at the size of his penis. According to this recollection, Zelda Fitzgerald had told her husband that he "could never make any woman happy . . . She said it was a matter of measurements."[33] Fitzgerald suffers a crisis in confidence in the size of his penis and seeks out his friend, Hemingway, for advice. Hemingway takes Fitzgerald into the men's room, inspects his genitals, and reassures him:

> "You're perfectly fine," I said, "You're OK. There's nothing wrong with you. You look at yourself from above and you look foreshortened. Go over to the Louvre and look at the people in the statues and then go home and look at yourself in the mirror." (190)

They actually *do* go to the Louvre in *A Moveable Feast*—although Hemingway disputes his own version in a letter[34]—and Fitzgerald, moderately reassured but still fretting, goes on his way to Hemingway's amusement. Some critics find in this absurd account little more than Hemingway jibing at his friend and rival and dubiously trumpeting his own physical endowment and setting himself up as a judge of the adequacy of others. Indeed, a mini-debate has ensued over the sizes of the penises of both Hemingway and Fitzgerald. In *The True Gen*, Barnaby Conrad claims that bullfighter Sidney Franklin told him that, "Hemingway's sexual organ was undersized" and that "[i]t was like that of a little boy."[35] In the same volume, former *Esquire* publisher Arnold Gingrich attempts to settle the dispute, declaring, "I happen to be in a position to give firsthand eyewitness observations in both instances of Hemingway's and Fitzgerald's sexual equipment. . . . In neither case were they undersized."[36] It is difficult to imagine anyone seriously arguing over the dimensions of the penis of almost any writer other than Hemingway. The irony of all the comments about Hemingway's remarks on Fitzgerald's alleged concerns and the interest in Hemingway's size lies in this author's negation of that organ in so much of his fiction.

Despite the literalness with which Hemingway displaces the male phallus in *The Sun Also Rises* and other texts, on another level his work does not seriously oppose Silverman's "dominant fiction." Silverman refers to "individual men who embraced lack at the level of their unconscious fantasies and identities" (52) and Hemingway conforms to this view. One can see the wound of Jake Barnes in *The Sun Also Rises* as a rejection of the patriarchal mandate, but through a groveling embrace of his suffering and emotional trauma, he endeavors to emerge as a newly reconstituted man. "The pain he suffers is an ultimate pleasure," says Deleuze of the generic masochist, "it confirms him in his inalienable power and gives him a supreme certitude" (39). Phillips echoes this remark when she writes: "A man does remain a man even after erotic humiliation, and men involved in masochism may symbolically endanger their masculinity in order to test and fulfill themselves as men" (30). Hemingway spent a good deal of his life testing and fulfilling himself as a man. Despite Jake's lack, he recuperates the function of the phallus. The mutilated hero emerges uncertainly triumphant at the end of the novel, vanquishing his genitally complete competitors by his ability to successfully negotiate the female Other in the person of Brett Ashley. Of course, this also means that he must submit to her, which he has been doing all through the novel anyway. Brett, both consciously and unconsciously, humiliates Jake from beginning to end of *The Sun Also Rises.*

But the submission to women comes fraught with ambiguity in Hemingway. Despite the undermining of the equation of the male genitals with phallic power, Hemingway keeps sight of the symbolic significance of their correlation. Hemingway's simultaneous longing for and fear of the phallic usurpation by women finds expression in *The Garden of Eden* in David Bourne's initial acceptance and subsequent rejection of his wife's appropriation of phallic authority. In the sexual sphere he acquiesces to her dominance but when it threatens to overwhelm him in the social domain, specifically in artistic expression, she becomes a feared, castrating presence. Hemingway's bedroom consciousness does not readily translate into social ideology. If patriarchal society demands that pleasure can only be experienced when the male retains control, Hemingway rejects this on the sexual level. But in the social sphere, he appears to embrace it.

That the sexual politics of Hemingway do not quite fit into Silverman's schema does not detract from her innovative analysis. Her generally convincing conclusions—arrived at through a selective investigation of psychoanalytical, historical, literary, and cinematic sources—one of which is that masochism poses a dangerous challenge to patriarchal values, cannot apply in its entirety to Hemingway because his character remains so elusive and contradictory. If Hemingway's masochism were self-consciously acknowledged and embraced, he would bolster Silverman's thesis, but then he would also have been a different artist and a different man.

Silverman advocates the need to determine the "libidinal politics" of cultural creations that demonstrate alternative masculinities (296). "We need to begin thinking seriously," she writes, "about the political implications of desire and identification" (296). The problem with her interpretation as it applies to Hemingway arises because of the opposition of his desire that subverts her "dominant fiction," and his identification that upholds it. This contradiction may explain the enormous appeal and influence of his work. His writings allow the solace of surrender inherent in masochism while reinscribing traditional canons of masculinity.

Silverman's analysis relies heavily on the Freudian tradition. She accepts the basic premises of most of the Freudian definitions of masochism and exerts great effort to locate the male masochist as a liberatory subject by attempting to use Freud against himself. She methodically elucidates some of Freud's often contradictory statements on masochism, including " 'A Child Is Being Beaten.' " What Sherwood Williams calls the "byzantine complexity"[37] of Freud's treatment of masochism, especially in this essay with its "constructed" second phase, is well known and there is no need to argue the logic of it here except to note that while the concepts lie within grasp, its application in constructing a coherent theory of masochism must always remain problematical. The complexity of the formula, together with the intuitive nature of its theoretical application makes it a questionable construct from which to analyze human interactions. We should take Freud at his word when he says: "Little light is thrown upon the genesis of masochism by our discussion of the beating phantasy" (XVII 193). The numerous attempts to apply " 'A Child Is Being Beaten' " to the study of masochism have led commentators to some maddening twists of logic. Silverman's negotiations of this essay yield engaging hypotheses. However, this forms the least convincing part of her argument.

Both Silverman and Bersani work within the psychoanalytic tradition and seek to use the words of Freud the theoretician to overcome the prejudices of Freud the Victorian gentleman. They reconceive some of Freud's most basic theories and apply them, as did Herbert Marcuse and Norman O. Brown a few decades earlier, to a philosophy of liberatory sexuality and progressive gender relations. Of such revisionist interpretations of Freud, Dollimore writes: "It could be argued that the susceptibility of psychoanalysis to being so imaginatively rewritten constitutes a limitation rather than a strength in that a theory which offers so little internal resistance to such diverse appropriations loses its force as theory" (203).

In contrast to Silverman's psychoanalytical interpretations, Siegel in her more literary study, *Male Masochism: Modern Revisions of the Story of Love*, suggests that critics should move beyond psychoanalysis for, as she points out, "Freud's theorizing about male masochism is a product of Victorian literature" (152). Freudian psychoanalysis in the classical tradition, upholds Silverman's "dominant fiction," as she, of course, is well aware. But while Silverman works within the psychoanalytical tradition to mount her critique, Siegel rejects the very foundations of Freudian interpretations of masochism because "[i]ts language predetermines the aim of treatment: to reduce the male patient's masochism so that he can (re)gain his masculinity" (152). This regaining of a prevailing view of masculinity constitutes the aim of psychiatry since at least Krafft-Ebing, who insists that masochism "is a manifestation of psychical characteristics of the feminine type transcending into pathological conditions, insofar as its determining marks are suffering, subjection to the will of others, and to force" (237). It is just such a characterization of supposed innate feminine masochism, later supported by psychoanalysis, that has provided a target for so much feminist criticism for decades. The masculinity that Krafft-Ebing and the Freudian tradition support, of course, reflects the post-decadent, triumphalist Victorian view of male dominance.

Through a selective examination of literary traditions that demonstrate male masochism, Siegel seeks to "reach a perspective from which we may look back, otherwise than psychoanalysis dictates, over the dynamics of power between men and women" (139). Siegel's survey touches upon such traditions as tales of courtly love, male and female troubadour poetry, Edgar Allan Poe, Charles Dickens, and Emily Brontë. She concludes with a discussion of the works of Kathy Acker and Angela Carter. Siegel maintains that literary interpretations of "the male masochist come[s] to us through the Victorian novel and the language of Freudianism, which have worked together to contain his rebellion within a conservative power structure" (141). Siegel criticizes Freud, and the Victorian tradition, for an "epistemological dependence on a particular, anti-courtly concept of gender difference" (152). Siegel advises:

> Critics who conceive of their own role oppositionally and work to disempower hegemonic ideologies might look to the figure of the male masochist as a model of transgression, whose willing inversion of patriarchal values, including a jubilant offering up of self, could unsettle the dominant discourse on masculinity. (141)

While some elements of Hemingway's fiction hardly seem transgressive of patriarchal values, his work does demonstrate the "offering up of self" by his heroes to dominant women even if it is not always unambiguously "jubilant," if they sometimes feel a sexual guilt, or "remorse," over such surrender. Hemingway also seems to embody another point that Siegel emphasizes in her critique of Freudianism.

> Freud misses what seems to be one of male masochism's greatest sources of pleasure: a temporary release from society's coercive descriptions of gender roles that enables a relaxation of the moral and physical tension of sexual responsibility. (152)

Hemingway's heroes seem, at times, to groan under the weight of the coercive tension of the patriarchal imperative and his dominant women characters provide the occasion for these protagonists to drop their traditional masculine armor. According to Smirnoff, masochism is not so much the yearning for suffering but the quest for a " 'state of well-being,' a state of diminished tension which initiates pleasure" (62). Hemingway's heroes often find this state of well-being in their submissive relationships with women.

In psychoanalytic terms, the burden of masculinity lies in the paternal superego. In masochism, according to Deleuze, "*The father's likeness represents both genital sexuality and the superego as an agent of repression: the one is expelled with the other*" (emphasis in original, 125). Studlar adds, "masochism repudiates the father, patriarchal law, and superego maturation" (112). We see this process at work in Hemingway's texts. The hero as subject shrugs off the pressure of genital sexuality and with it the patriarchal "law of the father." The temporal roots of this rejection of inherited norms of masculinity lie in the Great War that traumatized Western civilization, and with it, the symbolic role of the father. Many young men and women of that era rejected, in both real and symbolic modes, much of the legacy of patriarchy. Hemingway's "lost generation" characters share this rejection. Yet Hemingway's heroes seek to establish a new masculinity after rejecting both the old models and homosexuality. Part of this new model involves sexual submission to women.

Siegel asks the question: "do any of the meanings of the modern term *masochism* seem appropriate to the description of an active, heroic masculine love?" (10). She answers affirmatively and Hemingway's work also promotes this "heroic" and chivalric quality of heterosexual masochism. The Hemingway "code hero" has long been recognized by critics for his courage, endurance, stoicism, and sense of duty. These values, an inheritance from Victorian "muscular Christianity," held powerful sway throughout Hemingway's life and show remarkable resiliency even today. The ascendancy of these values left women in an uncertain position. Courage, stoicism, and duty were seen as masculine preserves. In addition, the legacy of chivalry and courtly love was undermined during the Victorian era, depriving women of what may have been a dubious privilege but a privilege nonetheless. The emergence of the New Woman coincided with the consolidation of a self-centered capitalist economy that became the preserve of men. Women were now treated as equals in theory, shorn of traditional privileges without of course, being granted equal rights. Men who opposed the new values, who clung to a now outdated devotion to women, became isolated. Male authors could not longer be taken seriously if their work featured heroes enslaved by love. As Siegel remarks:

> The late nineteenth-century grouping of certain sexualized desires together and their later stigmatization as masochism stand out as milestones in the representation of male sexuality. Having passed these milestones, readers could never again see as a hero the lover who yields without reserve to his passion for woman. (10)

As Siegel points out, women authors in the mid-Victorian era, such as George Eliot, could still portray a Ladislaw, hopelessly devoted to Dorothea, in *Middlemarch*. But the backlash against Eliot and her work began almost before her body was cold in its grave. Hemingway was born into this atmosphere. His heroes embody the cardinal late-Victorian virtues, extolled by Kipling and others, of courage, stoicism, and duty so strongly that little attention is directed toward these same characters' devotion to their women who sometimes embody these heroic qualities themselves. Part of Hemingway's enduring appeal is that he convincingly depicts the qualities of courage, stoicism, and duty in his male characters but couples them with a consuming and yielding passion for women that, considering his immediate popularity and despite Siegel's comment, readers must have missed in fictional heroes for two generations.

Laura Frost's work, perhaps more than Silverman and Siegel, locates masochism within a progressive tradition. As Frost notes: "Feminism and queer theory have been particularly effective in reading masochism 'against the grain' of the psychoanalytic model" (227). Frost sees heterosexual male masochism as essentially and self-consciously progressive, especially in the work of Joyce and Sacher-Masoch. Frost writes of the latter that he "is clearly considering the question of female empowerment" as he demonstrates "his erotic interest in relinquishing power to a woman" (238). Both Joyce and Sacher-Masoch, she writes, "imagine[s] a world in which female power does not cancel out sexual pleasure" (241) and in which "the 'thrill' of female domination is predicated on the inversion of women's subordinate status in patriarchal society" (242). This view sees the male masochist as involved in an inherently progressive social project. The application of Frost's theory to Hemingway yields very mixed results and in some ways it clearly fails. If, to use Silverman's phrase, Hemingway's "libidinal politics" are progressive, how does this translate into his social views? Hemingway certainly held some progressive views, reflected in his fiction most prominently in *To Have and Have Not* and *For Whom the Bell Tolls*. Yet he also upheld many prevailing values, especially those associated with gender. Frost writes: "There are many indications that the masochist is aware of the conflicting relationships of his sexual desire to his reformist project and to the status quo" (242). Hemingway may well have been aware of this conflict, aware that his sexuality implied a more progressive gender-political position than he was ready to fully embrace. Too often in his public life he favored the status quo over his politically radical sexuality.

HEMINGWAY AND THEORIES OF REACTIONARY MASOCHISM

Opposing those who we might call the progressive theorists, some scholars question heterosexual male masochism as an alternative position to patriarchal dominance. Sabine Wilke remarks: "The functioning of the male masochist's pleasure . . . rests upon the suspension of the woman's desire."[38] Angela Carter writes of the "spurious female dominance" of masochism because the woman "is not cruel for her own sake or her own gratification" (21–22). Suzanne R. Stewart, in *Sublime Surrender* (1998), agrees with Phillips and Deleuze that "[t]he masochist remains at all points the stage director of his fantasy" but she discounts any subversive potential.[39] The manipulative aspect of masochism can fit neatly into an analysis of Hemingway for he controlled his texts, and presumably his personal life, to accommodate sexually dominant women or women who became sexually dominant at his behest. But while some critics assert that male masochism represents empowerment for women, Stewart is disturbed by what she sees as yet another form of male control. And while she allows that masochism radically subverts "bourgeois liberalism," Stewart adds that:

> The relationship between the male masochist and modern culture
> was gendered, for in the masochistic universe modernity came to be

feminized: the adoration of and submission to the products of culture were also sexual; the male masochist perceived himself as subjected to a dominatrix, to a topos called the Cruel Woman. The masochist himself created this Cruel Woman as aesthetic object and in that move attempted to reassert control, both over the means of cultural production and over the woman's body. . . . [M]asochism subverted the contract (in its economic, civic, and political meanings) as well as the hitherto more easily maintained distinctions between male and female, public and private, consent and compulsion. And yet, such subversions remained politically ambiguous at best, for they were predicated on silencing women whose position as victims of a sexual hierarchy had been triumphantly usurped by a male claim to the margin that, once so claimed, became the new center. (13–14)

Hemingway's "claim to the margin" resonates in alienated characters like Jake Barnes and Frederic Henry. His "lost generation" characters echo Stewart's comments. Though Stewart confines her analysis to *fin-de-siècle*, Europe, predating Hemingway, she finds long-lasting effects from what she sees as masochism's role in preserving phallocentric hegemony. If, as she implies, her theory can be updated and can include Hemingway, his masochism emerges as a protected enclave of male domination in the guise of submission. Since he was actively involved in the construction of his macho image, his private masochism would not have reached into a larger social sphere and translated into a perception and endorsement of women's social equality.

Nick Mansfield's analysis, *Masochism: The Art of Power*, agrees in part with that of Stewart. Mansfield asserts that masochism represents a modern form of the doctrine of male superiority, dressed in a raiment of powerlessness and victimization. He states that masochism "creates a way for masculine hegemonic systems to confirm their own power, and annihilate the other, while performing a loud even self-mutilating powerlessness."[40] Mansfield points to masochism's fluid concept of gender and finds that "[m]anipulating gender categories is one of its most important types of play, but the appropriation of, or identification with, the feminine on the masochist's part is never at the expense of his masculinity" (xii). According to this theory, masochism "steals" the feminine identity to mask itself as victim, thereby concealing its own power. Mansfield maintains that, "the masochistic subject combines genders without deconstructing the opposition between them. The masochist wants to own the feminine without ever giving up anything masculine" (46). Mansfield finds a spurious transgression in masochism that hides an abiding sexism. "The gender-crossing of the masochist," he writes, "does not trigger an identical transformation in the woman, who must take on the role of his sexual partner and dominate him. Instead, she must become the conduit of the masculine principle that can never be absent from the scene" (46–47). Agreeing with many that the masochist controls his fantasy, Mansfield finds woman as the real victim. But in masochism, woman is not sacrificed upon an altar of male aggression. On the contrary, her central role in the masochistic scenario calls upon her to provide the aggression.

Mansfield's remarks here, while centering on gender and sexuality, raise masochism above the dynamics of physical desire where it must remain grounded. He neglects the importance of masochism's determination not to seek to physically dominate women but rather to submit the male body to the female body and affect an exchange of sexual power. As Seigel writes, "[m]asochism can, in essence, transform the male body from an instrument of punishment for women into a medium through which women can generate pleasure for both themselves and their partners" (119). Mansfield neglects the primary materiality of masochism in an effort to locate it ideologically. As Deleuze states, "[m]asochism in its material aspects is a phenomenon of the senses" (101) to which Seigel adds: "Deleuze's theory can attract a feminist reader because he envisions the body of the male masochist as the site of *both* the subversion of patriarchal law and its confirmation" (emphasis in original 111). Mansfield discounts masochism's sexuality and subversion and addresses only the confirmation and the law. As the work of Hemingway makes clear, masochistic artists can subvert certain patriarchal values, while upholding others. To see masochism one-dimensionally, solely as a tool of power, conforms it to a narrow political concept, missing its many nuances.

Even if we accept that Hemingway's gender politics leave much to be desired, he cannot be identified as the type of Machiavellian player that Mansfield imagines. Hemingway's embodiment of masochism was unacknowledged and may have operated at a subliminal level in much of his work, even if not in his personal life. And while he may have been aware of the contradiction between his sexual desire and his social views, Hemingway's attitudes were shaped by a variety of forces that have little to do with a subtle attempt to use masochism as a kind of smokescreen to disguise his more traditional values.

Masochism in Mansfield's view reveals itself as a reactionary social force. Mansfield's analysis inflates the "power" of masochism to an impossible degree. Masochism, it must be remembered, remains in essence a sexual practice, albeit one informed by powerful psychological forces. It cannot be reduced to a political philosophy. While claiming that "[m]asochism does not present itself as a high serious, philosophical address to the world, and should not have such expectations forced upon it" (16), Mansfield nevertheless attaches an excessive and misplaced ideological importance to it.

A more extreme argument in this direction occurs in David Savran's *Taking It Like a Man* (1998), in which he argues, following one thread of Freud's theory, that male masochism always builds upon a homosexual foundation, that the male masochist, in Freud's words, "evades his homosexuality by repressing and remodeling his unconscious fantasies."[41] Savran seems to agree that male masochists must necessarily be repressed homosexuals. Savran writes, "[m]asochism functions, in short, as a mode of cultural production that simultaneously reveals and conceals (through the mechanism of disavowal) the homoeroticism that undergirds patriarchy and male homosocial relations" (32). Savran accepts Freud's intuitive speculations involving the beating fantasy and finds that "the most significant component of the male fantasy . . . is its heterosexualization" (31). In this process, the masochistic subject substitutes the cruel mother for the punishing father and thereby "the fantasy, so heterosexualized, becomes tolerable for the subject" (31). This analysis represents a literal application of Freud's most unstable explication of masochism. Despite the wealth of material he presents, Savran scarcely discusses the classic masochism developed in *Venus in Furs*. Sacher-Masoch, for example, is only mentioned twice in this long book and Hemingway (in passing) only once. Instead, Savran draws on many examples from literature, theater, and cinema, but most of these do not relate to masochism as it has been classically represented but to Savran's own construction of it. Savran conforms these disparate elements to his overriding thesis, that contemporary white masculinity is informed by a masochistic sense of victimization and exhibits violently psychotic tendencies.

Similar to Mansfield's argument, Savran finds "that masochism functions as a kind of decoy and that the cultural texts constructing masochistic masculinities characteristically conclude with an almost magical restitution of phallic power" (37). Yet Hemingway's work consistently undermines the phallic signifier. Savran, whose agenda is ostensibly progressive, finds in male masochism a reactionary psychosis. He suggests that gay men and lesbians suffer from the supposed ascendancy of this chimerical, heterosexual, "reflexive" sadomasochistic construction (236). This view privileges the position of gay men and lesbians without giving any consideration to heterosexual male masochism, which has been likewise reviled, if not to the same extent, for at least a century. Both homosexuality and heterosexual male masochism have been labeled as "perversions," often for quite similar reasons. Savran's privileging of homosexuality needlessly results in the further stigmatization of heterosexual male masochism and his work implicitly undermines what should be common ground among gay men and masochistic heterosexual men in their common resistance to prevailing stereotypes of masculinity.

My argument for Hemingway's masochism focuses on sexual desires and practices rather than on ideological orientation. Hemingway's sense of alienation certainly differs in degree, if not in kind, from the sense of social victimization described by Savran. The analysis of the cultural texts of masochism for political ramifications employed by Stewart, Mansfield, and Savran in one direction and Silverman, Studlar, and Siegel in another has limitations in its application to Hemingway. While it cannot be denied that Hemingway held phallocentric views, a causal relation between these views and his masochism does not convincingly emerge. However, Stewart's analysis of heterosexual male masochism may come closest to defining some of the conflicts between Hemingway's desire and his ideology. Part of Stewart's thesis, that male masochism grants woman a pyrrhic victory of the will, conforms to the mode of Hemingway's art. He creates his dominant women to satisfy his desire but leaves all significant social action to his men. However, while Stewart's analysis may apply in some respects to Hemingway as an individual artist, it fails to credit masochism in general for its approach to a significant exchange of sexual power.

The very different interpretations of Siegel, Silverman, and other progressive theorists capture the diverse spirit of masochism including much that surfaces in Hemingway's work. But an attempt to apply these authors' theoretical models to Hemingway proves difficult or incomplete because he remains such a mercurial entity. However, on the basis of the explorations by Siegel, Mansfield, Studlar, Savran, Stewart, and Silverman, two varieties of "libidinally-political" heterosexual male masochism can be identified: one socially progressive, and the other socially conservative. The former works to create figures such as Wilde's *Salome* and Swinburne's "Dolores," who display independent wills. The latter invents characters like Wanda in *Venus in Furs* and Catherine in *The Garden of Eden*, whose will ultimately remains subordinate to the men who create them. However, both Hemingway and Sacher-Masoch have impressive progressive credentials: Hemingway's service to the Loyalist cause in the Spanish Civil War, and Sacher-Masoch's support of revolutionary movements in nineteenth-century Europe. Yet, if their masochism must be judged politically, it remains socially conservative in the matter of larger gender relations, despite the nonphallic erotic content of their work. However, Mansfield's view of masochism as a sort of Trojan horse in the war between the sexes strains credibility. While masochism may be clever—"a very intelligent perversion," says Phillips (2)—it remains essentially apolitical. As Frost correctly notes, "claiming male masochism as a 'revolutionary' feminist technique seems as erroneous as dismissing it as surreptitious misogyny" (242).

While conceding that some masochism may reveal itself as socially conservative if this judgment must be wrung from it, there can be little doubt that it represents an extremely nonaggressive male sexuality. If in the most negative view of heterosexual male masochism, the submissive man remains in power, the dominant woman at least shares this power. To see the conscious surrender of power by the masochist to the woman as an empty gesture in its totality, misunderstands the rationale of masochism. The socially conservative nature of that masochism that works at the expense of the suspension of woman's desire finds recognition in Siegel's comments on Deleuze's "vision of the masochistic puppet master and his doll-like torturer" (111). Hemingway's work contains no such explicit and ritualized masochistic scenarios. Yet the characterization of male masochism in Hemingway's texts assumes more prominence as it exists against a backdrop of conflicting themes and emotions and for this reason has probably remained so lightly touched upon in evaluations of his work. Yet, Hemingway, in the agency of authorship, can be seen, if only subliminally, as the "puppet master" that Siegel refers to. He invests his women with extraordinary latitude only to draw them in when they threaten male authority. Hemingway negates the phallus in sexual relationships and clearly depicts this negation in his work. Yet, he retains a heavy investment in other elements of phallic authority.

CHAPTER 2

ELEMENTS OF MASOCHISM IN HEMINGWAY'S WORK

Hemingway's depictions of masochism, by turns subtle and dramatic, abound in his most important works. This chapter discusses the most salient features of masochism as recognized by commentators, both those within psychoanalysis and those who question many of its premises. Among these are fetishism, humiliation, suspense, the contract, and pain. Sodomy, while it is inherently masochistic, may not be common to all masochists. Yet it *was* important to Hemingway and is discussed below. But I would like to begin by touching upon another theme common but not exclusive to masochism that runs throughout Hemingway's fiction: the desire of the male and female lovers to merge their identities into one, an idea that radically questions theories of sexual difference. This desire for a symbiosis has become an important element in recent theorizations of masochism. Hemingway's preoccupation with this theme merits some exploration.

SYMBIOSIS AND THE RESISTANCE TO INDIVIDUATION

Many Hemingway scholars have noted the numerous attempts of his male and female lovers to blur their identities into each other's. In a perceptive essay Gajdusek (writing of *The Sun Also Rises*) states: "without the cross-over into the always dangerous territory of the other, and a moment of psychic integration with the other, without the daring and surrender of self that take place when *two become one*, there is no possible redemption" (emphasis in original 40). Gajdusek suggests that Hemingway knows deeply "the male way to heterosexual love is through recognition that the 'otherness' is part of oneself, and the supremely necessary male act is to dismember and eradicate . . . the fear of it" (40). Gajdusek sees this process as a necessary step toward individuation that takes place in Hemingway's characters and in most "successfully" socialized heterosexual males. The idea of individuation is important to psychoanalysis and has been treated at length by Freud, Jung, Lacan, and others. Yet, one can make a case that Hemingway's characters dwell so excessively upon the idea of symbiosis that they resist individuation and seek defiantly to remain within the protective sphere of the Other.

In her cinematic study, Studlar remarks that, "[s]eparation is required by masochism's structure of desire, a desire that seeks to overcome individuation and restore symbiosis but cannot tolerate the danger of closing the gap" (180). She refers to "the fundamental human conflict of symbiosis/separation" and finds it at work in the films she discusses and in masochism in general (193). This view approximates Jacques Lacan's "myth of the lamella," which he adapts from Plato's *Symposium*.[1] In the *Symposium*, Aristophanes states:

> The sexes were not two as they are now, but originally three in number; there was man, woman, and the union of the two, having a name corresponding to this double nature, which had once a real existence, but is now lost, and the word "Androgynous" is only preserved as a term of reproach.[2]

Human beings who were of box sexes, according to the story, were proud and content but also so terrible that the gods feared them and so split them in two. Humanity was so unhappy at this disunion that life became a constant effort to re-achieve a unity with the self. The idea behind this myth is the basis of much of psychoanalysis. According to Lacan, "the search by the subject [is not] of the sexual complement, but of the part of himself, lost forever, that is constituted by the fact that he is only a sexed living being" (205). The striving for such symbiosis is a rebellion against the individual "sexed living being," the idea of sexual difference. This pursuit of the forever elusive union with the self is conducted through sexuality. In Freud (and Lacan) this sought-after unity has affinities with the desire to be one with the mother, to return to a pre-birth state, or even the desire for a sibling. To complement the story of Aristophanes related by Lacan, Eby finds a possible source of incestuous desire in an alternative take on the myth of Narcissus offered by Pausanias in the second century (170). According to his view, Narcissus was not in love so much with himself as with his sister. Upon her death, he saw her image in his own reflection in the water and in this he recognized that "part of himself," which he thought was "lost forever" in Lacan's words. Eby writes that this "would have sounded remarkably familiar to Hemingway" (170).

This desire for symbiosis contains elements of narcissism and the seeking of the subject's self in another, or a yearning to be at the breast or in a pre-birth stage. Individuals may attempt to satisfy this desire by many different means including masochism. The important point is that the goal of the drive is a union with a part of the self. This ideal union can be approximated through a desire for the pre-Oedipal "oral mother" as Deleuze contends. Or it can also take the form of a desire for a sibling. In the case of Hemingway, his aversion toward his mother precludes a conscious desire for her. Yet this aversion does not extend to his sisters with whom he was close. Hemingway's lovers often demonstrate a propensity to treat each other almost as brother and sister, or to attempt to merge their dual identities into one. This provides an example of the "symbiosis/separation" that Studlar describes. Such desire for this symbiosis/separation characterizes masochism. Of this desire, Smirnoff states: "The symbiotic relation, as found in masochism, makes use of suffering, pain, and humiliation, not in order to obtain pleasure, but as a symbolic representative of both the unattainable fusion with [and] the impossible separation from the primary sexual object" (72). Hemingway's lovers consistently seek this "unattainable fusion."

Many of Hemingway's depictions of sexual relationships between men and women demonstrate the couple's desire to merge identities: to "both be alike" (AFTA 299); "brother and sister" (FWTBT 67); "can't tell who is who" (GOE 17); or "Couldn't I be you?" and "I'm you now" (ARIT 146). In the early story "Soldier's Home," young Helen says to her older brother Harold, "Couldn't your brother really be your beau just because he's your brother?"[3] The posthumously published, "The Last Good Country," which Lynn calls a "filial love story" (57) centers on the travels of a young Nick Adams and his sister, Littless, who run away from home together. Littless cuts her hair short to match her brother's and at one point, "sat on his lap and held her arms around his neck and rubbed her cropped head against his cheek" while telling him an imaginary story about being a "whore's assistant."[4] After too much of this kind of talk, Nick tells her, "Get off my lap," (532) because as Lynn suggests, "he gets an erection" (57). Such explicit incestuous desire for a sibling indicates that although Hemingway wished to disavow the mother, he did not feel an alienation from the totality of the female sex. Hemingway's potential lovers in *A Farewell to Arms, For Whom the Bell Tolls, Across the River, The Garden of Eden,* and other works express the wish to merge identities as an approximation of such a pre-Oedipal symbiosis.

Lacan stresses "the essential affinity of every drive with the zone of death" (199). These pre-Oedipal desires can never be fulfilled in life. They seek an idealized possibility in death and represent *Thanatos*, the Death Instinct. Of masochism's flirtation with death, Studlar writes:

> In choosing death, an ambiguous, even illusory triumph is created, especially in masochism, where desire is secretly ruled by the infantile fixation. Death provides a victory over the limitations of repressive reality and the promise of a transcendence of socially bound identity. It offers the only possible liberation from the repetition of desire. (84)

Masochism's relationship with the Death Instinct finds expression in Phillips's comment that in masochism, "one gets a foretaste of mortality" (154). Studlar asserts that "masochism's obsession with death may be interpreted either as the expression of a universal urge or as the result of the masochistic wish for complete symbiosis with the mother and a return to nothingness" (123). Because the masochist does not, in reality, seek death, the apprehension of the object of desire can only be accomplished through some degree of fantasy.

In an alternative ending in the manuscript of *The Garden of Eden*, discussed by Robert E. Fleming, David and Catherine Bourne contemplate a suicide pact in an effort to affect a permanent symbiosis.[5] Catherine looks back with regret and says to David, "Remember when I used to talk about anything and everything and we owned the world? . . . All we had to do was see it and we owned it."[6] She is chastened now after her breakdown and confinement at an asylum in Switzerland. "If it goes bad again," she continues, "so I'd have to go back to the place, can I, may I do it the way Barbara did?"[7] Catherine is referring to the suicide by drowning of Barbara Sheldon after the death of her husband Nick in the same novel. She asks David, "Would you do it with me?" And he says, "Sure."[8] As Sacher-Masoch writes: "Nothing comes easier or more naturally to lovers than mutual suicide."[9] Eby finds that the provisional ending of *The Garden of Eden* "holds out the possibility of merger in mutual obliteration" and "acknowledges the fundamental loss masked by the fetish" (258). Dying together represents a fantasy of overcoming the separation and achieving a symbiosis and reunion.

FETISHISM

Another method of seeking what Smirnoff calls the "unattainable fusion with . . . the primary sexual object" (72) is through the fetish.

Studlar remarks that "children, regardless of sex, use *transitional objects* to ease the separation from the mother" (emphasis in original 40). According to some researchers and theorists, the fetish provides the tangible and very physical link between the child and the idealized mother and allows at least an illusory sense of reunion that can be realized through the agency of fantasy. Eby exhaustively explores the many manifestations of *Hemingway's Fetishism* and any attempt to add to his discussion presents a daunting task. The following brief notes build upon his work and hopefully complement it, even if occasionally disagreeing.

Deleuze writes that "there can be no masochism without fetishism in the primary sense" (32). Deleuze indicates Freud's view of the fetish that at the sight of the female genitals, the male believes the female has been castrated and finds comfort in "the image or substitute of the female phallus" (31). Studlar quotes Freud's assertion that the fetish itself "saves the fetishist from becoming a homosexual by endowing women with the characteristics which makes them tolerable as sexual objects" (209). Here again, Freud seems to assert that the masochist or fetishist does not realize that he actually is, or should be (or would be without psychoanalysis at any rate), homosexual. Psychoanalysis finds that the fetish, as an Oedipal phenomenon, allows the individuation and socialization of potentially dysfunctional males. Studlar again quotes Freud who wrote "the fetish is a penis-substitute for the missing penis of the mother and hence a means of defense against castration anxiety—and nothing else" (40). While not agreeing entirely with Freud's proposition, Deleuze nevertheless continues by identifying several characteristics:

> Fetishism is first of all a disavowal ("No, the woman does not lack a penis"); secondly it is a defensive neutralization [as opposed to a negation] . . . in the third place it is a protective and idealizing neutralization (for the belief in the female phallus is itself experienced as a protest of the ideal against the real; it remains suspended or neutralized in the ideal, the better to shield itself against the painful awareness of reality). (31–32)

Eby's compelling psychoanalytical portrait of Hemingway accepts the Freudian view of the fetish as the substitute for the mother's imagined penis. Yet Eby also states that the fetishist "disavows not only the penis-less state of women, he disavows sexual difference itself," (171) which represents a considerable broadening of Freud's more narrow approach to the fetish as "a defense against castration—and nothing else."

Anthony Storrs calls fetishism, not a perversion, but "a triumph of human imagination."[10] This imagining or "memory" of the female phallus forms the basis of Freudian explanations of fetishism.

Theories of masochism are divided on the issue of the female phallus. According to Deleuze, the imagining that goes into masochism ascribes a phallic authority to women that finds symbolic representation in the fetish. Silverman and Studlar appear to disagree though for different reasons. Silverman claims that "the castration which is synonymous with sexual difference is not endemic to the female body" and calls attention to "projection" by which "female subjectivity represents the site at which the male subject deposits his lack" (60). Other scholars discussed by Studlar dispute that the fetish must constitute solely the restoration of an imagined female "lack" and hold that if "the male child wants to be united with the first object of oral gratification and erotic stimulation as well as have the breast (and perhaps the womb) himself, then fetishization of the female reflects the child's disavowal of lack in relation to the mother" (41).[11] Paraphrasing some of these theories, Studlar, in agreement with Eby's comment above, notes that the fetish represents "the child's own wish to become both sexes" (40). Such a desire is incompatible with the revulsion and fear that, according to Freud, all males feel upon first viewing the female genitals. Studlar quotes John Ellis's point that pornography, with its "massive dissemination of images of female genitals," refutes Freud's view of "the fright of castration which probably no male human being is spared" at the sight of a naked woman (39). Studlar also quotes Erik Ericson's view that "it does not seem reasonable to assume that observation and empathy," qualities so well developed in Hemingway, "would so exclusively focus on what is not there" (39). Studlar remarks that "Freud failed to adequately acknowledge or investigate the role of the mother as an active, independent, powerful, and even threatening figure" (15). Deleuze and Silverman appear to accept the basic Freudian concepts even while revising them, while Studlar seeks to remove the idea of "castration anxiety" and a corresponding "penis envy" from the formulae of fetishism. In all three cases, they seek to expand upon the theory of the fetish and its importance.

Hemingway exhibits many fetishes, among them his near obsession with hair-cutting and salons, which lead inexorably to sexual adventures. Smirnoff remarks that "[t]he close relationship between fetishism and masochism has so far not been sufficiently explored" and adds that the idealized woman "is actually taking the place of the fetish" (70). In Hemingway, as Eby points out "*The hair is itself a symbolic 'female phallus,' and all of Hemingway's fetishized women are phallic women*" (emphasis in original 43). Often, but not always, Hemingway's women characters have short hair or talk about having it cut short. Brett Ashley in *The Sun Also Rises* exhibits "hair brushed back like a boy's" (22). When Marie Morgan in *To Have and Have Not* (1937), who sports a short coif, suggests that she may let her hair grow out, Harry tells her to "keep it like it is" (116).[12] Maria has a cropped haircut in *For Whom the Bell Tolls*, as do many women in the short stories. Catherine Barkley in *A Farewell to Arms* talks about cutting her hair short and Catherine Bourne, in *The Garden of Eden*, cuts hers very short. In contrast, Renata in *Across the River* has long flowing tresses that appeal no less to the colonel than do the short hairstyles of Brett to Jake or Catherine to David Bourne. Barbara and Janet, in the deleted sections of *The Garden of Eden* and *Islands in the Stream*, also have long, shoulder-length hair and they make over their men in their own image.

Hair, for Hemingway, serves as a gateway to transgressive sexuality. The Bournes' matching short haircuts along with their nude sun-bathing appear as part of an overall effort to transform their appearance, to sculpt their bodies to become almost interchangeable along the lines suggested by a sculpture by Rodin. Spilka and Burwell[13] discuss the importance of Rodin's statue, "based on Ovid's *Metamorphoses* and Baudelaire's *Les Fleurs du Mal*," that impressed the Bournes so greatly in a passage deleted from the published version of *The Garden of Eden* (Spilka 285). The statue depicts two naked women kissing and embracing and seeming to merge into one androgynous form. In bed together, Catherine reminds David of the Rodin statue and asks, "Are you changing like the sculpture?"[14] This deleted dialogue occurs immediately before Catherine sodomizes David for the first time, which corresponds to page 17 of the published novel. Hemingway depicts both Catherine and David as endeavoring to merge and each to become "both sexes."

Hemingway indulged his passion for hair by becoming an amateur coiffeur himself, cutting and dying the hair of his fourth wife, Mary. Eby makes the point that in the years following World War II, this passion became a compulsion and that Hemingway worked obses-sively, cutting and coloring not only Mary's hair but his own (201–203). He left behind a record of this in unpublished letters to Mary, in one of which he writes, "If a girl has a right to make her hair red I have—I've fought enough fights so no one can say anything to me. . . . So I will be a red-headed kitten when I see you."[15] And only with difficulty was Mary able to dissuade her husband from having his ear pierced and wearing an earring. Eby sees this as part of "Hemingway's transvestic impulses" (212). Though he is careful to say that he cannot imagine "Hemingway posing in front of the mirror, wearing lipstick, high heels, and an evening gown," Eby also "suspect[s] Hemingway occasionally imagined" such a "transvestic self-image" (212). While cross-dressing is not inherently masochistic, it has become a staple in many masochistic fantasies as "forced feminization."[16] Eby does not relate Hemingway's fetishism to masochism. Although no evidence exists to support the contention that Hemingway was an occasional transvestite, if as Eby suggests, he crossed-dressed in his imagination, this fits into the masochistic ensemble. And Hemingway, no doubt, had memories of his childhood when he was forced by his mother to wear little girls' outfits and this must have recurred to him painfully over the years. This may, indeed, be one of the reasons that he did not cross-dress even if part of him subconsciously wished to.

Another instance of fetishism—the amputee—occurs not only in *The Sun Also Rises* but also in a bedroom scene in *To Have and Have Not*. Harry has lost an arm in a gun battle. In bed with Marie, she tells him, "Go ahead. Go ahead now. Put the stump there. Hold it there. Hold it. Hold it now. Hold it" (114). Though not indicated in the text, the location of "there" can be surmised even without exclamation points which Hemingway disdains. In addition to Harry's missing arm, ruined limbs characterize Colonel Cantwell and, of course, Jake Barnes. Of the women these three characters love, Eby suggests, "the erotic attraction to amputees, seen in Renata, Marie Morgan, or Brett Ashley, is a classic sign of penis-envy" (56). The physical liabilities of Cantwell, Harry Morgan, and Jake serve better to illustrate Silverman's point that "the male subject, like his female counterpart, might learn to live with lack" (65). These characters embody lack as a permanent condition of their subjectivity. Rather than Renata, Marie, and Brett entertaining penis-envy, it seems more likely that Cantwell, Harry, and Jake wish to endow their lovers with the phallus. These Hemingway's heroes divest themselves of a phallic sexual agency and transfer it to their wives or girlfriends. Their women accept this agency as a gift, a masochistic tribute, rather than necessarily desiring it in the first place.

Toni Morrison sees the obsessive suntanning of the characters in *The Garden of Eden* as the "fetishizing of color."[17] She sees the efforts of David and Catherine to darken themselves as an example of "Africanization," a theme that her essay develops at length and that is discussed in Chapter 6. Fetishism also presents itself in *The Garden of Eden* when Marita leaves her martini behind at the bar and David "raise[s] it to his lips and found as it touched his lips that it gave him pleasure because it was hers" (127). Evidence of fetishism occurs in *A Farewell to Arms* in the hospital when Catherine Barkley penetrates Frederic's anus, as she administers an enema to him, which they both clearly enjoy. "There, darling," she says, "Now you're clean inside and out" (104). In case the reader has missed this, Frederic, as narrator, repeats on the next page, "I was clean inside and outside and waiting for the doctor" (105). The enema as fetish represents another common feature of masochism.

Another type of fetish appears in *A Farewell to Arms* in the description of Catherine in what seems almost a dominatrix outfit. She wears "hobnailed boots and a cape and carried a stick with a sharp steel point" (302)—a dream-image for a heterosexual male masochist seeking female domination. In Frederic's first meeting with Catherine, she carries a curiously fetishistic accessory. Frederic describes her appearance: "Miss Barkley was quite tall. She wore what seemed to be a nurse's uniform, was blonde and had a tawny skin and gray eyes. I thought she was very beautiful. She was carrying a thin rattan stick like a toy riding-crop, bound in leather" (18). This description of Catherine Barkley in her nurse's outfit holding a riding crop could fit a professional dominatrix in certain scenarios. It is impossible to know if Hemingway deliberately tries to evoke such an aesthetic image here but, whether intentionally or not, he clearly does so.

A pictorial representation of the beloved constitutes a ubiquitous fetish for the masochist. In the opening chapter of *Venus in Furs*, Severin's friend, the narrator, holds a long conversation with a marble statue of Venus. Lisa S. Starks, commenting on the masochistic aesthetic in Shakespeare's *Antony and Cleopatra*, writes of its "emphasis on the frozen scene of artistic contemplation."[18] Starks finds an instance of this "frozen scene' in the famous description by Enobarbus of Cleopatra on her barge. In a passage in *The Sun Also Rises*, Brett Ashley assumes center stage in a similar *tableau vivant*. The scene takes place during the fiesta in Pamplona before the running of the bulls. The local Spaniards, joined by tourists, revel in the street as Jake relates: "Some dancers formed a circle around Brett and started to dance. . . . Brett wanted to dance but they did not want her to. They wanted her as an image to dance around" (155). The crowd transforms Brett into a virtual statue and continues to revel with pagan abandon. This conjures up the image of woman as sacred and immobile, a representation of a goddess with the power to nurture or destroy. Deleuze finds that for the masochist, "women become exciting when they are indistinguishable from cold statues in the moonlight or paintings in darkened rooms" (69). Studlar echoes this point when she writes, "painting and statues, like masks and dolls, exemplify the iconic suspension of spatial and temporal laws, the delay of gratification, and masochistic contemplation in the art model" (153).

On a cold morning in Venice in *Across the River*, Colonel Cantwell asks Renata to pose: "Turn your hair sideways on top of this bridge and let it blow obliquely" (187), and as she assumes this position the colonel simply admires her impervious, statue-like radiance.[19] The colonel gazes helplessly upon the frozen beauty of his beloved. Later, Renata presents a portrait of herself to the colonel, her description of which—"I look as though I were rising from the sea without the head wet" (93)—recalls Botticelli's *The Birth of Venus*. The gift overwhelms the colonel and leads him to tell her, "I love you very much. You and you portrayed on canvas" (137). He props up the portrait in his hotel room and spends much of chapters XV–XVIII in conversation with this pictorial stand-in for Renata. Just as the narrator of *Venus in Furs* converses with the statue, Cantwell addresses the portrait: "I wish your mistress was here and we could have movement" (166). Earlier he suggests: "Portrait, keep your God-damn chin up so you can break my heart easier," but regrets his mild profanity and, "felt shame for having talked to the portrait roughly" (160–161). Apparently offended, " 'The hell with you,' the portrait said, without speaking, 'You low class soldier' " (161). Insults and verbal humiliation provide essential components of the masochistic encounter. Here, the colonel puts the deprecating words in the mouth of the portrait, further investing his masochism with fetishism. The colonel allows himself the luxury of such suspense in his time alone with the portrait. When he next meets Renata he freely confesses, "Last night, and at first light, I talked to the portrait as though it were you" (193). These chapters demonstrate an extreme form of devotion to a female subject by the notoriously macho Hemingway and highlight another aspect of a devotion already apparent in Jake Barnes and Frederic Henry.

HUMILIATION

Eby comments on the role of humiliation in the manuscript of *The Garden of Eden*. Referring to the unconventional hairstyles of Nick Sheldon and David Bourne, which they sometimes feel obliged to hide, Eby writes that the "very fact that the male protagonist needs to be coerced into wearing the fetish implies a reluctance on his part that is inseparable from an element of humiliation," and asks, "how, then, is humiliation related to the preservation of masculinity and how can humiliation excite?" (258). Eby answers his question in the following paragraph by citing a case history involving verbal humiliation and cross-dressing, without however, calling it masochism. Humiliation is as important to masochism as the ritualized suffering at the hands of the dominant woman.

Several similarities between *Venus in Furs* and *The Sun Also Rises* reveal themselves in the humiliation of the masochistic subject. Jake Barnes's near physical castration by a war injury and his psychic emasculation by Brett demonstrate acute examples of suffering. Brett's public affair with the young bullfighter receives Jake's humiliating acquiescence. She tells the adoring Jake: "I'm mad about the Romero boy. I'm in love with him I think" (182). Similarly, in *Venus in Furs*, when Wanda first lays eyes on the Greek she instructs Severin to "find out immediately about the man we saw. . . . Oh, what a man!"[20] At Brett's insistence, Jake helps arrange her love affair with Romero. She tells Jake, "Oh, darling, please stay by. Please stay by me and see me through this" (184). Brett and Jake sit at a table in the café watching the bullfighters and their entourage at another table. Brett gives Jake his orders: "Ask him to come over to have a drink" (184). This reprises the scene in *Venus in Furs* in which Wanda, arranging a rendezvous with another suitor, orders the adoring Severin to "Take this letter to Prince Corsini" (226). Reflecting on her cruelty, Brett muses, "I've always done just what I wanted," and "I do feel such a bitch" (184). Jake does as he is told and introduces her to Romero and even translates for the bullfighter when his imperfect English fails him. Brett then dismisses Jake and he leaves the café as "[t]he hard-eyed people at the bull-fighter table watched me go. It was not pleasant" (187). Twenty minutes later, Jake returns to the scene of his public humiliation and finds Brett and Romero gone.

The rival for the affections of the superior woman represents, according to Deleuze, "the hope of a rebirth of the new man that will result from the masochistic experience" (66). In *Venus in Furs*, this role falls to the character of the Greek because "when he is idealized he foreshadows the outcome of masochism and stands in for the new man" (66). In *The Sun Also Rises*, Romero provides this same model. Spilka, in an early essay, rightly sees Romero as one of "the few remaining images of independent manhood" to whom Jake attempts to measure up.[21] The humiliation of the subject in both *Venus in Furs* and *The Sun Also Rises* serves a higher purpose than degradation for its own sake. In both cases, it leads potentially to a renewed masculine awareness.

In the fantasy of *Venus in Furs*, Severin's final outrage at being whipped by the Greek with Wanda's encouragement leads him to reject his masochism, though many critics find a lack of sincerity in Sacher-Masoch's supposed "cure," including Smirnoff who calls the wish for such a cure an "absurd claim coming from a masochist" (66). Jake Barnes, on the contrary, does not disavow his masochism (or his pessimism) at the end of *The Sun Also Rises*. His masochism remains compatible with the "rebirth of the new man" that Deleuze describes (66). Through his suffering Jake achieves a rebirth of sorts as he rescues Brett Ashley and when she remarks on the "damned good time" they could have had, he replies, "Yes. . . . Isn't it pretty to think so?"—implying, perhaps, a willingness to continue with her and endure more suffering if she wills it (247). Hemingway actually wrote a few pages of a sequel to *The Sun Also Rises* in which both Jake and Brett appear, lending credence to the belief that the ending of the novel suggests possibilities for a renewal between them.[22]

Brett's attitude toward Jake differs markedly from the pity or contempt one might expect from a woman who has cuckolded her man. Brett is so assured of her dominance over Jake (and many of the other male characters) that she does not need to pity him. For she loves him and tells him, "I simply turn all to jelly when you touch me" (26). She is well aware of what he suffers for her throughout the novel. Jake's sexual lack is difficult for Brett to bear and she refers to her love for him as a "hell on earth" (27) because of her frustration over his physical condition. But as a woman with sexual needs she seeks satisfaction from others. Despite Jake's lack and his masochistic devotion to her, Brett both respects him and relies on him. He is the only man in the novel who she can trust. In this sense, Jake has become a new man by transcending his suffering and emerging cleansed and renewed through his masochistic relationship with Brett.

Earlier in the novel, when Jake asks Brett to live with him, she replies, "I don't think so. I'd just *tromper* you with everybody. You couldn't stand it" (55). Jake assures her that he could because "I stand it now" (55). As we have seen, the despotic woman who takes on other lovers in the presence of the worshipping masochist forms an essential part of the literary fantasy in *Venus in Furs*. Jake acknowledges his humiliation and accepts it, just as Severin does. Jake, as narrator and Hemingway's presence in the text, exhibits a superior attitude toward another lovesick admirer of Lady Ashley, Robert Cohn, who "follow(s) Brett around like a poor bloody steer" (142). This characterization follows a conversation describing steers as the hapless victims of the bulls in the *corrida*. Cohn refers to Brett as Circe "who turns men into swine" (144) and feels she is a "sadist." But Mike Campbell taunts Cohn and corrects him by saying, "Brett's not a sadist" (166) and indeed she is not for as we have seen, the dominant woman of masochism cannot be truly sadistic. Throughout the novel Brett's triumphs over men do not come about through sadistic impulses but rather through an overabundance of empathy and attempts, however misguided, at communion. Brett's humiliation of Cohn earns him Jake's contempt because Cohn cannot accept the suffering she metes out to him, unlike the masochistic Jake who wallows in it.

Suspense

Deleuze writes that "[w]aiting and suspense are essential characteristics of masochism" (70). He and others have remarked on the absence of an aggressive masculine impulse in masochism in favor of a deferred gratification heightened by suspense. This suspense works in two ways. First: the application and withdrawal of painful stimuli (which to the masochist is pleasurable) heightens the sense of anticipation and tension. The regular or irregular pauses that punctuate the lashes of the whip or the strokes of the cane would be one example of this suspense. The masochist waits for the punishment he is sure will come but the uncertainty of the timing gives rise to suspense. The other form of suspense occurs in the deferral of sexual gratification that, ironically, produces pleasure. We have seen this quality at work in the suspension of gratification that characterizes Colonel Cantwell's night in the hotel with only the fetish of Renata's portrait for company.

According to Studlar, "Masochistic pleasure does not reside exclusively in the whip or the kiss but also in the suspenseful anticipation of bringing the fantasy to life" (24). The deferral of male sexual gratification characterizes masochistic literature. Certainly, Jake Barnes suffers from this suspension of sexual satisfaction throughout *The Sun Also Rises*. He spends most of the novel in a state of suspended, deferred gratification, all the while longing for Brett and displaying a willingness to accompany her anywhere and even to introduce her to other men so long as he can remain in her presence. In *For Whom the Bell Tolls*, when Maria apologizes to Robert for being unable to have intercourse due to her pain, she proposes alternatives. Robert declines her offer, choosing to remain in suspense, to defer gratification, thinking, "I'll need all of that there is tomorrow" (369), implying a sublimation of his sexual energy into the heroic actions he must undertake the next day. Robert refuses to seek sexual release without satisfying Maria. His refusal of Maria's offer of some alternative sexual favor occurs shortly before he lapses into "a voluptuousness of surrender into unreality that was like a sexual acceptance of something . . . only the delight of acceptance" (370). Robert here, despite his disappointment, demonstrates that, in Studlar's words, "pleasure is taken in desire unfulfilled" (126). Siegel refers to this as "eroticized sexual frustration" (33). This escape into an unreality, an imagining, forms a crucial element in the masochistic aesthetic discussed by Studlar and Deleuze. Studlar remarks: "Stillness within movement creates a mystical suspension of time reflecting the ultimate masochistic entrapment of infantile fixation" (129). We have seen how, in *Across the River*, Renata controls the movements of the colonel, telling him when to move and when to keep still. He willingly submits to her commands and her entrapment of him in their erotic encounter in the gondola (141–147) and as Michael Reynolds notes, "Cantwell brings the young girl to a sexual climax" (216). Brenner suggests that the colonel "manually induced her [Renata's] orgasm" (161) although the text is unclear about the details.

In a perceptive reading of *Across the River*, John Paul Russo argues that in this scene, Renata "experience[s] three orgasms to Cantwell's none" (166). Russo, like Brenner (161), identifies the first orgasm at the point in which the narrator remarks that "the great bird had flown out of the closed window" (ARIT 144), which is not the first time that Hemingway has used a similar phrase as metaphor for sexual climax.[23] After this, while the colonel is eager to gratify Renata again she tells him: "But it is too soon now. Don't you know how a woman feels?" When *she* is ready, after the colonel pours her a drink, Renata asks/orders him: "Let's do it again, please, now I am in the lee" (145). The colonel and Renata cover themselves for shelter and at the point of her orgasm, "the girl had shifted too, under the blanket, with the wind getting under the edge of the blanket; wildly" (145). Afterwards, exalting in her satisfaction while appropriating the colonel's military identity, Renata triumphantly declares, "I just took the city of Paris" (146). Renata suggests the third orgasm when she asks the colonel: "Do you think we could once more if it would not hurt you?" (147).[24] The colonel places Renata's pleasure before his own and neither insists upon, nor is he offered, any corresponding sexual release as he remains in a suspenseful anticipation, which is gratification in itself. Like many women in contemporary erotic masochistic literature, Renata confirms, in Russo's words, her "sexual terror" over the colonel (167). As Russo puts it: "Renata has satisfied her selfish desire: She has experienced three orgasms, avoided sexual penetration, and refused orgasm to her partner" (167). The colonel gratefully submits to this treatment just as in much masochistic fiction the dominant woman declines genital penetration and denies orgasm to the submissive man. In Renata and the colonel, Hemingway renders characters who embody several of the qualities of the dominatrix and her slave.

THE CONTRACT

The importance of the contract to masochism comes, like so much else, from *Venus in Furs.* Severin and Wanda sign a contract giving her virtual power of life and death over him. The contract, or at least a verbal agreement, forms an important part of many masochistic relationships according to some of its adherents. Whether a written or verbal contract characterizes all such relationships is open to question but enough comment on this point has been offered that it should not be ignored. In the form of the contract, according to Deleuze, "the masochist aims not to mitigate the law but on the contrary to emphasize its extreme severity" (91). The contract, he suggests, represents a means of usurping patriarchal authority from the father and transferring it to the mother. Deleuze adds, "The masochistic contract excludes the father and displaces onto the mother the task of exercising and applying paternal law" (93) and "leads straight into ritual" (94). In Hemingway's work, both the mother and father are excluded as he elevates other women as objects of respect and reverence.

Jeffrey Jerome Cohen argues that "contractual gender" had become standardized by the twelfth century when Chrétian's romance of Lancelot and Guinevere was written.[25] Cohen reads this tale through the paradigm of the masochistic contract. Masochism disrupts traditional gender relations by undermining the historical function of the contract. By doing so, according to Tania Modelski, "the entire system is exposed as a mockery."[26] Deleuze writes that in "the contractual relation the woman typically figures as an object in the patriarchal system" and the very notion of the contract "is thereby implicitly challenged, by excess of zeal, a humorous acceleration of the clauses and a complete reversal of the respective contractual state of man and woman" (92). According to Cohen's analysis:

> By foregrounding agency within the paradigm of power, contractual gender opens up the dangerous possibility that sexual relationships could be figured otherwise [than "essential" norms of masculine and feminine]; even more disturbing, when a gender relationship is based upon a reconfigurable contract, it denaturalizes "sex," "gender," and

the power relationships of all kinds invested in imbuing these terms with their cultural meanings.[27]

Cohen, like Deleuze, emphasizes the importance of the social history of the contract. The masochist usurps, subverts, and parodies the use of the contract that had become almost a secular sacrament in bourgeois ideology.

The contract's centrality in many masochistic relationships seems important because of the element of ritual it provides and the partners' potential enjoyment of the formal exchange of power. Masochism can, of course, exist without any contract simply by mutual agreement. Nowhere in Hemingway's work, of course, can we find anything as explicit as a masochistic contract. But in *The Garden of Eden*, Catherine's assurances of discretion to David represent both his consent to her appropriation of the phallus and their verbal contract to protect their secret. Catherine gives her word to David, "We won't let the night things come in the day" (22). Later she tells him more explicitly: "I will only be a boy at night and I won't embarrass you," and adds, "Don't worry about it please" (56). Clearly she means to reassure him that she loves him, that in the daytime he can still be the man, and that she will not compromise him either in front of others or in his own eyes, but that in the evenings he belongs to her will. Catherine's remarks here imply the kind of discretion that Hemingway would have demanded in his own marriages, and constitute a version of the masochistic contract.

Phillips describes the contract as "a private game, a psychosexual adventure, primitive and sophisticated at once, relying on trust, humour, acting ability and emotional elasticity" (25). Her remarks highlight the theatrical aspect of masochism and the contract constitutes one of its major props. Phillips also emphasizes the sense of humor. To see the contract as the actual surrender of all agency from one person to another would miss its point as a self-conscious "act" and its sense of what Phillips calls "daring playfulness" (25). Catherine in *The Garden of Eden* certainly exhibits this "daring playfulness" as she brings a reluctant David into her sexual schemes. It is only when she moves outside of the sexual realm that she becomes a threat and David abrogates the contract.

PAIN, VIOLENCE, DEATH, AND EMPATHY

In addition to fetishism, suspense, humiliation, and the contract, we have seen how bodily pain features prominently in most Hemingway texts. Aside from his wounded heroes, he writes with obvious relish about the suffering and death of everything from soldiers and civilians to horses and bulls. Edward Said calls *Death in the Afternoon*, for example, a "studious rendering of the mechanics of ritualized suffering."[28] Hemingway's vision of life as malevolent and hostile demands a degree of surrender to its violent torrents. This surrender must take place on both the physical and psychic planes as the wounded body meshes with the wounded soul. In the masochistic worldview, woman as the natural force inflicts these wounds and this suffering. In turn, the nurturing of women gives the man strength to face his inevitable physical and emotional suffering. Hemingway's fiction is replete with wounded masculinity. Nearly all the novels feature a man in pain as the hero and many of the short stories are built around this theme including "The Gambler, the Nun and the Radio," "In Another Country," "The Capital of the World," "A Natural History of the Dead," and many others. Often the wounds are psychological, as in "A Way You'll Never Be," "Soldier's Home," and "Homage to Switzerland." A willingness to surrender to pain, physical or psychic, dominates Hemingway's texts. The idea of surrender is pervasive and sensual even when not directly involving sexual activity. But the important element remains the notion of surrender.

Many wounded figures stalk through Hemingway's fiction. Many of these characters experience a keen sense of psychological alienation as well. Commenting on masochism in the work of Sacher-Masoch and Richard Wagner, Stewart writes "men were viewed as already wounded or fragmented, subjected and enslaved to modern civilization by their own desires, which, of necessity, remained unfulfilled" (13). Many Hemingway characters, quintessential expressions of the "lost generation," combine both physical pain and thwarted desires, and fit Stewart's description. In Hemingway's world, pain presents itself as inevitable and he embraces it in its many manifestations. These range from the physical wounding of his characters, the painful submission to sodomy that brings sexual pleasure, and the general physical and psychological submission to women who alternately discipline, degrade, and sustain the suffering male.

Although the physical wounds in Hemingway's fiction do not, of course, result from masochistic sexual activity, their preponderance, together with nonphallic sexuality and passive sodomy, convincingly demonstrate masochism. According to psychoanalysis, masochism first becomes apparent in infantile sexuality when desire for an incestuous relationship with the mother or the father is repressed. The child becomes aware of the sense of guilt in association with the incestuous desire. The parent metamorphoses into the punishing authority rather than the loving nurturer. The desire for the incestuous relationship becomes a desire for punishment by the father. As Dorothy Hayden points out, "The fantasy of being beaten becomes the meeting place between the sense of guilt and sexual love."[29] Hemingway exhibits the sense of guilt in much of his work. Deleuze, however, questions the overall accuracy of the Freudian Oedipal model and presents alternative routes to masochism insisting that the father must be "disavowed," not transformed into the punisher. Hemingway goes one better and disavows both the mother and the father. Though he does not express "the fantasy of being beaten," he hardly needs to, given the variety of physical suffering to which he subjects his characters.

Masochism nearly always involves the application of some degree of violence, usually not very severe, or at least the threat of it. In the light of some revisionist interpretations of Hemingway's work, his cult of masculine violence needs reemphasis. Violent activity foregrounds the action in *A Farewell to Arms*, *To Have and Have Not*, *For Whom the Bell Tolls*, and *Islands in the Stream*, and many short stories. The memory of past violence informs both *The Sun Also Rises* and *Across the River*. The violence of blood sports forms the objects of scrutiny in *Death in the Afternoon* and *Green Hills of Africa*. Virtually the entire Hemingway *oeuvre* is invested with violence and a malevolent vision of the world. A disturbing aspect of this preoccupation reveals itself in not only the act of violence but also with the results of such acts, that is, dead bodies. Much of Hemingway's writing, from the very earliest to the latest, dwells on observations of death. Much of this dying is done by the animal victims of blood sports but primarily Hemingway presents human death. This near obsession surfaces abruptly in the collection, *In Our Time*, the book that established Hemingway's reputation. In the introductory pages, "On the Quai at Smyrna" (added when Scribners republished the collection), Hemingway presents wartime images of dead civilians, women clutching dead babies, corpses floating in the harbor, and crippled mules abandoned in the water of the bay. As Jeffrey Meyers points out, this vignette conveys Hemingway's empathy with both the human and animal victims of cruelty (101). Images of death and serious injury proliferate in *In Our Time*: German soldiers get picked off as if in target practice; revolutionaries hang six cabinet ministers; cops shoot down Hungarian "wops"; bulls gore matadors and horses; a man commits suicide by slitting his throat with a razor; a punch-drunk boxer receives blows from a blackjack; five prisoners are hanged. Edmund Wilson, in his introduction to *In Our Time*, points to the focus of Hemingway's work as the exploration of "[s]uffering and making suffer, and their relation to the sensual enjoyment of life."[30] This reflects Studlar's comment that "characteristic of the masochistic scenario of desire is the participant-players' assumption of various ego or superego positions, their shift in power positions from inflicting to receiving pain" (52). The remarks of both Wilson and Studlar imply sadomasochism but the quality of empathy lifts Hemingway's work above true sadism. Wilson sees this as "always in the long run, a losing game" (xi), further suggesting a type of moral masochism. Hemingway adopted the code of the sportsman as the best method (vague as it is) to negotiate the world. Accepting the inherent hostility of the world, one could at least play by its rules and view the suffering of others with empathy since such suffering could easily fall upon oneself.

Moral masochism, defined by Freud as one mode of this "perversion," occurs due to an "unconscious sense of guilt" and becomes apparent when "[t]he suffering itself is important" regardless of who or what brings it about (XIX 165–166). This has some relation to the "self-defeating personality disorder" that modern psychiatry had substituted for the term "masochism." Silverman defines moral masochism as occurring, "when the ego begins to enjoy and indeed to provoke the super-ego's severity" (160). It seeks an expiation of guilt and exists in some individuals who wish to suffer violence and a martyrdom similar to that of Jesus Christ and other Christian saints. Starks maintains

> [T]he representation of spirituality in terms of physical and mental anguish does not preclude the erotic; indeed, it indicates its involvement in the erotic. Physical and mental torments lie at the heart of the erotic fantasies underlying Christian mysticism and, in varying degrees, the discourses of medieval and early modern Christianity, a belief system that revolves around the central sacrifice of Christ.[31]

Although Silverman distinguishes between its "moral" and "Christian" varieties (197), both can represent a kind of masochism with a cause. But rather than fixate moral masochism as a species distinct from the other masochisms of psychoanalysis, it seems more appropriate to view it as merely an element often present in masochism proper. Hemingway and his characters accept their many injuries as an integral part of human experience and the best of them suffer these wounds as stoically as Christian martyrs. As H.R. Stoneback argues in detail, Hemingway took his Catholicism much more seriously than most biographers acknowledge and his embrace of this religion was neither "nominal" nor "bogus."[32] And while Stoneback may overestimate these religious convictions, Hemingway appears to have had a great respect for the Church throughout his life even if he did not practice the religion very faithfully and heaped scorn upon some of its representatives.[33] The sensuality inherent in Hemingway's view of suffering as both morally and physically redemptive, does not contradict his self-identification as Catholic.

More than one driving force works in the desire of the masochist. Commentators have suggested that the early Christian flagellants may have gratified the libido while mortifying the flesh. Krafft-Ebing cites examples of cases of "the excesses of religious enthusiasm" (212, 237). Clearly, the highly developed moral sense typical of the purer forms of Christianity would present itself to the religious flagellant. A sophisticated sense of compassion and empathy would accompany this highly developed morality. As Christopher Newfield points out, Hawthorne provides an example of a religious flagellant in Reverend Dimmesdale in *The Scarlet Letter*.[34] Newfield maintains that Dimmesdale's masochism serves no larger social purpose other than to expiate his own guilt. Yet, the expiation of guilt combined with a larger social compassion can reveal themselves in empathy. A belief in the sense of a guilt shared by all of God's human creations is, of course, a cornerstone of Christian belief. Hemingway's fiction secularizes this essential Christian empathy. The bodies of his characters provide the site upon which the punishments of fallen humanity are visited. His preoccupation with the suffering of others represents not a sadistic voyeurism but a relatively pure empathy toward those in physical or psychological distress. This is most apparent, perhaps, in *For Whom the Bell Tolls*, as the victims of both fascist and loyalist violence are portrayed with empathy.

Further violence occurs in the famous scene of the retreat from Caporetto in *A Farewell to Arms* in which Frederic Henry narrowly escapes a firing squad. Hemingway shows compassion for the hapless Italian officers forced to pay with their lives for the incompetence of their superiors. *To Have and Have Not* features graphic civilian violence among the smugglers and Cuban exiles of Key West. *For Whom the Bell Tolls* takes place, literally, in an armed camp. In the posthumous *Islands in the Stream*, hero Thomas Hudson methodically removes bullets from badly decayed dead bodies, victims of a massacre that occurred over a week earlier (322–326). These victims have been exposed to the ravages of tropical heat and scavenging land crabs but Hudson does not flinch as he stoically completes his grim task. The same novel contains a seemingly gratuitous reference to the dismembered corpse of a woman found in a river bed (240). This incident does nothing to advance the plot of the novel and seems to provide nothing more than another excuse to depict a gruesome corpse. Indeed, many of the episodes in *Islands in the Stream* seem disconnected and it has generally been regarded as an artistic failure though recent criticism, especially the work of Burwell, has somewhat altered this view. Yet Hemingway knew, as publishers have long known, that random visitations of scenes of mayhem jolt the reader and rivet attention. What allows Hemingway's work to rise above the sensational in such scenes is his enduring quality of empathy.

The short story "A Natural History of the Dead," consists, in part, of a taxonomy of death in which Hemingway seems to indulge a juvenile urge to shock his readers. Hemingway saw significant action in a noncombatant position in World War I when he was still little more than an adolescent. He covered both the Spanish Civil War and World War II in the role of a supposedly unarmed journalist. (However, Hemingway continually went about armed to the alarm and dismay of his fellow journalists.) He personally witnessed death at close range. He and Martha Gellhorn spent time in China during the brutal Japanese occupation. Even before American troops were committed to World War II, Hemingway organized, and got government backing for, a dangerous if somewhat farcical submarine-hunting expedition in the Caribbean. Hemingway's portrayal of violence in nearly all of his work indicates almost a morbid interest in the death and dying he so often witnessed. He was wounded in World War I and suffered many physical injuries throughout his life, from gunshots to plane crashes. His literary expressions of extreme violence seem remote from the much more mild forms of violence usually associated with masochism. Yet the propensity to absorb violence as both observer and recipient marks the Hemingway code hero and this heroic quality is consistent with personal masochism. As Siegel states, "what is generally called heroism involves the conscious choice of suffering. To this extent all literature exists in reference to an intertext that connects masochism with a kind of idealized masculinity" (33). Hemingway, more than most authors, embodies this intertextuality as his characters willingly endure suffering and even certain death, as does Robert Jordan when he chivalrously sends Maria to safety in an act of individual heroism in *For Whom the Bell Tolls*. Robert's act presents itself as all the more unselfish as he places the security of Maria and his comrades above his own. Robert's heroism is not unrelated to his self-denial, his "pleasure taken in desire unfulfilled" (in Studlar's words) in his lovemaking with Maria. This sensual quality of his heroism does not diminish it.

At times, some of Hemingway's battered characters express pleasure in receiving their injuries. An unnamed alcoholic vet in *To Have and Have Not* confesses to the "secret" of how he can take so much punishment. "It don't hurt," he says, "Sometimes it feels good" (203). While this comment comes from a marginal but sympathetic character and not from a Hemingway hero, the expression of the correlation of pleasure with pain can be seen as a reflection of the author's feeling. Hemingway often spoke and wrote of his many injuries with obvious pride. The sensual pleasure in the endurance and toleration of this pain combined with both guilt and empathy are essential to masochism.

Few of Hemingway's leading characters provoke violence, though Harry Morgan in *To Have and Have Not* constitutes a notable exception. But neither do most of these characters shrink from violence, usually considering it a duty especially in war. This conforms to the long-standing Christian theory of the just war and with Victorian ideals of Muscular Christianity, though Hemingway, of course, secularizes these ideas. Hemingway's own personal acts of aggressive violence occurred during his hunting and fishing expeditions. His most serious violence toward human beings occurred in World War II, according to biographers, when some say he almost certainly killed some German soldiers in a couple of skirmishes in France (Meyers 400). More recently, William E. Coté questions the veracity of these accounts.[35] Hemingway's boastful letters with exaggerated kill counts, varying from 26 to 122, are regarded as unreliable (88). Coté concludes that "it is not clear that he killed anyone, or if he did, he did not kill twenty-six people, much less 122" (102). Coté also notes that even if Hemingway did not participate actively in killing human beings, he certainly at least observed it and suggests that this may account in part for his postwar depression and his psychological deterioration during the 1950s (103). Aside from these wartime incidents, most of Hemingway's violence took the form of modest fisticuffs with friends or rivals, some of which were given wide play in the press. In general, Hemingway's primary response to victims of violence, other than his own, appears as empathy. In all his writing about men at war and even in his accounts of his hunting experiences, the reader never encounters anything resembling true sadism in the Hemingway hero. The passage in *For Whom the Bell Tolls*, in which Pilar recounts the massacre of the "fascists," engineered by her amoral man, Pablo, contains such implicit empathy with the victims that when the novel was published Hemingway was criticized by communists and other volunteers who served in the International

Brigades. Even in his stories of hunting a concern, often receiving explicit statement, surfaces for the fate of a suffering animal. Abandoning a wounded animal to bleed to death, rather than pursuing it to administer a merciful kill shot, violates Hemingway's sportsman ethics. He advocates the same for humans in especially desperate circumstances in *For Whom the Bell Tolls* (162–163). Having suffered numerous wounds himself, he endows his characters with a tremendous capacity for pain. The avoidance of necessary pain represents cowardice. The acceptance of necessary pain represents courage, the primary virtue of the Hemingway code hero.

The many Hemingway heroes who suffer physical wounds highlight his masochistic vision. Frederic Henry receives shrapnel in his leg in *A Farewell to Arms*. Harry in "The Snows of Kilimanjaro" contracts gangrene. Harry Morgan has his arm shot off in *To Have and Have Not*. The dying Richard Cantwell, in *Across the River*, has both a bad leg and a bad hand. And in the most dramatic wound, Jake Barnes has lost a good portion of his genitals in *The Sun Also Rises*. In the same novel, Count Mippipoulous exhibits for Jake's admiration the arrow wounds he has received in "seven wars and four revolutions" (60). But in addition to wounds caused by violence, by the penetration of bullets and shrapnel, Hemingway's male heroes occasionally get penetrated in the bedroom as we shall see.

Chapter 3

Desire and Denial

Sodomy and Homophobia

Though sodomy can be variously defined as any of a number of different "unnatural acts," the sense in which the term is used here refers to anal penetration. Bersani's explorations of Freudian theory reveal a strong link between masochism and sodomy. Bersani's work suggests that the position of the passive partner in consensual sodomy is inherently masochistic and experienced as such. Submitting to sodomy can be both painful and accompanied by an aura of humiliation, what Bersani calls "a self-debasement."[1] Heterosexual sodomy with the man in the passive role forms an integral element in much contemporary erotic masochistic literature.

Hemingway's relentlessly expressed homophobia precludes him from entertaining the idea of submitting to sodomy from a man. D.H. Lawrence in *The Rainbow* and *Lady Chatterley's Lover* presents sodomy as appealing so long as it is performed by the man on the woman. In Lawrence's view sodomy on the man (on himself at least, despite some overt homosexual impulses) would represent a violation of the "phallic consciousness" and appear akin to blasphemy. Hemingway, for all his affirmation of male values and his hostility to homosexuality, does not present a phallic consciousness and he endorses sodomy on the male if performed by a female. Much of his work seems to dethrone the male phallus, as we have seen most dramatically in the character of Jake Barnes. And though he celebrates sodomy on the man, Hemingway remains consciously opposed to homosexuality. So often does Hemingway display this aversion that he sometimes seems to invent scenarios in which he can indulge his distaste for male homosexuals. This homophobia can be seen as a self-defense to deflect his own even more aberrant (to him) sexuality of masochism. Bersani calls homophobia, "the vicious expression of a more or less hidden fantasy of males participating, principally through anal sex, in what is presumed to be the terrifying phenomenon of female sexuality."[2] This may approximate Hemingway's route to homophobia. His awareness of his alternative sexuality led him to associate it with both female sexuality and with homosexuality and part of him shrank from this.

Sodomy cannot be designated as either specifically heterosexual or homosexual. Certainly it constitutes a common practice among many gay men but it can also appeal to lesbians and to both heterosexual men and women. According to a leading feminist publication, *The New Our Bodies, Our Selves*: "The anus can be stimulated with fingers, tongue, penis or any slender object. For many of us, it is a highly sexually sensitive area."[3] Of the broad appeal of sodomy across lines of sexual preference, lesbian writer Susie Bright, comments:

> [T]he popularity of anal sex has become outrageous. . . . particularly with men who want their female lover to fuck them in the ass. . . . of course for a man to say he likes anal sex—to be penetrated—well, socially the stigma is: he's saying that he's really not a man, that he's effeminate . . . most of the men who want to get fucked put out a very "masculine" facade—they're not the kind of person who walks into a room and you say to yourself "I know that man wants to get fucked in the ass!"[4]

That description can apply to Ernest Hemingway.

Sodomy from both male and female points of view is the subject of the essays in Jonathan Goldberg's *Reclaiming Sodom* (1994). Although gay perspectives (including Dorothy Allison's essay recounting lesbian experiences) predominate, Goldberg introduces the volume with a discussion of an example of female-on-male sodomy from the perspective of the woman who initiates the encounter. Referring to Foucault's reference to sodomy as "that utterly confused category" (101), Goldberg asserts that "the act of sodomy enables the productive confusions and rigorous questioning of a range of presumptions and conventions governing gender, sexuality and the relations of fantasy and acts."[5] One of these presumptions equates sodomy solely with male homosexuality. Columnist Tristan Taormino writes: "It's a falsehood that *all* gay men have anal sex, and it's equally mythic that gay men have more anal sex than straight people or lesbians."[6] Regarding a man's desire to be sodomized by a woman and a woman's desire to penetrate a male lover, Goldberg finds that "the possibility of desiring 'the same' has to do with the fact that men and women both have anuses, can locate their desires there (hence, the woman's fantasy about penetrating a man also lights on the anatomical place both genders share as sexual site)" (1). Goldberg's point, that anal sexuality demonstrates in a singular manner what men and women have in common, rather than what divides them, is one that merits further study. In this sense, we can see how men and women can attempt to approximate the common experience of nongenital sexuality that characterizes Hemingway's work, however elliptically. This reflects Moddelmog's comment on *The Sun Also Rises*: "The text asks us to suspect, and finally to critique, those systems of representation that are insufficient and hence disabling to efforts to comprehend the human body and its desires" (99–100). Hemingway's explorations of these desires form a compelling, if misunderstood, part of his work.

Despite the attraction of sodomy, Hemingway easily maintains his public claim to a manifestly heterosexual masculinity. Clearly, Hemingway's attraction to sodomy should not lead to the conclusion that he was homosexual, latent or otherwise, despite the efforts of some critics to impose such a gay, or almost-gay, sensibility upon him. When Moddelmog asserts that "homosexual desire was among the desires he felt and depicted," she is not so much making a case for Hemingway's homosexuality as questioning the validity of the hetero/ homo binary as the only viable index for organizing sexual desire (85). Whether Hemingway felt homosexual desire, as she and other critics have suggested, remains a point of debate. That he never, apparently, acted upon such desires is more substantiated by evidence. In any case, sodomy remains a polymorphous practice that transcends categories of sexual preference.

While male-on-female and male-on-male sodomy both have long literary traditions, novelists seldom portray female-on-male sodomy as the mode of sexual conduct between the characters in their fiction. Hemingway's overt use of such sodomy as the means of expression of the physical love between Catherine and David Bourne in *The Garden of Eden* remains remarkable because of this rarity. Because Deleuze's concern lies with the heterosexual, female dominant/male submissive scenario made famous by *Venus in Furs*, sodomy is unimportant to his thesis. Even though the master text of masochism does not explicitly discuss sodomy, Freud sees one characteristic of masochism in the desire of the man to "be copulated with" (XIX 277), and while we can reject his insistence that this desire is necessarily "feminine," it does point to a salient feature. Sodomy has come to occupy a prominent place in the erotic literature of hetero- as well as homosexual masochism. Jean Genet depicts male-on-male sodomy throughout his work. Lawrence, features male-on-female sodomy in *Lady Chatterley's Lover* and

The Rainbow. Joyce presents a rare instance of female-on-male sodomy in the form of fisting in *Ulysses* (440).[7] And Hemingway's depiction of the lovers in *The Garden of Eden*, although the mechanics remain unclear, undeniably includes female-on-male sodomy.

To further explore the nature of sodomy as an essential component of Hemingway's masochism, it is useful to look at Bersani's comments on sodomy and its relation to his view of a "self-shattering *jouissance*." Bersani's primary interest lies in gay male masochism but his argument has broader applications. In a review of Bersani's *Homos* (1995), Patrick Paul Garlinger suggests that, "The strict alignment of sodomy with homosexuality as a subversive practice privileges homosexuality and forecloses the possibility of any corresponding heterosexual acts having a similar effect."[8] Yet while Bersani may claim a privileged position for sodomy within homosexuality, his argument does not deny this "self-shattering" to women or to heterosexual men. For he writes (in basic agreement with Freud) that: "The investigation of human sexuality leads to a massive detachment of the sexual from both object-specificity and organ-specificity" (39). Bersani asserts that *masochism serves life* and that it "developed as an evolutionary necessity" (emphasis in original 39, 41). Elsewhere he refers to masochism as an "evolutionary conquest."[9] When, in *The Freudian Body*, Bersani claims that *masochism serves life*, he refers to a "gap between the period of shattering stimuli and the development of resistant or defensive ego structures" (39). Masochism, he contends, fills this gap between the stimuli and the defenses and thus allows the human organism to mature. Bersani continues by asserting: "Human sexuality is constituted as a kind of psychic shattering, as a threat to the stability and integrity of self—a threat which perhaps only the masochistic nature of sexual pleasure allows us to survive" (61). This idea comes very close to the French euphemism for orgasm—*le petite mort*. Masochism, Bersani believes, lies at the very core of all sexuality. Further he says, "Sexuality—at least in the mode in which it is constituted—could be thought of as a tautology for masochism" (39). Concurring, Laplanche writes that "we are led to emphasize the privileged character of masochism in human sexuality."[10] Bersani arrives at his findings through a radical but logical reassessment of *Three Essays on the Theory of Sexuality*, *Civilization and its Discontents*, and other writings by Freud and sums up the essentially nonverbal nature of what he attempts to describe: "We desire what nearly shatters us, and the shattering experience is, it would seem, *without any specific content*—which may be our only way of saying that the experience cannot be said, that it belongs to the nonlinguistic biology of human life" (emphasis in original 40). If, as Bersani contends, following the tradition of psychoanalysis, both sexual object and organ are nonspecific, the desire to be sodomized can be either heterosexual or homosexual, and any similarly shaped object can serve as well as an erect penis, depending on the desire of the male or female individual involved. This primacy of the desire of the passive participant in consensual sodomy demonstrates that "sadomasochism" occurs at the instigation, and therefore with the consent, of the masochist.

A heterosexual man's experience of consensual sodomy ought to be permitted its own heterosexual reactions. David Bourne's reaction to sodomy in *The Garden of Eden* approximates Bersani's "self-shattering *jouissance.*" Bersani's suggestion that for many gay men sodomy "has the terrifying appeal of a loss of the ego, of a self-debasement"[11] can apply just as easily to heterosexual men. With regard to Hemingway, what remains important in Bersani's analysis is the emphasis on the masculine. Here, perhaps, we can discern an affinity, if not a conjunction, between Hemingway's sexuality and homosexuality. Moddelmog suggests that by "[p]laying the woman's role during sexual relations, especially by being the recipient in an act of sodomy, David aligns himself with the common conception of the homosexual man" (73). Yet Bersani writes that for the homosexual "[i]t is not a woman's soul in a man's body" that matters but rather "the incorporation of woman's otherness."[12] Hemingway's incorporation of woman's otherness into his sexuality does not decrease his masculine identification any more than it does for Bersani's gay man. The heterosexual David Bourne shares the masculine identification that prevails in much of Bersani's view of the gay man. Hemingway, of course, also identified himself most emphatically with the masculine and with phallocentric power arrangements as well which should counter some arguments about his "feminine" sensibility.

Revisionist critics such as Spilka, Brenner, and Eby have tried to establish a feminine "side" to Hemingway. Moddelmog refutes such revisionism for its inclination to impose an old-style essentialism when she writes:

> Hemingway critics and biographers have been unable or unwilling, to break from conventional societal codes in their efforts to reconstruct Hemingway. This constraint has enabled them to dress the old Hemingway in new clothes without leaving anyone to utter the words "transgendered" or "queer." (35)

The suggestion of a queer homosexual sensibility in Hemingway remains as problematic as the assertion of a "feminine side." However,

Moddelmog's use of "transgendered" may be more helpful although the concept of what it constitutes is still, apparently, evolving. If, as many maintain, "transgendered" reflects a mental attitude or state of mind without necessitating a physical and medical "gender reassignment," then Hemingway could well fit this model. Some formulations still define "transgender" as a synonym for "transsexual," which implies the use of, or the desire to use, surgery and/or hormone treatments to change one's biological sex, and this does not, of course, apply to Hemingway. However, many now use "transgendered" more broadly to describe a greater variety of people than those who seek to change their biological sex. Author and activist Leslie Feinberg accounts for the broadening of the term when she writes that "more people are exploring this distinction between a person's sex—female, intersexual, and male—and their gender expression—feminine, androgynous, masculine, and other variations," and adds that: "Transgender people traverse, bridge, or blur the boundary of the gender expression they were assigned at birth."[13] Hemingway's work crosses gender boundaries repeatedly while he consistently maintains a heterosexual preference. Gay activist Ramon Johnson adds to the definition of transgender: "The sexual preference of a transgender person often varies."[14] According to this corollary, Hemingway's sexual preference for women can coexist with a designation as transgendered. Writing in 2003, Taormino states that "dialogue and diversity within LGBT communities . . . [have] ushered in a new identity: the Queer Heterosexual." As Taormino notes, a new openness characterizes much contemporary queer theory. She writes: "Once staunch separatists, queer people are flaunting our fluidity when it comes to gender and identity. . . . The roles of active initiator and penetrator are no longer solely the domain of men, nor are the qualities of receptivity and passivity for girls only."[15] Clyde Smith speaks of a "redefining of transgender" and he defines "queer" broadly (quoting Kate Bornstein's words) "as anyone who cares to admit their own gender ambiguities."[16] If we can identify Hemingway as heterosexual but not quite straight, we can do worse than refer to him as a queer heterosexual or as transgendered even if he never cared to or dared to admit it himself.

One of the great strengths of Moddelmog's study is that it clearly identifies the desire of the critical and commercial endeavors to preserve the traditionally masculine Hemingway legend but she never fully confronts this author's enduring homophobia or his misogyny. Some recent critics overstate Hemingway's obvious interest in homosexuality by making him seem both hostile and desirous of it, making him in other words the classic "latent homosexual" of psychoanalysis. What Hemingway does in *The Garden of Eden* and elsewhere is to affirm the patriarchal social mandate while undermining it in sexual relationships. Hemingway's male characters often engage in subversive sexual practices but they usually reaffirm other patriarchal values and always reject homosexuality. As Moddelmog argues, Hemingway's ideological identification conforms to the compulsory heterosexuality demanded of men (and women) in twentieth-century America, while his desire integrates more fluid notions of sexuality.

While homosexuality can never present a viable option to Hemingway, it is too facile to call his stance a simple denial. Even if Hemingway felt homosexual desires but willed himself straight, we have to accept the results of his own personal project.[17] Hemingway's characters engage in many alternative forms of physical love and the variety he presents is both exciting and innovative enough in itself without having to label it reductively as inherently homosexual especially when the erotic object choice is always female. Hemingway continued to identify with many traditionally masculine values and it would be wrong to think that he did not internalize those values in a meaningful way, that he only adopted them to provide a smokescreen to hide his alternative sexuality. To satisfy his alternative sexual longings, Hemingway has his characters submit to women in situations where it does not threaten his otherwise traditional values. David Bourne surrenders to Catherine where it is safest—in the bedroom—to the maintenance of the traditional order.

Hemingway sustains traditionally male and female societal roles but subverts these roles on the sexual plane. Hemingway's men dominate in the world. His women often dominate in the bedroom. While Bersani admits "the practice of S/M depends on a mutual respect generally absent from the relations between the powerful and the weak," he finds that "S/M is nonetheless profoundly conservative in that its imagination of pleasure is almost entirely defined by the dominant culture."[18] In this sense, *The Garden of Eden* appears less subversive than some scholars, like Spilka, believe. Hemingway, after creating Catherine as a representative of a subversive sexuality, intervenes on David's behalf to destroy her. In the manuscript, as Eby (33, 248–249) and Moddelmog (65) point out, Marita takes Catherine's place in gender crossing but while she assumes the sexual role of "the boy," she does not threaten David by taking on other prerogatives of the phallus in the social realm.

Marita, despite her radical sexuality, is submissive to David outside of the bedroom. Indeed, her character is unbelievable and as dead as wood compared with the vitality the author invests in Catherine. In the unpublished manuscript, Marita continually strokes David's ego after he has worked on his writing comparing him to a "great wonderful horse." These remarks come after David has rewritten some of the material in the manuscripts that Catherine had destroyed. Marita stays out of David's way in this restoration work. The narrator emphasizes that Marita is entirely supportive but that David remains "detached and separated from her" by his efforts at restoration. So great is his concentration that Marita is "afraid to enter in any way" into his work. But David compliments Marita on her supporting role assuring her that her presence has "helped enough." The narrator relates that both David and Marita are so "proud" of the work he is doing that they do not need to talk about it.[19]

Confined to a silent and supporting role, Marita muses on their sex life in an interior monologue: "I can give him everything that Catherine does . . . and do it better."[20] By "it" Marita may be referring to her role as "the boy" or the dominant, phallic woman but she knows her place in the overall relationship is subservient to David. At one point when she has assumed the role of the boy, Marita asks David, apparently jokingly if he would mind if they could be "social equals."[21] David, apparently realizing that the suggestion is out of the question and was obviously said in jest, does not even bother to answer her. In one of his own interior monologues, David compares Marita to the departed Catherine and thinks, "Christ it was good to finish today and have her there." He is relieved that Marita shows "no damn jealousy of the work" and that she understands what David is "reaching for" in his writing.[22] Clearly, while some deleted portions of the original manuscript portray radical sexuality, which could threaten Hemingway's image, other sections demonstrate his investment in traditional male superiority.

Hemingway's construction of Catherine in *The Garden of Eden* can be compared to Sacher-Masoch's creation of the dominatrix Wanda in *Venus in Furs*. Sacher-Masoch in effect created the women who dominated him throughout his life. He and his mistress (and the model for Wanda in *Venus in Furs*), Fanny von Pistor, signed a "contract" in which Sacher-Masoch would serve as her slave for a period of six months; then, as if scripted, she left him. Pistor performed her role with Sacher-Masoch financing the project. His fictional *Venus in Furs* is based, more or less, on this real-life experience. Subsequently Sacher-Masoch became involved with another woman, who took the name of Wanda from the character in *Venus in Furs*, and performed the role of the dominant in their long relationship.

The difference between Sacher-Masoch and Hemingway lies in the latter's creation of Catherine as a work of the imagination, with no acknowledged basis in fact. In *The Garden of Eden*, Hemingway obviously identifies himself with David, the young writer. David consensually puts himself at the disposal of his audacious wife, never sure where her sexual whims may take them but these are, after all, Hemingway's sexual whims. This sexuality involves the switching of traditional sexual roles and sodomy performed on David by Catherine. David enjoys the adventure for a time, but finally he and Hemingway rebel not at Catherine's domination of the sexual relationship, but at her intrusion into the male domain of art. As Comley and Scholes note: "Hemingway has done all he can to make Catherine an interesting figure . . . but he cannot allow her into his own preserve of masculinity" (62). Hemingway's desire demands a dominant woman yet his code of masculinity reins her in if she crosses social boundaries. How he balanced this in his private life, we will probably never know with any certainty.

Hemingway's domination of his wives in his public life (excepting the strong-willed Martha Gellhorn whom he failed to control) could have been part of a tacit understanding, as in the agreement between Catherine and David in *The Garden of Eden*, in which she assures her husband of her discretion. According to this understanding, the woman agrees to sexually dominate the man privately but submits to him publicly, and this again demonstrates a version of the masochistic contract. According to biographer Peter Griffin, Hemingway's fourth wife, Mary, claimed he was involved "in androgyny in more than one of his marriages,"[23] which suggests that he would have demanded a large measure of discretion in each of them. In her memoir, *How It Was*, published long after Hemingway's death, Mary Hemingway refers to an entry in her diary of "Papa clowning an interview . . . with an imaginary reporter from an imaginary magazine." She reports the following "exchange":

Reporter: "Mr. Hemingway, is it true that your wife is a lesbian?"
Papa: "Of course not, Mrs. Hemingway is a boy."
Reporter: "What are your favorite sports, sir?"
Papa: "Shooting, fishing, reading and sodomy."
Reporter: "Does Mrs. Hemingway participate in these sports?"
Papa: "She participates in all of them. . . . you must distinguish between the diurnal and the nocturnal sports. In this latter category sodomy is definitely superior to fishing."[24]

These remarks combined with the characterization of "androgyny" go a long way toward confirming active-female/passive-male sodomy in Hemingway's fourth marriage and suggest it in previous ones.

MISOGYNY

The accusation of misogyny has been leveled at Hemingway for decades. It contains enough truth to preclude a convincing denial. Many readers still remember Judith Fetterly's conviction that for Hemingway, "the only good woman is a dead one,"[25] and as Rena Sanderson points out, even today, "some women readers refuse to read him."[26] Yet, Hemingway often demonstrates in both his life and his work the ability to relate to women as equals, and in his sexual desire to elevate them to superiors. His friendships and intellectual relationships with Gertrude Stein, Katy Smith, Jane Mason, Duff Twydsen (the model for Brett Ashley in *The Sun Also Rises*), and with all of his wives confirms this. Lynn (320–323) and Brenner[27] provide details about Hemingway's friendships with many lesbian women in Paris in the 1920s, such as Sylvia Beach, Djuna Barnes, and Natalie Barney. Lynn remarks "How numerous were the lesbians of Hemingway's acquaintance! How numerous, how intelligent, how high-spirited!" (321). Burwell writes that "Hemingway was intrigued by the freedom that lesbians had achieved in their lives during his Paris years" (108). Hemingway demonstrated obvious respect for their artistic and intellectual abilities and an attraction to their status as "sexual outlaws." In spite of this, Hemingway still accepted, perhaps at times insincerely, the social norm of male superiority yet here were women who shared the same sexual object choice as himself. Did he thus elevate them to the status of men? For a time, perhaps he did but he severed his relations with several of these remarkable women. Yet he continued to counter in much of his fiction and, in all probability, in his personal sexual relationships, the male chauvinism that was so much a part of his heritage. His fiction demonstrates the gap between consciousness and ideology that Silverman discusses. As Silverman states this contradiction, "ideological belief operates at a level exterior to consciousness . . . the subject can continue to 'recognize' itself and its desires within certain kinds of sounds, images, and narrative paradigms, long after consciously repudiating them" (48). Hemingway's inherited values remained within Silverman's "dominant fiction" because of the "conservatism of the psyche—with its allegiance to the past" (48). Yet Hemingway learned new values in the transitional era between the two world wars but never convincingly shook off all the old ones, and even internalized them especially during his years in Key West from the late 1920s to the late 1930s.

Once in Key West with fame, Pauline's fortune, and (perhaps most importantly) far from the tolerant and ambiguous gender atmosphere of Paris, Hemingway was free to launch his super-macho persona. Key West may have seemed to him a town of "Men Without Women" as it was peopled by immigrants, political refugees, adventurers, and disenfranchised veterans of World War I. It was a very masculine setting that provided Hemingway with a rich environment in which to enact his personal patriarchal project. It was in Key West that he began to become known as "Papa," a term he enjoyed and encouraged. It is unusual for a man, barely into his thirties, to wish to be known as "Papa." Lynn reports that Hemingway actively encouraged this nickname as early as 1926 when he was just 27 (346). Hemingway played his role well. He adopted a young male fan, Arnold Samuelson, in 1934, and employed him on his boat and lectured him about writing, fishing, and other manly pursuits (as he lectured his readers in *Green Hills of Africa*, *Death in the Afternoon*, and in his journalism of those years). Samuelson's 1986 memoir, in which he writes, "E.H. was like a father to me" is rich in stories of Papa being Papa.[28] Thwarted to a degree in Paris, perhaps, in his wish to be a patriarch, Hemingway was now free to create his own world of "Men Without Women" in Key West. The suicide of Hemingway's father in 1927 played no small part in his wish to create his version of patriarchy. Though father and son were never close after his childhood, a case can be made that Hemingway's subsequent construction of a personal and exaggerated masculinity, which was only in part sincerely felt as we can see in his often remarkable portraits of women, can be attributed to feelings of restitution to his dead and pitied father. In his later years, Hemingway retreated significantly from such an unquestioning acceptance of his Key West values.

Hemingway's acceptance of the ideology of patriarchy and with it the phallic signifier and the power it implies, often finds itself at odds with the negation of the male phallus in his fiction. For many admirers of Hemingway's work, his moving accounts of the traditionally masculine virtues of courage and stoicism form, perhaps, the greatest elements of his appeal. Yet the celebration of those virtues need not have accompanied an intellectual acceptance of the prevailing norms of male social supremacy. And while Hemingway never appears to question such supremacy, he consistently violates one of the central tenets of this worldview in his submissive sexual posture toward women. It is not necessary to believe that Hemingway was either dissembling (although at times he proved himself capable of prodigious lying) or unaware of the contradiction between his ideology and his consciousness. As an artist he did not need to feel bound by consistency in this regard.

Because of Hemingway's ability to wear the armor of traditional masculinity and because the study of literature was largely a male domain, critics of his work in the past were usually men and usually focused on his male heroes until the publication of *The Garden of Eden*. Even before that novel's publication, some had already begun to question Hemingway's perceived chauvinism. As early as 1984, in *Cassandra's Daughters*, Roger Whitlow concludes a study of the portrayals of women in Hemingway's texts with these lines:

> From the penetrating and compelling portrayals of female trauma . . . to the victimized women . . . to the deeply loving women . . . Hemingway has presented interesting, dramatic characters, who offer a vision of life that is more humane and decent than that offered by the "heroes" with whom they spend—and often waste—their lives.[29]

But especially since the publication of *The Garden of Eden* and because of the obvious gender issues raised by the novel, female scholarship on Hemingway has increased to around a third of the total critical output. Lawrence R. Broer and Gloria Holland cite this statistic, provided by Beegel, in their recent edited volume of essays, *Hemingway and Women*.[30] Kathy G. Willingham calls for "a revaluation of Hemingway's literary treatment of women" that would "call[s] into question previous critical charges of misogyny,"[31] and several essays in *Hemingway and Women* do just that. Amy Lovell Strong makes a convincing case that Hemingway, "wittingly or unwittingly" created a feminist character in Catherine Bourne in *The Garden of Eden*, a character who "wishes to inhabit the unstable territory between binaries" and "to subvert fixed notions of gender identity."[32] Clearly, Catherine might be called a Third Wave Feminist far ahead of her time and Hemingway's ability to create such a character, like his earlier creation of Brett Ashley, demonstrates his personal appreciation for the kind of woman who does not conform to stereotypes that he accepted in the larger social world. Strong calls attention to this conflict by remarking on Hemingway's need to create, in contrast to Catherine, Marita whose "submission is so extreme, in fact, it almost becomes a parody of itself."[33] The novel certainly presents Catherine as the more vibrant of the two women, yet she must suffer for her independence. And in spite of the provisional and alternate endings in the unpublished manuscript that Strong cites, Hemingway clearly depicts Catherine, despite his enthusiasm for her sexuality, as a threat to his social ideology. Nancy Comley states, in her essay in the same volume, that "Hemingway conceived of sex and gender as a binary system [but] was fascinated with the possibilities of experiencing a shift in genders."[34] Yet she finds that for him only certain "sexual positions are sanctified by Western culture" (212). Indeed, this is what causes both David and Nick "remorse" in *The Garden of Eden*—their enthusiasm for alternative forms of heterosexual behavior that have the appearance (to them) of homosexual acts. This conflict makes Hemingway's portrayals of sexuality so enduringly fascinating but in the end, no matter which conclusion we choose for *The Garden of Eden*, Hemingway could never completely make the leap that would have broken the link to his late Victorian childhood with all the cultural baggage that came with it. His work unabashedly celebrates transgressive forms of sexuality yet he cannot fit this into his ingrained worldview. It is intriguing to imagine that if Hemingway lived a few years longer and seen the "sexual revolution" of the 1960s, he may have been able to "come out" in his own way.

CHAPTER 4

HEMINGWAY AND THE
FEMININE COMPLEX

An attempt to trace the origins of Hemingway's attitudes toward gender and sexuality calls for a look at some biographical details, most of which are already well known. Hemingway accepted the mystique of late-Victorian-influenced American masculinity very early in life in response to various environmental factors. Spilka convincingly demonstrates how Hemingway's boyhood reading of imperial adventure stories by Kipling and Captain Marryat, and of the Muscular Christianity in Dinah Craik's *John Halifax, Gentleman*, reinforced the views of his parents and played a significant role in his early development.[1] Spilka also emphasizes that Hemingway was fond of Emily Brontë's *Wuthering Heights*, and Mark Twain's *Huckleberry Finn*, novels far more subversive of Victorian values, but presented then (and now) as part of the bourgeois cultural legacy. What Hemingway gained from Kipling and Marryat was an appreciation of adventure for its own sake. And while what he took from Brontë and Twain fed his more expansive and sensitive side, the influence of Kipling and Marryat remained significant throughout Hemingway's life and he internalized many of those values in his persistent search for adventure and experience.

But as if to confound some of his youthful reading, as a child Hemingway witnessed the domination of his father by his mother, and as a young man he determined to escape a similar fate. This explains in part why he eventually created a persona of ultra-masculinity. Hemingway came to pity his father, who later took his own life, and blamed his mother for the suicide feeling she had emasculated her husband (SL 670). Deleuze asserts that part of the aim of masochism lies in a "disavowal of the father" and in "obliterating his role and his likeness in order to generate a new man" (99). Hemingway, in many respects, attempts a similar project to create a new masculinity to obliterate the weakness of his own father. Yet, unlike Deleuze's model, he also attempts to disavow the mother and divorce himself from all feminine qualities. However, as we have seen, Hemingway did not feel an estrangement from women in general and he consistently sought to have it both ways with them. He wanted to be "masculine" and protect his women, yet he also needed to submit to them sexually. His life and work reflect extremes that alternately reinforce and undermine the prevailing gender values of the era into which he was born.

As a child, Hemingway enjoyed the outdoor masculine activities, especially hunting, that he shared with his father. As Meyers puts it, the senior Hemingway "incited Ernest toward an endless destruction of fauna: if it moved, they killed it" (9), a practice he continued with his own sons. These moments of father–son camaraderie, perhaps the only times the young Ernest witnessed his father behaving like a "real man," led him to emulate and exaggerate these masculine qualities. The compulsive hunting along with Hemingway's early wartime experiences gave him a life-long tolerance for the sight of blood and gore. But he took this beyond tolerance into an actual enthusiasm for the observation of death or the possibility of death. In *Death in the Afternoon*, he finds the disemboweling of the horses at bullfights "comic" (6). Robert Cohn is ridiculed in *The Sun Also Rises* for almost becoming sick at this sight (165–166). Hemingway once tried to provoke the poet and publisher Robert McAlmon by accusing him of cowardice because he shrank from gazing at a dead, maggot-infested dog.[2] Stephen Spender recalls that in Spain, Hemingway referred to him as "too squeamish."[3] Hemingway's ability to tolerate, even to relish, scenes of suffering and death may provide examples of an aggressive impulse, socially useful according to Freud, which can, he asserts, transform itself into sexual sadism and, when accompanied by a heightened sense of guilt, can turn into masochism.[4] Though as we have seen, many commentators now question the link between sadism and masochism, the element of guilt remains essential. Hemingway's hunting forays with his father can represent a socializing of the aggressive impulse. The guilt would develop later in his life.

Away from his wife, Hemingway's father acted assertively but in the home the mother ruled. Grace Hemingway grew dependent upon a female companion, Ruth Arnold, a development that began to unnerve her husband. Ruth had taken voice lessons from Grace and soon accepted an invitation to become a live-in, part-time housekeeper at the Hemingway home. Speculation exists that Grace initiated a lesbian relationship with Ruth who had moved into the Hemingway home at the age of 12 when Hemingway was just nine years old, and she stayed for over a decade.[5] Grace was still in contact with her as late as

1950 (SL 675). According to Gajdusek, "Hemingway came at last at 19 to a full and shocked awareness of his mother's lesbian relationship with Ruth Arnold" (47). According to these speculations, Hemingway, throughout his formative years as he developed a sexual awareness, may have witnessed his mother in a lesbian relationship. This could have helped to produce the gender confusion and the consuming interest in female sexuality that Hemingway carried into full adulthood and that he suppressed beneath his public image. The relationship of Grace and Ruth may have provided the model for the wife and girlfriend in "Mr. and Mrs. Elliot." Hemingway's own father, rendered redundant by the presence of Ruth, conforms to Mr. Elliot as the useless husband of that story. If the suggestions of lesbianism or even the appearance of it are accurate, Hemingway could have developed a perplexity over assigned gender roles.

Earlier in his life, Grace Hemingway, as if to punctuate her domination over her children, wrote in her son's baby book: "He gives himself a whipping with a stick when he has done wrong so mama does not have to punish."[6] This bizarre comment suggests the cruel mother of masochistic fantasy. In addition, as many biographers have noted, Grace dressed the young Ernest and his older sister Marcelline as twins, sometimes in boys' and sometimes in girls' clothing.[7] Hemingway critics and biographers correctly make much of this "twinning." Brenner suggests that as a child, Hemingway witnessed new additions to the family, all of them welcomed by his parents and all of them female (his brother Leicester was not born until Ernest was 15), and may have felt an inferiority as a boy because "the successive arrival of siblings . . . persuaded him that girls were a preferred commodity" (19). As Eby remarks: "The little boy who had been twinned with his sister and forced to wear his hair exactly like hers grew up into an adult who could imagine nothing more erotic than twin-like lovers with identical haircuts" (259). Such identical haircuts, or conversations about them, appear in *A Farewell to Arms*, *Islands in the Stream*, *The Garden of Eden*, *A Moveable Feast*, "The Last Good Country," and other Hemingway texts.

This twinning with his sister may have led Hemingway to that desire that, as we have seen, Lacan describes as the "subject's claim to something that is separated from him, but belongs to him and which he needs to complete himself" (195), and that can manifest itself in a desire for the mother or for a sibling. We have seen how so often Hemingway's depictions of sexual relationships between men and women show the couples' desire to merge identities. Spilka has remarked on Hemingway's youthful reading of *Wuthering Heights* (138). Hemingway may have been especially struck by the passage in which

Catherine Earnshaw says, "I *am* Heathcliff! He's always, always in my mind: not as a pleasure . . . but as my own being."[8] Such comments can represent a resistance to separation and individuation and may have had great resonance for the young Hemingway. In his youthful imagination, he may have felt comfort and validation in the thought that his sisters felt the same identification with him. Though as adults Hemingway and Marcelline kept a distance, he may have displaced his early closeness with her and his other sisters onto other women and onto the characters in his fiction.

Hemingway grew to loathe his mother. "I hate her guts," he wrote, "and she hates mine" and he did not see her in the last 20 years of her life (SL 670). While accepting the notion of Grace's domination of her husband and children, commentators may occasionally underestimate the extent of the resentment this engendered in her oldest son. In one of their case histories, Kerry Kelly Novick and Jack Novick report on a child who exhibits a "discharge of aggression against the hated mother," and they note that: "Masochists are highly receptive and are ready to take in any stimuli from the outside world, ranging from subtle shifts in mother's moods to what one homosexual patient described as his desire for a 'fist-fuck.' "[9] As a child, Hemingway saw many "shifts in mother's moods" and his later characters sometimes exhibit a desire similar to that referred to by the Novicks' patient. As an adult, Hemingway vented feelings of rage against his mother regularly. A mother who toyed with the psyches of her children the way Grace Hemingway apparently did, should perhaps have expected her son's resentment in his later life. In childhood, Hemingway maintained close relationships to and was protective of his sisters and did not transfer his aversion toward his mother to all females.

Hemingway grew up in the company of women and despite ambivalent feelings toward them sought their society throughout his adult life. His fourth wife, Mary, in her autobiography *How It Was*, reveals a passage certainly never intended for publication. Hemingway wrote in an entry in Mary's journal: "She loves me to be her girl, which I love to be," implying an imagining of a mother and daughter, or perhaps two sisters, or two lesbian lovers (467).[10] He adds, "I have never cared for any man and dislike any tactile contact with men" (467). Psychoanalysis could interpret this as a loathing for the company of men as a result of contempt for the father, a feeling of comfort in the presence of women, and a desire for a return of the mother in spite of Hemingway's visceral objections to her. The comment also might reflect Hemingway's hostility toward male rivals, demonstrated in his frequent attacks on contemporary authors and his resentment toward any man who ever performed a kindness for him. It also indicates his submissive posture to women. While he had many long acquaintances with men, few seem characterized by a true friendship. Accustomed as he was to the company of women, Hemingway *did* make many female friends, including the many lesbians of Paris mentioned above, writers Dorothy Parker and Lillian Ross, and, of course, his four wives.[11]

Since it is a classic psychoanalytical formula, the dominant mother, passive father, and the early enforced cross-dressing has led to speculation that Hemingway was homosexual or bisexual, but no evidence supports this view. Agnes von Kurowsky, his first serious love, tells of convincing the young Hemingway not to accept an invitation to spend a year in Europe with a wealthy male acquaintance, who seemed to her to be after more than friendship from the young writer. Bernice Kert quotes Agnes as saying that Hemingway "was fascinating to older men."[12] But to Hemingway's homophobic imagination, this generic older man might be anyone from a tramp bent on rape to a cultivated person who exhibits an apparent altruism until he reveals his intentions and tries to use persuasion or force (MF 18–19). In *A Moveable Feast*, Hemingway claims that he told Gertrude Stein that he was prepared to kill any man who attempted to molest him sexually (18). Some men were indeed attracted to Hemingway, but we have no evidence that he ever reciprocated on a sexual level. Matthew Bruccoli mentions that "several weeks are unaccounted for" in Hemingway's life immediately following World War I when his activities are unknown to biographers (an indication of just how thoroughly his life has been researched) and some speculate that this period found him sexually involved with the same man, James Gamble, that Agnes had warned him against.[13] But there seems to be no solid evidence that Gamble was homosexual either. Brenner concludes that "Hemingway was latently homoerotic" on the basis of readings of his texts (19). Moddelmog is "willing, even eager, to explore the possible existence of 'queer' desires and their potential significance in Hemingway's erotic makeup" (42–43). Others, like Comley and Scholes, have stressed the author's many negative references to homosexuality, suggesting that they represent an almost obsessive interest in the subject. But without positive references or any biographical evidence, it remains specious to try to make a case for Hemingway's homosexuality. His fiction presents an argument that rather than homosexuality, Hemingway with his ardent love of women had an unconventionally submissive and masochistic side to a heterosexual nature.

Hemingway married four times. His marriages were consecutive with no appreciable gaps of time between them. His relationships with a future wife overlapped for a short period of time with a present wife. All of Hemingway's wives were cosmopolitan women. None of them could be described as prudish. All the wives were devoted to him in varying degrees and, with the exception of Martha Gellhorn, would likely have indulged his sexual appetites. As Kert notes, Hemingway's wives "dedicated their considerable energies to creating the kind of environment he needed and demanded" (9). Hemingway and Hadley lived a bohemian lifestyle in Paris, where they came into contact with many people who practiced alternative sexual lifestyles and as J. Gerald Kennedy notes, they had their own secret language to discuss their intimate transgressions.[14] Martha, by far the most independent of the Hemingway wives, had her own writing career that was bound to create problems with her husband who wanted her to write under the name of Martha Hemingway.[15] She refused this, to Hemingway's irritation, and maintained her professional independence, often traveling on assignment without him. This engendered a degree of jealousy and resentment on the part of her husband. He missed Martha's company and resented her successes in what he considered the male preserve of writing. Some biographers have cited undisclosed sexual problems between Hemingway and Martha. Kert notes that "the degree to which they were not sexually compatible" constituted a major cause of their estrangement (381). Amy Lovell Strong points out that Martha "seems to have refrained from the gender experimentation Hemingway enjoyed with his other three wives" (203). Burwell agrees, citing Martha's refusal to participate in "the gender-bending antics he found erotic" (212). Their marriage did not survive World War II in Europe where Hemingway met his fourth wife Mary, a reporter for *Time*. Mary performed the role of Hemingway's most faithful and loyal wife until his death in 1961. Hemingway dominated all of his marriages with the exception of his third to Martha who was the only wife to leave him. The other women, despite their considerable talents, accepted their role as the subservient partner in the marriage if not in the bedroom. This acquiescence to Hemingway's wishes and demands probably extended to his sexual appetites. If Hemingway wished to engage in masochistic sexual activities, these women would, no doubt, have played the role of the dominant to indulge him. Perhaps they enjoyed this role. We simply have no way of knowing with the presently available evidence.

Despite his four wives and several affairs, which do not seem nearly as numerous as is sometimes believed (and as Hemingway claims in conversation and letters), his biographers generally maintain that Hemingway was basically monogamous and, according to Meyers, "disliked casual sex" (244). Hemingway counted many women among his friends and as Kert asserts, "his personal world was alive with bold, resourceful, imaginative women whom he admired and very often married" (9). Other relationships with women remained platonic despite sexual overtones. Katy Smith and Duff Twydsen offer two examples. Gertrude Stein, a friend and mentor in his early Paris days, provides another. Hemingway's serious sexual relationships came one at a time, or sometimes two overlapped for a short period causing him guilt and grief. Even in freewheeling, pre–Castro Cuba, where he spent most of the last 20 years of his life, Hemingway does not seem to have frequented Havana's many brothels or lived the fast life as had Graham Greene, another expatriate and imperfectly Catholic convert often associated with Cuba.[16] Hemingway occasionally hired the services of prostitutes and of one of these Lynn remarks:

> [T]here was far less infidelity involved in these relationships than appearances often implied, for appearances seemed to be what mattered most to him. Even when he summoned an eighteen-year-old Havana whore, whom he nicknamed Xenophobia, to have dinner with him at the Finca [his home], Mary being in Chicago at the time, he was probably motivated by a wish to boast about his dinner partner to accomplished womanizers like [friends] Mario Menocal and Winston Guest, rather than any serious intention of taking Xenophobia to bed. (534)

To maintain that he was not a womanizer does not mean to suggest that Hemingway had a respectful attitude toward women. As Jamie Barlow points out, Hemingway intentionally injured two of the women closest to him in *The Sun Also Rises*, noting that they "suffered as a consequence of inclusion in the novel for Duff and of exclusion for Hadley."[17] And Wagner-Martin, while granting Hemingway's great gift for the erotic, what she calls his "romance of desire," nevertheless writes that he "would kill off troublesome women, leave them pregnant, erase them to imaginary and idealized images, or label them deviant" (69). In *Green Hills of Africa*, in a thinly veiled reference to Gertrude Stein, Poor Old Papa says, "she was damned nice before she got ambitious" (66).[18] Hemingway did not like ambition in women and writes in *A Moveable Feast*, also of Stein, that there is little "future with truly ambitious women writers" (117). Despite this, he married one, Martha Gellhorn, unsuccessfully. In *Across the River*, Cantwell and Renata discuss the ambition of the colonel's ex-wife (in a clear reference to Martha). "She had more ambition than Napoleon" says the Colonel, "and about the talent of the average High School Valedictorian" (195). Hemingway uses this occasion to demean ambitious women and to draw a comparison between Martha and his then-present wife Mary. The colonel tells a shocked Renata that his ex-wife was a journalist and her response is: " 'But they are dreadful!' the girl said" (196). But the blow to journalists is softened when Renata, in disbelief asks: "But you couldn't have married a journalist who kept on being that?" (196). The implication is that Mary, a former journalist, has given up her career to be a full-time Mrs. Hemingway. Martha threatened to sue Hemingway and successfully suppressed several more negative references to her in *Across the River*. Despite his contempt or condescension toward women in general, Hemingway elevated individual females to an almost divine status as objects of devotion.

A visitor to Hemingway's home in Key West in 1934 described his wife: "Pauline Hemingway came to the door wearing slacks, with her black hair brushed back in a boy's haircut. She was built like a boy and wore no makeup."[19] Pauline's sister, Jinny, was a lesbian and according to biographers, Pauline herself had "lesbian tendencies," which she acted upon after her marriage with Hemingway was over.[20] During his marriage to Pauline, Hemingway and Jinny were close friends and Kert notes that he considered dedicating *Men Without Women* to her (206). He was no doubt intrigued by his sister-in-law's sexual orientation and he admired her intellectual abilities (276–277).[21] Lesbianism fascinated Hemingway, and he writes of it often, though with an obvious lack of authenticity. He would seem to agree with Gertrude Stein, who he quotes as saying:

> the act male homosexuals commit is ugly and repugnant and afterwards they are disgusted with themselves. . . . In women it is the opposite. They do nothing that they are disgusted by and nothing that is repulsive and afterwards they are happy and they can lead happy lives together. (MF 20)

Hemingway's approval of this attitude finds expression in his many negative references to male homosexuality and his generally more tolerant and curious view of lesbianism.

Hemingway's fascination with lesbianism provides another example of his curiosity about the sexual lives of women. This curiosity ran so deeply that he likely tried to experience, as closely as he could, his conception of female sexuality. Though an experience of female sexuality remains foreclosed to a man, this imaginative endeavor put into practice can mean alternative sexual behaviors that seek to approximate the sexuality of women. Some varieties of masochism and of homosexuality seek to assume a female sexual posture. However, contrary to stereotype, most masochists and gay men are not effeminate and do not consider their sexuality feminine. Hemingway's alternative sexuality shares this masculine identification even as he seeks to approximate the experience of female sexuality.

Opposing Hemingway's masculine identification, Spilka writes of *The Sun Also Rises* that, "in accord with the oddly common attraction for men of lesbian lovemaking, the imagining into it that exercises suppressed femininity, and indeed the need for such imagining, such identification in the original nurturing sources of love—he [Jake] wants Brett in a womanly way" (204). But Hemingway would have rejected this idea, and he would have been right. For how, specifically, does a man desire a woman in a womanly way? One of Hemingway's descriptions of a man imagining female sexuality occurs in his novel of the Spanish Civil War, *For Whom the Bell Tolls*. The republican forces lie in wait to ambush a fascist patrol. A Loyalist, Augustin, compares his urge to kill to "a mare in the corral waiting for the stallion" and later adds "the necessity was on me as it is on a mare in heat" (309). Augustin assures hero Robert Jordan, the American leader of the Loyalist guerrillas in the mountainous Spanish countryside: "You cannot know what it is if you have not felt it" (309). This constitutes a crude Hemingway image of a man experiencing a conception of female sexuality. Is this reference to "a mare in heat" compatible with "desire in a womanly way" or is it a sexist characterization, an imagining based on male sexual drives? Spilka's remark attempts to elevate Hemingway but instead reduces his attitude to a parody of female sexuality and reinforces gender constructions that many critics have sought to undermine in recent years.

One answer to the question posed by Spilka's remark could be Bersani's contention that "the homophobic male must be 'remembering' a lost jouissance (that is, female sexuality as a male body has in fantasy experienced it)."[22] Bersani's view precludes a truly feminine perception in a man. He refers to men's ideas of female sexuality as experiences in fantasy that must necessarily remain indistinct and incomplete at best. To call Hemingway's sexuality feminine conforms it to a caricature of gender. Eby writes of Jake's desire for Brett in *The Sun Also Rises* that, "this part of Hemingway felt like it *was* a lesbian" (204). However, Hemingway's attitude toward androgynous women, perhaps like Duff and the lesbians he knew in Paris, is better reflected in a letter, in which he claims, impossibly, that he had had a sexual affair and "fucked a lesbian . . . with magnificent results" (SL 795).[23] This represents more the false bravado of the macho, who claims to be so manly that he can even "turn" a lesbian, than a man with a lesbian self-identification who desires "in a womanly way." Moddelmog finds in the readiness of some critics to graft a lesbian sensibility onto Hemingway a defensive reaction of those heavily invested in Hemingway's embodiment of traditional masculinity. Moddelmog writes, "it is safer to make Jake a lesbian because he can never really be one" (33), a position that thereby neutralizes any significant threat to the macho image.

Yet Hemingway's early story, "Up in Michigan," (1923) demonstrates empathy as he presents an often convincing portrayal of a woman's view of an impersonal, somewhat brutal heterosexual encounter. Hemingway, often crude but nearly always with a remarkable sensitivity, may have rendered this story through the eyes of one of his early "conquests." In this story, the sexually experienced Jim Gilmore seduces Liz Coates, a willing virgin. The narrator relates that "She was frightened but she wanted it. She had to have it but it frightened her"[24]—which conforms roughly to the "mare in heat" cited above. But after these awkward lines, the story proceeds to show that after they have had sex, Liz finds herself distressed, "uncomfortable and cramped," (62) pinned under the sleeping bulk of Jim. Though written in the third person, "Up in Michigan" presents more the perspective of Liz than of Jim. As Alice Hall Petry points out, "the story is told essentially from Liz's point of view" and depicts "the glaring disparity between male and female attitudes toward love and sex."[25] Liz tells Jim: "It's so big and it hurts so," (62) which demonstrates that to Hemingway, penetration involves pain. Despite some clichés, the narrator attempts to sympathetically relate Liz's point of view.

Hemingway probably never cared for a woman with the same adolescent passion that he felt for Agnes, who jilted him in 1919 when he was just 20, dealing a serious blow to his self-esteem. This emasculating experience finds expression in Jake Barnes's debilitating wound in *The Sun Also Rises*, which can be seen as a metaphor for the loss of the ability to love as well as the erosion of the phallus. Bruised by the experience, Hemingway regained some of his masculine self-respect when he married Hadley. But his feelings toward her became compromised by the imposing presence in his psyche of his own mother, his rejection by Agnes, and the single-minded pursuit of him by Pauline, Hadley's erstwhile friend. Spilka emphasizes Pauline's role in Hemingway's breakup with Hadley:

> Certainly it was Pauline who had served him so aggressively in his passivity, as to lead him to betray himself. Thus, with Pauline especially, the wounds of war and peace had crystallized as the wound of androgyny, the wound that is of identification with women and with the female within oneself, felt now as an almost intolerable vulnerability, a hidden emasculation, a secret loss of male identity, a self-betrayal—as that delayed time-bomb, *The Garden of Eden*, would eventually, in its own personally metaphoric ways, reveal. (222)

Spilka's remarks call for some elaboration. Whatever the extent of Pauline's aggression, it should be remembered that Hemingway did not "betray himself" nearly so much as he betrayed Hadley. And what Spilka refers to as the "identification with women and with the female within oneself" may amount in this case, at least partially, to an unscrupulous financial consideration. Hemingway's attraction to the wealthy Pauline began around the time that Hadley's trust fund was cut in half through bad investments or theft.[26] Is this a coincidence? In any case, up until the time when he became financially secure in the 1940s after the great success of *For Whom the Bell Tolls*, there may have been elements of both money and a sexual understanding involved in his relationships.[27] One can speculate that the androgynous-looking Pauline was willing to support him and perhaps to engage in nonnormative sexual practices to a greater degree than Hadley had, which is not to imply that Hadley was prudish in the least. If Pauline, as Spilka asserts, "served him so aggressively in his passivity" (222), she could in return have expected to call herself the wife of the great Ernest Hemingway, and to have earned that right. This is not to say that Hemingway and Pauline did not have a deep affection for each other or that he imposed his sexual desires upon her and thrust her into the role of the dominant woman against her will. These speculations merely suggest a possible trade-off, which may be part of the story.

Hemingway's submissive sexuality had its roots in the domineering personality of his mother and the weakness of his father. Hemingway's knowledge of his passive sexual nature must have seemed as injurious to his masculine identity as being homosexual would have been. His code of masculinity abhors homosexuality, but it also demands a man who is sexually dominant in relationships with women. His submissiveness may have been reinforced by his relationship with Agnes, his nurse when he was wounded in World War I. She, as the physically healthy nurse caring for him in a debilitated state when he could not even walk unassisted, may well have furthered a passive sexuality that coexisted with a macho mentality. Most biographers dismiss the possibility that he and Agnes had a sexual relationship (although Griffin disagrees). And with Agnes's own later denials, we have only Hemingway's boast that "it takes a professional nurse to know how to make love to a man with his leg in a splint."[28] So whether in fantasy or reality if Hemingway was still bedridden from his wounds and the two made love, it would have involved her taking charge—"being the man"—by moving both him and herself into position. And she, a nurse and dressing the part, would have lent a fetishistic air to these scenes. Even if this scenario did not take place in reality, it undoubtedly played itself out in his imagination.

Hemingway received his leg wounds while serving in a noncombatant position in the Red Cross attached to the Italian Army.[29] After his discharge and return home to the United States, he seriously intended to marry Agnes until she broke off the engagement leaving him devastated. Biographers agree on the traumatic effect this rejection had on Hemingway. But he transformed the pain he suffered in the aftermath of this relationship into some of his finest work. He first wrote of Agnes, bitterly, in "A Very Short Story" in *In Our Time* (1925), and he kept returning to her, especially as Catherine Barkley in *A Farewell to Arms*, who in some ways anticipates Catherine Bourne in *The Garden of Eden*.

1930S: GUILT IN LIFE AND ART: "THE SNOWS OF KILIMANJARO" AND *TO HAVE AND HAVE NOT*

Though his attitude toward women remains chauvinistic, especially in the Key West years of the 1930s, Hemingway often evinces through his work a bad conscience about it, particularly in "The Snows of Kilimanjaro" (1936) and *To Have and Have Not*, which appeared the following year. These two works manifest elements of Hemingway's dissatisfaction, later turning into emotional paralysis or fear and then guilt. This guilt may serve as an important element in Hemingway's masochism, the purpose of which is, according to Deleuze, "to resolve guilt and the corresponding anxiety and make sexual gratification possible" (104). Hemingway often sought to expiate guilt in his work.

Hemingway's creation of "The Snows of Kilimanjaro" corresponds to his ebbing days in Key West. His ever-present pessimism pervades this story, perhaps because his marriage to Pauline was collapsing as he wrote it. Although Hemingway's meeting with Martha, who was to become his third wife, did not take place until December of 1936, his predisposition to welcome her advances caused him guilt.[30] His affair with Martha, virtually right before Pauline's eyes, recalls his earlier affair with Pauline, of which his first wife, Hadley, was well aware. Hemingway's breakup with Hadley cost him dearly in guilt and self-pity as did the subsequent decline of his marriage to Pauline, as his work of 1936 and 1937 indicates.

In "The Snows of Kilimanjaro," the dying Harry, a successful writer, reflects that he had feared failure and resents that he had relied on the fortune of his wife Helen to provide a safety net. Hemingway dwells on this point, a point absent in *Green Hills of Africa*, his nonfiction account of his 1934 African safari. Pauline accompanied her husband on that safari and her uncle financed the adventure that provided the genesis of the short story. In it, Harry's relationship with Helen can be viewed in part as an autobiographical account of Hemingway's dying marriage to Pauline. Hemingway, through the narrator, depicts Harry as cruel and irritable as he reflects on his crumbling relationship with Helen as his life ebbs away from him and he also demonstrates ambivalence and a guilty conscience in regard to his wife. The narrator reveals Harry's feelings toward Helen as she hunts game in the distance: "She shot well, this good, this rich bitch, this kindly caretaker and destroyer of his talent."[31] But he immediately corrects this: "Nonsense. He had destroyed his talent himself. Why should he blame this woman because she kept him well?" (45). Even though Hemingway's affair with Martha had not yet begun, he increasingly experienced guilt in these days as his reliance on Pauline's affections declined and his resentment grew at his continuing financial dependence on her. Despite his artistic success he still relied on Pauline's money, as he had earlier on Hadley's trust fund. As he told a friend in 1934, "I was broke when I came back from Africa this spring."[32] Pauline had supported him through his lean years and still supported him in his extravagance.

In the pitiless depiction of Harry in "The Snows of Kilimanjaro," Hemingway presents feelings of desolation in the reflection of a wasted life. Harry views his life as one of missed opportunities, squandered talent, and sellout. As Harry lays dying, he remarks, "Love is a dunghill . . . And I'm the cock that gets on it to crow" (43). J. Gerald Kennedy comments that "Harry's remark betrays more than self-contempt: he represents love as a site of filth, implying disgust with his own emotional and sexual tendencies."[33] As he was writing this story, Hemingway had fallen out of love with Pauline. He may have felt that he had badly used her, had "corrupted" her by drawing her into his masochistic sexual fantasies. He may have felt that by placing Pauline into the role of the dominant, "the boy," that he had caused her sexual "remorse" or guilt, which in turn caused these in him. In this, he expresses the same sentiment as Catherine in *The Garden of Eden* when she tells David, "You didn't feel remorse?" And David's answer, relayed by the narrator is: " 'No,' he lied." Catherine is relieved and says, "I couldn't bear it if you had remorse."[34] Hemingway himself may have felt an affinity with his later creation of Catherine since both play the role of the corrupter and cause remorse and guilt to their lovers and ultimately to themselves. In "Snows," Hemingway, through Harry, lashes out at the spurned and wealthy wife, reducing her to tears by telling her that he never loved her (41) or truly enjoyed her company except when hunting (43). But Harry quickly blames himself for his outbursts, as when he tells Helen, "You're a fine woman . . . Don't pay attention to me" (49). Hemingway's emotional turmoil and sexual guilt must have been so great during the writing of this story that he may not have realized how confessional it appears.

Going further than "The Snows of Kilimanjaro," *To Have and Have Not*, in a subplot, presents what appears an even more self-critical account of the slow, painful dissolution of the author's marriage, as James McLendon points out (173–174). Though Harry Morgan acts as the hero of this unusual novel, other characters reveal Hemingway's guilt and remorse. One of them, Richard Gordon, is portrayed with what Phillip Young calls "savage disgust aimed at a successful writer."[35] In much of his work, Hemingway targeted other authors but in *To Have and Have Not* he may well have been writing about himself. In the novel, Richard Gordon has an extramarital affair. His wife, once again a Helen, discovers it and informs him that she will leave him. An emotional scene follows in which Helen tells him, "You wouldn't marry me in the church and it broke my poor mother's heart as you well know" (185). This may reflect some of Hemingway's own experiences. Pauline, from a devout Catholic family, risked her parents' disapproval when she planned to marry Hemingway who as a divorced man was off-limits. However, as Stoneback points out, when Hemingway formally converted to Catholicism in Paris in 1927—primarily to accommodate Pauline—he was granted "all dispensations" (including his divorce of Hadley) by the Archbishopric.[36] This enabled him to marry Pauline in the good graces of the Catholic Church. With his references to "remorse" and his apparent penitential feelings, Hemingway made a very passable if imperfect Catholic. In *To Have and Have Not*, Helen continues:

> "I broke my own heart, too. It's broken and gone. . . . Love was the greatest thing, wasn't it? Love was what we had that no one else had or could ever have? And you were a genius and I was your whole life. . . . Slop. Love is just a dirty lie. . . . Love is that dirty aborting horror that you took me to. Love is my insides all messed up. It's half catheters and half whirling douches. I know about love. Love always hangs up behind the bathroom door. It smells like Lysol. To hell with love." (185–186)

The references to abortion, though clear enough, remain unelaborated, and Hemingway's attitude seems to imply disapproval as does his 1927 story, "Hills Like White Elephants," but in each case he lays the blame squarely upon the man. Helen's outburst and the intensity of her attack show how merciless Hemingway could be in depicting himself in an untenable situation. He remained paralyzed emotionally for a couple of years, torn between his guilt and his new infatuation with Martha. Hemingway's actions, or rather his inability to act decisively during these years, were cowardly and destructive. He failed to act "manfully" and simply confront Pauline with the hard truth, and he thereby prolonged both her agony and his own.

In *To Have and Have Not*, Hemingway even criticizes his own instincts as a writer if we can assume that the character of Richard Gordon represents a part of himself as McLendon suggests (174). That character's reading of Marie Morgan demonstrates a profound failure of perception. Gordon sees Marie as "a heavy-set, blue-eyed woman, with bleached blonde hair showing under her old man's felt hat, hurrying across the road, her eyes red from crying" (176). In his role as writer and observer of humanity, Gordon feels he has captured a character for his fiction and imagines a scenario in which Marie is a disgruntled and repressed woman who makes her husband's life miserable and barely suffers his sexual advances. However, Hemingway's descriptions of the bedroom intimacy between Harry and Marie Morgan depict a lusty couple, proving Richard Gordon's perception badly lacking. By extension, Hemingway may be saying the same thing of himself. These truly confessional scenes bespeak a paralysis in his ability to create during stressful times. A final statement of remorse and self-pity occurs in the last glimpse of Richard Gordon who Marie now judges, in a reversal of his gaze, as she sees him staggering home from a night of drinking in Key West. Her reaction, in ironic counterpoint to his estimate of her, is, "Some poor goddamned rummy" (255). Hemingway drank heavily throughout his life, and he himself, along with his character Richard Gordon, may serve as the object of Marie's pity.

In *To Have and Have Not*, many contemporary readers may have felt the brave but reckless Harry Morgan presented an extension of the author's persona, but they may have failed to recognize Richard Gordon, a weak and unpleasant character, as another side of Hemingway. The novel evolved over a period of years. The opening chapters, which establish Harry's character, appeared in 1934 as a short story, "One Trip Across." The later chapters in which Richard Gordon appears were written during the crisis in Hemingway's marriage some years later. The portrayal of Harry as a rugged, rough-living, hard-drinking sailor and of Gordon as a sniveling, two-timing, "poor goddamned rummy" of a writer, reflects how Hemingway's self-image (if not his public image) changed in a few short years. It gives the novel a slightly schizophrenic quality. In the later chapters of *To Have and Have Not*,

Hemingway performed a sort of self-exorcism with his art. It remains a brutally honest and morally self-lacerating performance. Harry in "The Snows of Kilimanjaro" also wrestles with guilt but remains more philosophical. He has not led an admirable life, but he does not repel the reader as Richard Gordon does. Both characters demonstrate a sense of guilt, largely based upon their mistreatment of women. Hemingway accompanies these portraits of guilt with strong elements of self-pity and an implicit desire to be punished, which both relate to his masochism. The two works can be read as humiliating public confessions.

Hemingway's empathy with the women depicted in these works, while no doubt sincere, sometimes takes on the appearance of a self-serving catharsis. "Guilt and expiation . . . are genuinely and deeply experienced by the masochist," writes Deleuze but he emphasizes that "[t]he depth and intensity of a feeling is not affected by the uses which it may be made to serve" (100). It follows from Deleuze's assertion that "anxiety and guilt . . . are distorted and parodied to serve the aim of masochism" (91), that the masochist may truly experience guilt yet connive with himself to expiate this guilt pleasurably or in a self-serving manner. As Jacqueline Tavernier-Courbin points out, Hemingway sometimes uses a "disingenuous" "self-criticism" to try to make himself appear more sympathetic, but that "these examples of self-criticism are not meant to be taken seriously by the reader" (101). Hemingway's characters often admit to guilt without appearing to suffer much from it, or perhaps they feel they have already suffered enough and expiated their guilt. Despite this ambivalence, Hemingway's artistic achievements in these confessional writings, and the continuing popularity that reinforced his confidence in his honest and "true" writing, may have justified him in the belief that he had atoned for his sins against his wives.

But these sins apparently returned to haunt him in later life, according to Burwell, as he was preparing *A Moveable Feast* for publication. This book deals, of course, with his Paris years where he experienced such intimacy with both Hadley and Pauline. Some months before his death, Burwell writes that Hemingway belatedly "saw with blinding sight the part he had played in destroying the two personal relationships that he now believed had been the most sustaining of him as a writer and most indicative of his integrity as a man" (183). Hemingway may have worked off his guilt through his art of the 1930s but the remorse returned to torment him in his final days.[37]

CHAPTER 5

DEFYING THE CODE

MASOCHISM IN THE MAJOR TEXTS

In one of the most quoted lines in *The Sun Also Rises*, Jake Barnes as narrator tells the reader, "Well, it was a rotten way to be wounded" (31), referring to the World War I injury that severely damaged his genitals, leaving him sexually dismembered. Concerning this injury, which never receives a full description, Hemingway later claimed that he carefully tried to demonstrate that the "important distinction is that his wound was physical and not psychological."[1] Hemingway, in this intention stated three decades after the novel appeared, wants to leave Jake's psychic masculinity intact. But Jake certainly exhibits psychological wounds as well. Already, in this early novel, Hemingway's choice of a nearly castrated hero who yet remains a decidedly masculine, if mangled, presence highlights a personal crisis in masculinity.

In addition to the dislimbed Jake, this novel of American expatriates in France and Spain introduces Brett Ashley, the first fully developed dominant woman in Hemingway's fiction. Early in the novel, Jake says, "Brett was damned good-looking. . . . her hair brushed back like a boy's" (22). She is tall, long-legged and "built like the hull of a racing yacht" (22). Many Hemingway heroines have a similar appearance— tall, well-built, with short hair. Jake longs for Brett and weeps over her (31). Here, in a divide between his public persona and his art, Hemingway presents a refreshingly honest depiction of a man unafraid to show emotions. Indeed, many of the characteristics of both Jake and Brett play against traditional gender formations. Brett often refers to herself as "a chap" (22, 32, 57). That Hemingway created this androgynous and promiscuous "chap" as the love interest of the sexually disabled Jake has led critics to wonder about the nature of their relationship.

Some scholars have speculated that, against the odds, Brett and Jake manage to consummate their relationship during "gaps" in the seventh chapter of the text, but differ as to how. The insertion within the dialogue of the word "Then" and the phrase "Then later," each followed by a colon, suggesting the passage of some time, comprise the "gaps" and remain the only indication that something sexual transpires (55, 56). Lynn suggests that when Brett sends Count Mippipopolous away from the flat, she and Jake "make love in a fashion often associated with lesbian as well as heterosexual intercourse," (324) implying oral sex. Spilka, satisfied that Jake and Brett merely exchange "fervent kisses," disagrees and asserts that Hemingway would not have been "ready, at this early stage of the sexual revolution, for those oral-genital solutions that recent critics have been willing to impose upon him" (203). While Spilka may be correct that an "oral-genital solution" does not take place here, his remark seems to advance the untenable idea of oral sex as an invention of the late twentieth century. More convincingly, J.F. Buckley holds forth "the possibility of masturbation, oral sex, or other expressions of desire," one of which could include sodomy.[2]

The episode is suggestive and open to interpretation. The words "She stroked my head" (55) appear, leading some to suggest that Brett manipulates with her hand the remains of Jake's genitals to give him an orgasm. However, this interpretation fails to take into account that Jake apparently lacks the "head" in question. Just after the gap— "Then later:"—Brett asks Jake, "Do you feel better darling? Is the head any better?" (55). This conveys the idea of Brett inquiring about a headache or Jake's psychological or emotional state rather than an allusion to his genitals. The "gaps" occur early in a chapter (VII) that consists almost entirely of dialogue. Readers must glean what they can from the characters' conversation without the narrator's intervention. Yet just before a crucial gap, Jake as narrator, tells the reader: "I was lying with my face away from her" (55), which affords another possible reading. This position can suggest either the manual manipulation by Brett's hand or Brett's anal penetration of Jake, using her finger(s) or some object, anticipating the more explicit scenes in *The Garden of Eden*.

Discussing this passage Wolfgang E.H. Rudat makes a case that Jake, despite his wound, retains the ability to engage in "anal homosexual intercourse" and implies that Hemingway created a gay, or at least a gay-friendly, character.[3] But Rudat ignores the possibility of anal heterosexual intercourse with the man in the "passive" role, which the passage suggests. No other man is present here as Brett has already sent the count away, so homosexuality is not an immediate issue. In 1926, Hemingway could not, or chose not to, make the sexual content clear. As Lynn points out, an "artful vagueness" conceals what actually takes place here (324). But certainly, Hemingway does not present Jake as homosexual (or gay-friendly, either) but rather as almost heroically and defiantly heterosexual in his devotion to Brett. If we choose to interpret Brett as one of the precursors of Catherine Bourne in *The Garden of Eden*, sodomy becomes a logical explanation.

In the character of Jake, we can perceive how Hemingway's sexual desire is at odds with his traditional masculine identification. Ira Elliott, referring to Jake's hostility to the gay men in the early chapters of *The Sun Also Rises*, writes that "inasmuch as Jake considers himself to be heterosexual, the novel posits the site of sexuality in gendered desire rather than sexual behavior."[4] Jake's self-identification as heterosexual combined with his crippling wound, limits his choices for sexual fulfillment. Elliot writes that "what distinguishes Jake from the homosexual men is gender performance and erotic object choice" (86). Jake "performs" traditional masculine gender that includes the choice of women as erotic object but his performance of sexuality subverts this paradigm so that the woman must possess the phallus so he can receive it. Elliott also refers to two incidents in which women, Brett and the prostitute Georgette, "press" against Jake's body in relatively nonsexual situations, and surmises that Jake "desires more than he can do; he wants not just 'pressing' but penetration" (90). Elliott suggests that Jake desires to penetrate women. However, Hemingway's creation of this character implies the opposite, that Jake was written without a complete penis precisely so he could *not* penetrate but only be penetrated, and only by women, thereby retaining a heterosexual masculine identification. Forter writes convincingly of "Hemingway's commitment to masculinity as a principle of penetration" but suggests that on another level the novel hints at "the loss of phallic manhood in the name of a recovered capacity for receptivity" (33). Such receptivity can find physical expression in the act of sodomy.

Hemingway provides a relatively explicit description of sodomy in a dream sequence in the posthumous *Islands in the Stream*. Earlier in that World War II era novel, hero Thomas Hudson, after losing his wife and three sons to accident and war, receives a surprise visit from his movie star first ex-wife (called simply "Tom's mother" in the published novel but identified in deleted portions of the manuscript as Janet or Jan), when she turns up unexpectedly in the Havana bar he haunts. Meyers (484) and Lynn (418) both report that Hemingway based this character on his longtime friend, Marlene Dietrich, who according to Studlar collaborated with Josef von Sternberg on some of cinema's most striking examples of "the masochistic aesthetic" in films such as *Morocco* and *Blonde Venus*.[5] Still in love, Hudson and Tom's mother repair to his villa, called here the *Finca* (the name of Hemingway's home on the outskirts of the Havana). Hudson and his ex-wife continue their reminiscing conversation as he carries her to the bed. They apparently make love but the reader gets no description of this other than the single word, "Afterwards" (307), followed by postcoital dialogue. The couple have little time together as she must catch a flight to continue entertaining the troops as part of her volunteer duties for the USO (another apparent reference to Dietrich). But she reappears to Hudson in a dream while he's on patrol searching for German U-boats. The dream sequence constitutes a quite singular example of Hemingway's submissive sexuality and it is worth quoting at length:

> He dreamed Tom's mother was sleeping with him and she was sleeping on top of him as she liked to do sometimes. . . . Her hair hung down and lay heavy and silky on his eyes and on his cheeks . . . Then he lay under her weight with her silken hair over his face like a curtain and moved slowly and rhythmically. (332–333)

In the dream, Hudson asks Jan, "Who's going to make love to who?" She answers him: "Both of us. . . . Unless you want it differently." Hudson then says, "You make love to me. I'm tired." To which she responds, "You're just lazy. Let me take the pistol and put it by your leg. The pistol's in the way of everything" (333). (Hemingway heroes often sleep with their pistols. Here, Jan wants to move it.) The description of the obviously phallic pistol as "in the way" can be interpreted as another example of Hemingway's dismissal of male genital sexuality as an aggressive force. But Hemingway goes further here.

Hudson suggests that Jan "Lay it [the pistol] by the bed. . . . And make everything the way it should be." Then Jan asks, "Should I be you or you be me?" Hudson gives Jan "first choice" and she says, "I'll be you." To which Hudson responds, "I can't be you but I can try." She tells him, "It's fun. You try it. Don't try to save yourself at all. Try to lose everything and take everything too" (333).

During this dialogue some unspecified activity transpires and since this occurs in a dream an exact interpretation is impossible. But one plausible explanation is that Hudson has not laid the pistol on the table but rather that Jan sodomizes him with it. She asks, "Are you doing it?" He responds, "Yes. . . . it's wonderful." Then she asks him, "Do you know now what we have?" Which can mean—do you know now what we women feel when we are penetrated? Hudson replies, "Yes I know. It's easy to give up." Finally he asks Jan to "hold me so tight it kills me?" He awakens from the dream to feel "the pistol holder between his legs" (333–334). In light of all this, the possibility that Hudson's ex-wife sodomizes him with the pistol does not seem outlandish. For Hudson had already "moistened the .357 Magnum and slipped it easily . . . where it should be," (333) which is apparently "between his legs" (334).

Islands in the Stream forms an important part of Rose Marie Buwrell's study, *Hemingway: The Postwar Years and Posthumous Works*, which argues that all the late writings form part of one great urtext and are unified by several themes, including "the male artist's distrust of women and the feminine aspect of his own creative imagination," and a preoccupation with "writing as an isolated and onanistic act" (4). Burwell asserts that if Hemingway "were to function as a creative artist, and as a heterosexual male . . . he would find himself in conflict with women" (32). Hemingway demonstrates a distrust of individual women in the late works but he also idealizes women in many of the characters and the works seem to represent an effort to submit himself to these women, despite his life-long identification with traditional male values. There is indeed a conflict in Hemingway's late work, but the conflict is with the patriarchal value system as much as with women, a conflict he would never resolve. The similarities in the characters and motives of Barbara and Catherine in *The Garden of Eden*, Janet in *Islands in the Stream*, and to some extent, Miss Mary in *True at First Light*, do indeed support much of Burwell's argument.

Hemingway's portrayal of his male characters' submission to women becomes much more pronounced in the later works. The preoccupation with hair, present from the very earliest texts, becomes a near-obsession in the work of the 1950s in which women more dramatically gain sexual control over the male characters. And the gateway through which these female characters pass on their way toward domination over their men often leads straight through a hair salon. Why Hemingway's curious fascination with hair leads to female domination is much less important than the fact that it does so. Eby and others have explored in depth Hemingway's fetish with hair and found that this fixation opens up other alternative areas of his sexuality. Hemingway's fetishism goes hand-in-hand with his masochism. The importance of haircutting as a corollary to the transgressive sexuality of David and Catherine in *The Garden of Eden* is well known. Eby discusses the incident in which Hemingway cut and dyed the hair of his wife Mary on their 1953 trip to Africa (201–203). Eby also covers the less well-known hairstyling activities of Thomas Hudson and Janet in *Islands in the Stream* and Nick and Barbara Sheldon in *The Garden of Eden*, passages deleted from the published versions of both novels.

In a deleted section of *Islands in the Stream* Janet convinces Thomas Hudson to allow her to cut his hair without letting him look in a mirror (an important prop in many Hemingway texts). Hudson, who narrates this passage, describes how Jan cuts his hair "boldly with a plan." He admits that he is "bored" at first but that it is "nice to have your girl play with you in any way."[6] Jan refuses to let him watch her progress as Hudson's boredom turns to apprehension about how she is styling his hair. She is transforming him into a modified version of herself although at this point her hair is still much longer than his. But she shapes his hair so it will grow out to resemble hers. As she continues to cut, Hudson feels disconcerted and both he and Jan are "excited," indicating that they are becoming aroused during the procedure. When she is finished, Jan looks at him and calls him "my new slain knight." This metaphor may not be as curious as it first appears for with its allusions to both battle and chivalry it emphasizes Hemingway's continuing concern with wounded masculinity and devotion to women. Jan wants to show off her man and convinces him to accompany her to a restaurant where people can see the results of their secret bond thereby making their "secret" public. Hudson at first does not like his haircut and hesitates to go out in public but finally agrees and afterwards says that it was "excellent training" in his domestication by Jan. He tells her, "Thank you very much for making me brave"—brave enough, that is, to let people see that Jan is now feminizing him after her fashion. "The people really look at us," Jan observes, "But they look with envy"—implying her belief (and, it appears, the author's) that many men and women would similarly like to transgress gender roles.

Later in bed, Hudson feels "a strange hollowness and desperation" and Jan asks him, "Do you feel it . . . our thing coming in so that nothing can stop it." The "hollowness" that Hudson feels suggests a receptive desire to be filled, and the "desperation" may represent a forbidden desire that he cannot, or refuses to, identify. Hudson claims to be baffled by whatever it is he feels and says, "But cutting people's hair can't make all these things." Jan tells him not to think and "kiss me and be my girl" and "my girl has to be a boy." Hudson then feels "a weakness [that] was concentrated forward from the base of his spine" and he feels "weak and destroyed inside himself"—a vivid description of the experience of passive sodomy. At this point, Jan again tells him to "lie back" and not to think and then she swings "her silken hair over him and kissed him hard." After she has apparently sodomized him, Jan assures Hudson that tomorrow in the daytime he can be the boy again and she will be the girl. Even though she has publicly exhibited his feminization at the restaurant, she assures him that he can still play the role of the man most of the time.

The activities of Jan and Hudson suggest Hemingway's increasing need for a woman to dominate him sexually. His explorations in his fiction in the 1940s and 1950s of women who actively attempt a project aimed at the feminization of their men represent a maturity in this conviction that was already hinted at broadly in the earlier works. It is important to remember that the haircutting activities are always instigated by the female characters. If Hemingway's sexuality was more traditional and he also happened to have a hair fetish, it is likely that male characters would occasionally initiate haircutting adventures. There is nothing inherently perverse about a man with a weakness for women's beautiful hair, whether long or short. But in Hemingway's work, it is always the woman who initiates the man into hair-play and that serves as a gateway to their domination of these men. Jan's wish to dominate Hudson comes across clearly when she calls him "my plaything" and tells him that he must do "whatever I want you to," to which Hudson simply replies, "All right." [7]

Hudson later refers to these "strange and untellable pleasures"[8] and in the published version of the novel he asks his handgun, "How long have you been my girl?" (327), which relates to Thomas Hudson's dream of his ex-wife sodomizing him with his own pistol (333–334). At least two other Hemingway protagonists sleep with a pistol. At least three times in *For Whom the Bell Tolls* (76, 279, 389), Robert Jordan is awakened and immediately feels "the butt of the pistol that lay alongside of his bare right leg" (389). When Maria first joins him in the robe/sleeping bag, she feels the pistol below Robert's waist and he feels her "relax" as she, apparently thinking it is his erection, prepares to be penetrated. Robert laughs and tells her, "Do not be afraid. This is the pistol" (77). In the posthumous fictional memoir, *True At First Light*, Papa, the autobiographical narrator, describes his sleeping companions:

> I lay in the cot with the old shotgun rigidly comfortable by my side and the pistol that was my best friend and severest critic of any defect of reflexes or of decision lying comfortably between my legs in the carved holster that Debba had polished with her hard hands and thought how lucky I was to know Miss Mary and have her do me the great honor of being married to me and to Miss Debba the Queen of the Ngomas.[9]

In this curious impressionistic passage, Hemingway relates guns to the women in his life. The "rigidly hard" shotgun reflects Debba's "hard hands." The pistol as a "severe critic" corresponds to Miss Mary who has deigned to marry Papa. Both Debba and Miss Mary become phallic women as they are equated with weapons. Hemingway ends the passage with Papa reflecting that "I could decide what was a sin and what was not" (281). Debba, Papa's African mistress, appropriates the holster to the pistol that "she truly loved" (281) and the narrator often describes her as pressing it hard (248) or holding it tight (278). Many of the women in the African stories—Helen in "The Snows of Kilimanjaro," Margot in "The Short Happy Life of Francis Macomber," and Miss Mary in *True at First Light*—handle guns with ease and precision and the narrators express admiration for this skill. Hemingway's appreciation for women with guns can be seen as another sign of his bestowal of the phallus on dominant women.

The question of the role of the dominant woman in the masochistic scenario has vexed scholars for some time. Siegel and Silverman find progressive and empowering qualities for women within male masochism. And as Taormino writes: "As women, since we are already positioned as the receptive, penetrated partner, we need only reorient ourselves to focus on the *other* orifice" and adds that this gives men the chance to "know what it's like to give it up."[10] Her comment echoes Thomas Hudson's remark in *Islands in the Stream*: "It's easy to give up" (334). Transgendered author and activist, Pat Califia, agrees with Taormino when she writes: "It's wonderful to fuck someone in male persona," but adds that "it is difficult even for polymorphous perverts to create top/bottom roles that do not share the worst characteristics of polarized, dichotomous genders."[11] What concerns Califia is "top/bottom roles" rather than "top/bottom" positions. These comments demonstrate that "top" and "bottom" may be meaningless designations except as adjectives describing sexual positions. The top does not necessarily correspond to the one who has social power. The bottom, especially as it reveals itself when the masochist retains control, does not correspond to a loss of power.

In Thomas Hudson's dream, his ex-wife "was sleeping on top of him" and "her hair hung down" in his eyes (333–334). Hemingway had earlier employed the sexual perspective of the bottom from the man's point of view in *A Farewell to Arms*. On the lovemaking in this novel, Spilka remarks:

> As no one has yet puzzled out, he [narrator Frederic Henry] would have to lie on his back to perform properly, given the nature of his leg wound, and Catherine [Barkley] would have to lie on top of him. This long-hidden and well-kept secret of the text is one Mary Welsh Hemingway implies about married love with Ernest and even quotes

him on in *How it Was*, one Ernest seems to imply about himself and Hadley in *A Moveable Feast* and makes fictionally explicit . . . in *The Garden of Eden*. . . .[That] Hemingway could not articulate that secret in *A Farewell to Arms* indicates the force not merely of censorship in the 1920s, but of chauvinist taboos against it. The interesting thing is that Hemingway—for whom the idea of female dominance was so threatening—could so plainly imply the female dominant without being understood or held to his oblique confession. . . . But that Hemingway could overcome his own and everyone else's fear of female dominance—could give it tacit public expression—seems to me remarkable. (213)

One must question Spilka's characterization of this discovery as a "long-hidden and well-kept secret" that "no one" before him had "puzzled out." Brenner discusses this passage (32) in a book published seven years before Spilka's. What's more, the novel explicitly describes the position of the lovers. Catherine places herself above Frederic and he, as narrator, says, "she would dip down to kiss me" (114). Frederic loosens the pins in Catherine's hair and "it would all come down and she would drop her head and we would both be inside of it" (114). Though he may not have been the first to divine this rather straightforward passage, Spilka makes his point about passivity as Frederic remains on his back with Catherine above him. Even more importantly, Spilka acknowledges "female dominance" in Hemingway's work three times in this passage. But when Spilka speaks of the "chauvinist taboos against" depicting this kind of sexuality, it must be remembered that Hemingway fully endorsed this kind of chauvinist thinking in nearly every area outside of his own bedroom.

But as an often-honest writer Hemingway was compelled to deal with his sexuality on some level. However, he must have felt he was too honest for his own good in *The Garden of Eden*, which can explain why he never actually finished the novel to the satisfaction of the image he felt compelled to serve. Lynn remarks that "Perhaps one of the factors that caused him to withhold the book from publication was a feeling that its audacity was more than the public taste at the time could cope with" (541). Burwell writes that Hemingway "clearly did not feel comfortable about disclosing," even in his letters, the content of this work-in-progress (97). He could not project this passive side of himself too obviously because of the public image he had cultivated. He had always exaggerated his macho traits and downplayed his submissive response to women, but in his work he needed to find a way of dealing with this response. Comley and Scholes say: "One solution that he found—possibly the most important one—was to make his women more like himself and to make his men . . . more feminine" (62). This comment is perceptive but it, too, seeks to impose a feminine identity on Hemingway, something not easily accomplished. It might be more accurate to say that Hemingway was willing to portray women as aggressive and men as passive and felt some discomfort in doing so, which may explain the characters many references to "remorse." Hemingway never seems sure of how far he can go in such descriptions of gender or of how much "remorse" to assign to transgressing accepted constructions of it.

Hemingway defies the code of masculinity again, as we have seen, in his enthusiasm for hairdressing, a cliché of unmanliness. Catherine Barkley in *A Farewell to Arms* wants her hair cut short. Near the end of the novel, anticipating Barbara Sheldon and Jan in unpublished sections of *The Garden of Eden* and *Islands in the Stream*, she tells Frederic Henry that she wants him to let his hair grow "a little longer and then I could cut mine and we'll be just alike" (299). A bit later, she returns to this idea: "We'll go together and get it cut or I'll go alone and come back and surprise you, . . . You won't say I can't will you?" Frederic answers, "No, I think it would be exciting" (304–305).

In *For Whom the Bell Tolls*, Maria sports a boy's haircut and Robert Jordan loves to run his hand through it and feel "the silky roughness of the cropped head rippling between his fingers" (73). She has small breasts and a long, slender body, "slim and long and warmly lovely," (283) a possibly phallic description. She echoes Samuelson's description—"built like a boy"—of Hemingway's wife Pauline (16). Robert often refers to Maria's "cropped head" as do the other guerrillas. Robert and Maria fall in love with each other almost immediately. They make love and the earth moves. The wise Pilar tells them that this shattering experience (to use Bersani's term) occurs only three times, with luck, in a lifetime. But aside from her boyish appearance, little about Maria presents itself as masculine or assertive unless we consider her long body itself as a symbolic phallus. When Robert goes on his last dangerous mission, Maria implores the Virgin Mary to bring him back safely because: "There isn't any me" (Catherine Barkley uses this exact phrase in *A Farewell to Arms* [111]), she prays, "I am only with him" (484). She remains submissive and compliant to Robert and loves him so much she would follow him anywhere. She wants to stay and die with him after he is mortally wounded, but he will not allow it, making his character more heroic. So, despite her androgynous looks, she does not fit the Hemingway formula of a dominant woman. The love scenes involving Robert Jordan and Maria are understated, as if Hemingway's descriptive powers fail him when a man makes love to a subservient woman. Yet Hemingway beautifully captures the emotional state of the mutual love of Robert and Maria while he skirts the purely physical. He provides physical descriptions leading up to the act, whether out in a field or in Robert's robe but slips into the shorthand of "Then afterwards" (284) to introduce the postcoital dialogue. Hemingway clearly means to convey the impression that Maria remains totally subservient to Robert Jordan throughout the novel. After the guerrilla camp receives the early morning surprise of a fascist invader, as he leaps into action to meet the threat, "Robert Jordan could feel Maria against his knees, dressing herself under the robe. She had no place in his life now" (288). Maria, like many Hemingway women, exerts a powerful sexuality but lacks social agency.

By way of contrast, the character of Pilar, in the same novel, has many masculine characteristics—she possesses a large and imposing physique, she uses foul language, and she temporarily takes command of the guerrilla band from her man, the amoral Pablo. Despite these masculine qualities and a scarcity of traditionally feminine traits in beauty and comportment she represents another recurring type of Hemingway woman who often assumes the role of a potential lover. Marie Morgan in *To Have and Have Not* and Honest Lil in *Islands in the Stream* provide two more examples. This type of woman, often portrayed as both motherly and as the whore-with-the-heart-of-gold, receives positive treatment in Hemingway's work. She often performs a traditional literary role as the all-knowing interpreter of thoughts and actions and also provides important background information. Pilar provides the narration of the massacre of the fascists that became so controversial when the novel was first published. She intuitively senses the mutual attraction of Robert Jordan and Maria and facilitates their sexual relationship.

Several critics have commented that Pilar represents a fictional version of Grace Hemingway. Brenner remarks that Hemingway's "hatred of his mother" may have been balanced by "his secret admiration of her Pilar-like dominance" (19). Others, such as Comley and Scholes (46) suggest that Pilar is modeled on Gertrude Stein, another large woman who, like Pilar, dispensed wisdom and sound advice, and who some see as a surrogate mother figure to the young Hemingway in his early days in Paris. Allen Josephs, however, points out that Pilar has been positively identified "not as Gertrude or Grace but as the flamenco dancer and singer Pastoria Imperio"[12] (94). Pilar may be a composite based in unequal parts upon several people and drawn from Hemingway's imagination. In any case there is a direct reference to Stein in *For Whom the Bell Tolls* when Robert says, "A rose is a rose is an onion . . . a stone is a stein is a rock" (312). If Hemingway looked to Stein as a mother figure, she also exerted an erotic influence on him and, according to some biographers, he was sexually attracted to her (Griffin 15). If Hemingway's own mother had lesbian tendencies, Stein's open relationship with Alice B. Toklas, who Hemingway also befriended, must have seemed something like *déja vu* but, in contrast to his hatred for his mother, Hemingway greatly enjoyed and benefited from his relationship with Stein, although they later ended their friendship.

Accusations of misogyny toward Hemingway must be tempered by his obvious empathy with women who lack the physical attributes of classically defined beauty. Hemingway finds an intangible quality, a definite comfort, and even a beauty in such women and he portrays them often. When Hemingway renders this type of woman in his fiction, she often appears as a prostitute though the author repeatedly demonstrates respect for the women in this trade. In *Islands in the Stream*, Thomas Hudson remembers a mass deportation of European prostitutes from Havana and how the crowds thought it was funny. The narrator relates Hudson's thoughts: "Why whores should be funny he had never understood" (246). In *To Have and Have Not*, Marie Morgan at 47 is described as "a big woman, long legged, big handed, big hipped, still handsome" (116), and Harry worries how she will be provided for after his death as "she's too old to peddle her hips now" (175), confirming his knowledge that she used to do so before she met him. Earlier, describing some other Key West women, Albert, the narrator of chapter nine, says, "the hardest working married women in town used to be sporting women" (99).

Erotic attraction to a big-bodied prostitute finds expression in the enigmatic story, "The Light of the World." The unnamed narrator (probably Nick Adams since this story fits his character) is over-whelmed at the sight of Alice who he estimates to weigh 350 pounds: "She was the biggest whore I ever saw in my life and the biggest woman."[13] Later Nick says, "she smiled and she had the prettiest face I ever saw" (297). Nick and Alice do not have a sexual encounter in this story as his friend Tom shuffles him away. But clearly Alice represents a potential love object.

A similar type, the aging, overweight prostitute, Honest Lil, appears in *Islands in the Stream*. Thomas Hudson and Honest Lil have long been friends and occasional lovers in Havana. The narrator describes her

> She made her stately progress to the far end of the bar, speaking to many of the men she passed and smiling at others. Everyone treated her

with respect. . . . She had a beautiful smile and wonderful dark eyes and lovely black hair. . . . She had a skin that was as smooth as olive-colored ivory . . . with a slightly smoky rose-like cast. . . . There was this lovely face looking down the bar at him, lovelier all the time as she came closer. (266–267)

A conversation between Honest Lil and Hudson, showcasing Hemingway's ongoing gift for dialogue, takes up some thirty pages of the novel. Hudson is grieving the death of his son, Tom, and finds comfort in Honest Lil's conversation, though he stoically refrains from discussing his grief. Hudson and Lil entertain each other with stories of their pasts, their thoughts on love and family, and Lil comments on the sexual appetites of many of the men she has been with, some of whom enjoy "piglike things" in bed (269). She exempts Hudson from this category though this conversation provides no details of his sexual tastes or of what constitutes "piglike things." They make plans to meet later in the evening but the unexpected arrival of Hudson's ex-wife takes precedence. Honest Lil serves a minor function in the novel, but she provides an instance of a type of woman that Hemingway returns to often and portrays with affection. There may be something in the commanding physical presence of such women, combined with worldly knowledge, and societally condemned sexuality that appeals to Hemingway. These women project an alterative point of desire for Hemingway, away from the long-legged beauties and the short-haired androgynes.

To return to Pilar in *For Whom the Bell Tolls*, she also serves as the vehicle to introduce another brief discussion of both lesbianism and a return to the brother–sister theme. When Pilar confesses her jealousy of Robert to Maria, the younger woman responds, "It was thee explained that there was nothing like that between us" (169). To which Pilar responds: "There is always something like that . . . something that there should not be. But with me there is not. . . . I want thy happiness and nothing more. . . . But now it gives me pleasure to say thus, in the daytime, that I care for thee" (169). Pilar's almost simultaneous affirmations and denials of attraction for Maria show her ambivalence in acknowledging lesbian desire. This brief passage reveals Hemingway's continuing need to insert a lesbian theme. In an earlier scene, Pilar also makes a reference to sibling relationships. She says to the lovers, "You could be brother and sister. . . . But I believe it is fortunate that you are not" (73). This reference to incest represents Hemingway's continuing interest in sibling-like relationships between his lovers in which identities and genders are blurred.

Hemingway proves quite capable of lofty descriptions of heterosexual love even when not depicting the man in a submissive role but these renderings of physical love also lack an aggressive male presence. The lyrical description of love finds its most compelling example, perhaps, in *For Whom the Bell Tolls*. Robert Jordan and Maria find several opportunities to be alone in their four days together, even within the restricted confines of the guerrillas' perimeter. The opening pages of chapter thirteen (173–174) find Robert and Maria returning with Pilar from the camp of their compatriot Sordo. Pilar deliberately walks ahead to leave the lovers time to be alone. Holding Maria's hand, Robert Jordan feels "as though a current moved up his arm and filled his whole body with an aching hollowness of wanting" (173). Maria, who had been gang-raped by fascist soldiers before being rescued by the guerrillas, wants Robert to help restore her ability to love. As he opens her shirt and touches her breast, she wishes to do the same with him: "Everything as you." She wants to emulate his masculine advances but he tells her, "Nay. That is an impossibility" (159). They proceed to make love. Hemingway presents the perspective of Robert Jordan as he proceeds psychically down "a dark passage which led to nowhere, then to nowhere, then again to nowhere" and he is "borne once again always and to nowhere, now beyond all bearing up, up, up and into nowhere, suddenly, scaldingly, holdingly all nowhere gone and time absolutely still and they were both there" (174). The constant repetition of "nowhere" represents a desire for psychic annihilation in sex, or as Studlar calls it, "a return to nothingness" (123). Robert and Maria "felt the earth move out and away from under them" (175). They both experience the *petite mort* and afterwards, Robert says, "I feel as though I wanted to die when I am loving thee." Maria agrees, saying, "I die each time. Do you not die?" (175). Robert Jordan experiences love as sacrifice, the "nowhere" representing his abandonment before and submission to the female presence. For her part, Maria refers to sex with Robert as "La Gloria" (411) investing it with almost religious significance. These passages reveal Hemingway at his most lyrical. Hemingway presents the love of Robert Jordan and Maria in eminently tasteful and powerful descriptions throughout the novel. The couple behave altogether as young lovers and Hemingway captures this beautifully. These scenes of sexual love, expressed metaphorically, comprise the most moving such passages in Hemingway's fiction. He conveys the feeling of love without caring to dwell on the act of penetration, which obviously occurs here. Hemingway celebrates heterosexual love without also celebrating the genital-phallic imperative.

While Maria maintains the role of submissive woman to Robert Jordan's hero in *For Whom the Bell Tolls,* Catherine Barkley in *A Farewell to Arms* presents a different case. Some critics have maintained that Catherine presents an essentially submissive woman, unhealthily devoted to and dependent upon Frederic Henry. While Frederic certainly exercises more social agency in the wider world than does Catherine a closer reading of the novel reveals that Catherine, much more than Frederic, defines the parameters of their personal relationship. Frederic relates his first amorous advances: "I leaned forward in the dark to kiss her and there was a sharp stinging flash. She had slapped my face" (26). Later, when she is ready, she kisses him and warns him of their future together telling him, "we're going to have a very strange life" (27).

Catherine suffers from loss and feels isolated since the death of her fiancée, killed at the front in the battle of the Somme. She attaches herself to Frederic to ease the sense of grief and guilt. She experiences guilt because she had denied sex to her boyfriend despite his entreaties in the period just before his death. In a very real sense, she uses Frederic to compensate for this loss. Her suffering is so great that she's willing to submerge herself into a single identity with him as if to diffuse the pain. Throughout the novel, she professes her undying love for Frederic and he reciprocates but Catherine engulfs his identity into her own. As Eby points out, "Catherine's plea is a demand for *recognition* and an attempt, however lovingly expressed, to commandeer her lover's body" (original emphasis 206). She makes numerous statements regarding the merging of her identity with Frederic's, such as: "There isn't any me. I'm you. Don't make a separate me." (111) and "We're the same one" (285). Remarks such as these disguise the fact that it is Frederic who surrenders himself to Catherine, after initially trying to resist falling in love with her. As narrator, he often speaks of Catherine's courage and at one point he says, "If people bring so much courage to the world the world has to kill them to break them so of course it kills them . . . It kills the very good and the very gentle and the very brave impartially" (239). These words foreshadow Catherine's fate. Hemingway also endows Catherine with one of his most important male characteristics—the ability to face death without fear. As she lays dying, Catherine tells a weeping Frederic, "I'm not afraid. I just hate it" (315). Hemingway reverses stereotypical, gender-specific character traits—in this case, courage and tears. Courage constitutes the single most important element of the Hemingway code hero and here Catherine embodies this virtue while Frederic weeps helplessly. Sandra Whipple Spanier asks, "Why has

Catherine, the only character besides Frederic who inhabits this novel from beginning to end, been so consistently ignored as a model of the Hemingway code?" She answers her question with: "The simplest explanation is that it probably never occurred to most readers that the 'code hero' could be a woman."[14] (13). Hemingway invests Catherine with the masculine qualities that he considers essential and that he gives these attributes to a woman demonstrates how he consciously subverts traditional values.

Hemingway's creation of the character of Catherine Barkley has received criticism for its lack of depth. Spanier remarks that Catherine "has been attacked or dismissed for her simplicity" (14) but adds that "the code hero usually *is* a simple character" (14). Although Hemingway never develops Catherine's character fully enough, depriving the reader of the opportunity to better understand her psychology, she possesses certain traits that establish her in the Hemingway *oeuvre* almost as a code hero in her own right. She conforms to other "lost generation" types that Hemingway depicted throughout the 1920s. She experiences the same sense of loss and emptiness. Her boyfriend has been killed, she has lost her religion, and feels no ties to her native England. She appears just as emotionally adrift as Jake Barnes and Brett Ashley in *The Sun Also Rises*. She meets Frederic Henry and essentially takes over his life. In many ways, Frederic's motives, though he acts as narrator, remain as vague as Catherine's. His chief drive, aside from self-preservation, consists of his love for Catherine. When she tells him, "We're the same one" (285), she imposes a unity onto their relationship, a unity quite similar to that which both Catherine Bourne and Barbara Sheldon attempt to impose on their husbands in *The Garden of Eden*. In *A Farewell to Arms*, Catherine Barkley tells Frederic, "there's only us two and in the world there's all the rest of them" (134) and Frederic, as narrator, relates: "we were alone together, alone against the others" (238). Both David Bourne and Frederic Henry accept the limits placed upon their social relations and their confinement in interpersonal relationships imposed upon them by the two Catherines. The major difference, apart from the explicit sex of *The Garden of Eden*, lies in Catherine Barkley's lack of participation in the larger world outside of her relationship with Frederic, and Catherine Bourne's determination to involve herself and her husband in the fulfillment of her will in that world in the form of the narrative of their gender transgressions. Frederic, therefore, remains faithful and devoted to Catherine Barkley to the end, while David and Catherine Bourne undergo a traumatic rupture.

CELEBRATING THE DOMINANT WOMAN
IN *THE GARDEN OF EDEN*

Hemingway did much of the writing of *The Garden of Eden* in the years just after World War II. The more provocative nature of the love scenes may be due in part to the relaxation of censorship over the course of the mid-twentieth century. But it is also fair to surmise that Hemingway's sex life with Mary, who he married in 1944, became more eventful than previously and developed certain areas more fully. Meyers reports that 800 pages of the novel were completed in the first half of 1946 (436). In a recent essay, John Leonard reports on his exhaustive research into the chronology of the composition of *The Garden of Eden* and concludes that Hemingway composed the better part of the novel during a "late flowering period" from 1957 to 1959 and that it represents a "fully-achieved narrative written very late in the life of a great American author" (80). With revisions throughout the 1950s, the manuscript numbers some 2,409 total pages according to Burwell (99), remaining unfinished at the author's death though with "provisional endings." The novel, as published, presents a number of themes, chief among them a submissive male and aggressive female sexuality, which in Book One receives such a celebratory treatment as to leave little doubt of the author's feelings. Hemingway's unambiguous portrayal of such sexuality may well explain why he never sought to publish this work. The exigencies of his image may well have restrained him from sharing his art. The character of Catherine Bourne presents an accumulation of traits inherited from many of her predecessors and amounts to a quantitative and qualitative synthesis. A dynamic character who despite her youth is self-consciously decadent and eager to experiment, Catherine's personality presents at least two sides. One consists of the devoted wife and another the initiator of forbidden love.

When Catherine has her hair cut short for the first time, she arrives triumphantly at the hotel and tells her author-husband, David, "I'm a girl. But now I'm a boy too and I can do anything and anything and anything" (14). David reacts ambivalently, repelled and attracted at the same time: "Her hair was cropped as short as a boy's. . . . It could mean too much or it could only mean showing the beautiful shape of a head" (14, 16). This comment conveys David's contradictory reactions to the newly androgynous Catherine. Even earlier, as if to warn him, Catherine had told David, "I'm going to wake you up in the night and do something to you that you've never heard of or imagined" (5). Her terminology suggests a violation and marks her as the aggressor and implies that consent is not required (though it is expected), that she will impose her will.

Later, in bed, David calls her "girl" and she quickly corrects him: "Don't call me girl." Then she begins to "take" him sexually and forcefully from the top, saying; "Now you can't tell who is who, can you? . . . You're changing . . . Oh you are. You are. Will you change and be my girl and let me take you?" She continues, "I'm Peter. You're my wonderful Catherine . . . You were so good to change" (17). Catherine's appropriation of the phallic name Peter gives some indication of what transpires here. Hemingway provides more:

> He [David] lay there and felt something and then *her hand holding him and searching lower and he helped with his hands* and then lay back in the dark and did not think at all and only *felt the weight and the strangeness inside* and she said, "Now you can't tell who is who can you?" (Emphasis added, 17)

The next night the scenario repeats itself and Hemingway is even more explicit:

> [S]he made the dark magic of the change again and he did not say no when she spoke to him and asked him the questions and *he felt the change so that it hurt him all through* and when it was finished after they were both exhausted she was shaking and she whispered to him, "Now we have done it. Now we have really done it." (Emphasis added, 20)

"The strangeness inside" which "hurt him all through" could conceivably be a description of David's thoughts. But clearly Hemingway describes not mental anguish but physical pain—the penetration by Catherine using her hand or an object held in her hand. The dialogue from the original manuscript after this nontraditional sexual act makes it more clear as when Catherine says, "It isn't everybody who has someone that's half boy and half girl."[15] Catherine has assumed the phallus both figuratively and literally. She becomes "the boy" Peter, and David is now "the girl" Catherine.

This description remains uncharacteristically explicit for Hemingway. A crossed-out phrase in the unpublished manuscript contains more graphic detail describing how David feels "something that yielded and entered."[16] What "yielded" can only be David's spinchter and what "entered" refers to the device—her finger(s) or some object—that Catherine uses to penetrate him. Yet even the toned-down language of the published version leaves only the instrument that Catherine uses to the imagination of the perceptive reader. Though the narrator does not make it clear, Hemingway may have felt he had gone quite far enough in his depiction of sodomy on the man by the woman. David Bourne accepts the transformation engineered by his wife to the point of willingly submitting to sodomy. He accepts the traditional role of the submissive female and even tacitly agrees to a form of feminization. Indeed, he must accept his feminization to avoid a self-identification as homosexual because of the common association then (as now) of sodomy and homosexuality. David's strongest resistance to Catherine's assumption of the role of "boy" comes when, after psychically assuming this role, she asks David if she can kiss him. He replies, "Not if you're a boy and I'm a boy" (67).[17] This remark demonstrates David's acceptance of a *de facto* consciousness of feminization at the hands of the dominant woman without an accompanying homosexual identification. David assumes the role of the "girl" whenever Catherine chooses to be the "boy" and have sex with him as such. At one point he even says to her, "Thank you for letting me be Catherine."[18] The motif of forced or voluntary feminization of the submissive man reenacts itself throughout the explicit literature of masochism. David's implicit acceptance of such feminization comes about through Catherine's assumption of the role of "boy," which threatens his psychic investment in the male body. The dread of homosexual identification leads to David's voluntary feminization. If he will be penetrated, it must be as a "girl."

As Catherine takes the initiative, Hemingway as the author manipulates her. Catherine controls David's sexual will, but the author controls hers. The text represents a masochistic fantasy that bears more resemblance to Sacher-Masoch's *Venus in Furs* than may initially seem apparent. The difference lies in the narrative device. In the text-within-the-text that forms the story of *Venus in Furs*, the narrator acts as enthusiast for the action. In *The Garden of Eden*, the narrator remains neutral, simply reporting the scene. But this very reportage comes close to placing the narrator in the role of participant. In many respects, David represents Hemingway as much as Severin stands in for Sacher-Masoch. David reluctantly submits to a dominant woman while Severin, in *Venus in Furs*, initiates his own surrender but both assume the role of the submissive male. The different devices produce a similar effect—sexual submission to a powerful woman.

In *The Garden of Eden*, the spouses have reversed traditional sexual roles in bed and they have both enjoyed it—David, to his surprise. At this point David seems quite happy to be submissive before his wife's sexual dominance. Perhaps more than anything else, David's delight in placing himself as the object of Catherine's will demonstrates

Hemingway's depiction of male masochism. David resists but only mildly, allowing Catherine full control, saying quietly to her as she sleeps, "I'm with you. No matter what else you have in your head, I'm with you and I love you" (20). This is the traditional feminine and submissive response of a wife to a husband and Hemingway turns it around. All this occurs in Book One before the appearance of Marita and before Catherine's displays of jealousy, first over David's writing, then over his growing involvement with Marita. Catherine deteriorates mentally as the novel progresses, and Marita replaces her in David's affections.

While the story of David, Catherine, and Marita is unfolding, the unpublished portions of the manuscript develop a second plot involving another young couple, painters Nick and Barbara Sheldon, and their own sexual transgressions. This subplot also involves another writer, Andy Murray, who in some sections of the manuscript assumes the role of narrator. The paths of all six of these principal characters— Catherine, David, Marita, Barbara, Nick, and Andy—cross several times in the unpublished manuscript. It is largely because of the wholesale deletions of so many important pages that touch on these interrelationships that many feel the published novel to be unconscionably eviscerated.

In a cold Paris apartment, Nick and Barbara Sheldon try to keep warm in their bed. They have already made passionate love and feel heady and "in a strange country."[19] Both wish to continue the moment but it is Barbara who directs their activities: "[J]ust shut your eyes," she tells Nick, "Be asleep and don't think at all,"[20] which recalls how David "did not think at all" (GOE 17) while Catherine sodomizes him, and Jan's instructions to Thomas Hudson, "Lie back and don't think about anything."[21] After Barbara's admonition, the narrator relates how Nick follows Barbara's directive as he tries not to think. After some modest foreplay by Barbara, Nick becomes aware of the bedcovers "rising and falling" and then feels "the entering, aching hard gentle then firm," and he feels "two firmnesses, the inner that was both" as well as breasts and body held tightly against his own.[22] At this point, Barbara tells Nick to keep his eyes closed. However, he opens them to see her arch her back then suddenly she moves forward and he feels her hair swing "forward like a silken curtain."[23] Nick closes his eyes again and he and Barbara continue to move. Hemingway then uses the familiar "Afterwards" to indicate that lovemaking is over and Nick and Barbara slowly begin to breathe more quietly as they feel the beat of each other's hearts.[24]

Barbara and Nick have made love in an unconventional manner. It is important for both of them, especially for Nick, that he keep his eyes closed and that he does not "think at all" as Barbara attempts to feminize him. Nick, like David, can only accept this if he shuts his eyes to it and does not dwell upon it. There is no question that Nick enjoys the physical sensations with Barbara, as David does with Catherine, but the psychological implications are too much to bear if he does not detach from them. Eby refers to this half-blind acceptance of feminization as "transvestic hallucination" as he describes: "In each passage, the male protagonist enters a state of 'not thinking' and then, aided by fetishistic/transvestic ritual and some form of anal penetration, hallucinates that he is *physically* transformed into a 'girl.' "[25] Barbara and Nick make love with "the blankets rising and falling," and she is obviously on top, which in itself is not unusual. It is unlikely that Nick would have had to detach himself if they were merely making love with the woman on top. But there is the discussion of the "entering, aching hard gentle then firm," and this must describe not just an erect penis since "there were two firmnesses," which implies that Barbara penetrates Nick while he penetrates her. Though the passage is poetic and not easy to decipher, the narrator's comment that Barbara's breasts are pressed against Nick suggests an external firmness that Nick can feel on his body, while the phrase "the inner that was both" suggests that both lovers have a firmness inside of them. To visualize the lovers together like this with Barbara on top of Nick suggests that she is sodomizing him either with her fingers or an external object, both certainly physical possibilities. This kind of action might be somewhat difficult if Barbara's breasts remained pressed firmly to Nick's chest but the passage suggests movement and there is no reason to believe she remains static in this position in which it would also be difficult to swing her hair forward. Again, as in the scenes with David and Catherine, the reader cannot be certain what device the woman uses to open and enter the man although with David at least the reader knows that he "helped with his hands" (GOE 17). And Barbara certainly makes love to Nick from the top as is made clear when her hair swings down over him "like a silken curtain," an image constantly repeated in the later works, such as *Islands in the Stream* (333), and recalls passages in earlier works such as Frederic Henry's comments in *A Farewell to Arms*.[26] Hemingway's male lovers often surrender themselves completely to the physically aggressive desire of the women they love and feel a sense of security beneath the "silken curtain" of their hair.

Nick Sheldon, despite his acceptance of Barbara's sexual directives, is not without some misgivings—or as the narrator and the characters themselves refer to it, "remorse"—about her increasing control of his sexuality. These qualms become more pronounced after Barbara cuts his hair to match hers, without following the close-cropped and stark hairstyles dictated by Catherine Bourne in her marriage. Barbara first makes Nick grow his hair longer to approximate her own shoulder-length tresses, just as Jan does with Thomas Hudson in the manuscript of *Islands in the Stream*. Then Barbara, in the same freezing Paris apartment, begins to trim Nick's hair so it will grow out to match her own. Just before cutting his hair, Barbara assures Nick that it will be in his interest to let her do so because she will then let him be "the boy" and she will be "the girl," suggesting to the reader that Nick is presently her girl and she is the boy. After this initial and radical haircut, Nick "felt strange and empty but very excited."[27] We have seen how both Nick and Thomas Hudson feel "empty" or "hollow" and "excited" at the same time. The excitement can relate to an anticipation, a longing to be violated, entered, and filled within their bodies, and represents a heightened state of receptivity. Sodomy, performed by their female lovers, can fulfill this desire and it seems to be what Hemingway is so often invoking in these passages. In the excised section of *The Garden of Eden*, just discussed, Nick has become totally dependent upon Barbara's sexual direction, has *become* her in a very real sense, and wants to experience what Jan teasingly asks Thomas Hudson in *Islands in the Stream*: "Do you know now what we have?" (334) as women, which in both cases can only mean the capacity to be penetrated.

Barbara plots her transformation of Nick (and herself) methodically. She knows enough to expect some resistance but she perseveres, sure of her own will. In contrast to Catherine and David, Barbara does not bully Nick or overpower him with her aggressive sexuality. She builds upon their already strong relationship as she decides to become the dominant force within it. In an interior monologue in an unpublished section of the manuscript, Barbara makes several intriguing observations on her increasing domination of Nick. Barbara muses about who will be "the one," which refers to who will be the "top" in the act of love. She thinks about how her hair comes down "over his [face] when I'm the one." She knows well that Nick, as a biological male, "can always be the one" but stops and thinks, "no I can too."[28] Barbara has rationalized her domination of Nick much more thoroughly than Catherine has in her relationship with David. Catherine acts almost by pure instinct while Barbara reasons her position.

Catherine's actions seem selfish compared to those of Barbara, who wants to control her husband's sexuality but seeks to persuade and convince him that her dominance is for their common good.

Over time, Barbara eventually sculpts Nick into an image of herself. In the unpublished manuscript when Catherine first lays eyes on Nick and Barbara she tells David, "I'm frightened," by their androgynously matching appearance.[29] The four sit together and have drinks as the narrator relates that Catherine, observing Nick's unusual haircut, feels "very strangely." After she composes herself, she tells Barbara how frightened she was at first. Barbara asks her why she was afraid and Catherine replies that she felt it was "something abnormal" and that she became disoriented because she enjoyed it. But on reflection she tells Barbara that she feels it was "just people being brave enough to do what they wanted." But Barbara corrects Catherine: "What *I* wanted," she insists, indicating publicly that she is the dominant partner and that Nick wears his hair in a feminine hairstyle for all to see because she wills it (emphasis added).

Similarly, in another discarded chapter, Andy Murray recalls a meeting with Barbara and Nick at the beach in Hendaye as they wear "Basque fishermen's shirts and shorts."[30] In the published novel Catherine and David also wear matching "striped fishermen's shirts and shorts" (GOE 6). Andy notes how both Nick's and Barbara's hair is long and styled in the same shoulder-length fashion. Andy expresses shock at the sight of the couple and tells Nick that he was "startled" and compares his surprise upon seeing them to, "[l]ike seeing unicorns."[31] After listening to Nick's explanation that it "means a lot" to Barbara to appear this way, Andy, like Catherine, reconsiders and admits that they do, indeed, look "wonderful together."[32] Barbara wants Andy to join them in their "secret" by cutting his hair like theirs, but Andy demurs, saying, "I'd be spooked," which is followed by Nick's response: "That's part of it . . . I was really spooked. Wasn't I Barb?"[33] Nick here confides his ambivalence to Andy while nevertheless admitting, in Barbara's presence, that he has obeyed her will. Nick in these passages (and David in others) seems to want to have it both ways—to affirm publicly his feminization at the hands of his wife, and to retain a masculine self-image that is not "queer."

Alone later with David, Catherine tries to explain away her nervous reaction by telling him that their own close-cropped hairstyles are much more fashionable than those of the Sheldons. She tells David that hers was "a real invention. You'll see. Everybody will do mine and nobody will do hers but queers."[34] This demonstrates the rivalry between the two dominant women of *The Garden of Eden*. Both have feminized their men but they disagree over who has done so most artistically or stylishly. Despite the undertone of male homosexuality, Hemingway remains hostile to it with the continual references to "queers" from the lips of both his male and female characters. In another passage, Andy discusses his friendship with the Sheldons with an unnamed woman who, puzzled, asks about Nick if there was anything "queer about him?" Andy assures her that there was not but later says that Nick and Barbara were "primitive."[35] To Hemingway's characters, "primitive" is acceptable, even attractive, but "queer" never is. In conversation with Andy, Nick expresses his misgivings about his transformation. "Everybody thinks we're queer," he says, "But who cares?" He then asks Andy directly, "Do you think I look like a bloody sodomite?" Andy assures him that he does not and asks who thinks that. Nick replies, "I do."[36] Nick may ask his friend if he looks like a "bloody sodomite" because he knows that he secretly *is* one, and a passive heterosexual one at that. Nick enjoys the sensual pleasure of this act, but he feels "remorse" and does not want his friend to think he indulges in it, although Barbara "outs" him at every turn.

Shortly after this dialogue takes place, Barbara decides to expand the prerogatives of her sexual power. On a walk on the beach with Andy, he relates how she "put her hand in my pocket very naturally as if it was her own."[37] Almost inevitably, shortly afterwards, Barbara succeeds in seducing Andy, enjoying it as his voice gets "thick" and touching the side of his face with her foot although afterwards she feels "remorse."[38] But what is important about this infidelity is that it apparently comes with Nick's acquiescence as he tells Andy that he is so busy with his painting that "I don't keep her good enough company,"[39] which essentially gives Andy leave to make love with Barbara. Nick virtually bows before the will of the dominant woman as she takes another lover with his knowledge.

The relationship of Barbara and Nick Sheldon, absent from the published pages of *The Garden of Eden*, displays perhaps more elements of masochism than that of David and Catherine Bourne. Barbara has feminized her husband in her own way and has cuckolded him and led him to doubt his own masculinity by making him fear that he is "queer." It is the last of these, the allegations of homosexuality, that most disturb both Nick and his author. Both Nick and his creator, Ernest Hemingway, obviously enjoy the passive role in sodomy but neither of them fully wants to admit it. Both affirm it as a heterosexual practice in part to avoid the dreaded epithet "queer."

While Hemingway exhibits homophobia against gay men, he remains fascinated by lesbianism. The lesbian encounter between

Marita and Catherine in *The Garden of Eden* is only acknowledged and mentioned as having taken place. Similarly, Barbara's attraction to Catherine is not significantly developed in the unpublished sections of the novel. This is totally unlike the relatively explicit heterosexual passages in the first two chapters. The theme of lesbianism had been covered by Hemingway before, most directly in an early story, "The Sea Change" (1931). This short tale takes place in a Paris café and centers around the conversation of a young couple, Philip and his unnamed girlfriend. They have both returned from a holiday and are suntanned and "her hair was cut short and grew beautifully away from her forehead."[40] She is about to go off on a lesbian tryst. Philip is jealous and cannot accept it at first, just like David Bourne in *The Garden of Eden*. But later he sends her off, apparently with his blessings. He then goes to the bar and feeling like a new man he tells the bartender, "I'm a different man, James . . . Vice is a very strange thing" (305). Some critics have viewed this story as a Hemingway endorsement or even an admission of homosexuality, when more likely it suggests a typically male fascination with lesbianism, not gay sex in general. The similarities to *The Garden of Eden* are obvious. An androgynous-looking woman is initiating "forbidden" sex. The man is at first angry and calls it "perversion" (304) but reluctantly comes to accept it and experiences a freedom he had not known before.

The theme of a woman drawing a man into a forbidden area of his sexuality can be seen in much of Hemingway's work, from his earliest stories through *The Garden of Eden*. Catherine Barkley tells Frederic in *A Farewell to Arms*, "I want to ruin you" (305) and two or more decades later Catherine Bourne says to David: "You aren't very hard to corrupt and you're an awful lot of fun to corrupt" (150). She also had warned him early on that, "I'm the destructive type . . . and I'm going to destroy you" (5). In addition, in another deleted passage, *The Garden of Eden* refers directly to "The Sea Change." David is thinking about "corruption" just as Philip (coincidentally, perhaps, the name originally given to David's character in the early drafts of *The Garden of Eden)* refers to "vice." "She [Catherine] changes into a boy and back to a girl carelessly and happily and she enjoys corrupting me."[41] Referring to their nighttime sex and daytime nude sunbathing, David continues, "The sea change was made in the night and grows in the night and the darkness that she wants and needs now grows in the sun."[42] Eby notes how these lines "read like a gloss of Hemingway's 1931 short story" (158) and Kennedy remarks that David's "experience seems an elaborate revision of Phil's predicament in 'The Sea Change.' David's participation in Catherine's erotic reversals—doing the 'devil things'—perhaps indicates his *own* androgynous interest in the female experience of intercourse" (emphasis in original, 133). And just as in "The Sea Change," in *The Garden of Eden* an attractive young woman with her hair "cut short" goes off to enjoy a first-time lesbian relationship.

Catherine does not initiate the lesbian experiment with Marita. She allows herself to be seduced by Marita, who claims to have done this reluctantly and only because she thought Catherine wanted it. The revelation of this "off-page" lesbian encounter occurs only in sketchy dialogue between Catherine and David. Hemingway wisely refrains from an explicit description such as he provides in the heterosexual episodes in the first three chapters. The lesbian relationship between Catherine and Marita never really comes alive. Catherine offers a few remarks about how when driving with Marita to Cannes, she "pulled out from the road and into the brush . . . I kissed her and she kissed me and we sat in the car and I felt very strange" (113). In the manuscript version, David later asks Marita about her interest in girls and she replies: "Girls are nothing if you're not that way" but adds that "[i]t's better than nothing."[43] But despite her radical sexuality, Marita presents an updated version of the Victorian angel-in-the-house in her submissiveness to David. By bringing the relatively lifeless Marita into the novel, Hemingway initiates Catherine's gradual loss of control. Catherine never intends for Marita to take her place. Catherine is not necessarily unbalanced to begin with. Events that she (through the agency of the author) sets in motion drive her crazy but there is nothing inevitable about it. Indeed to Burwell, "Catherine's actions seem not so much madness as healthy anger" (114). The traditional masculine in Hemingway made him feel he had to destroy his monstrous female creation of Catherine.

Hemingway often said that he never wrote with a specific plot in mind: "Sometimes you think you know how a story is going to end but when you get to writing it, it turns out entirely different."[44] This is no doubt the case here. Book One opens up a world of sexual possibilities. If one can imagine the book as written in anything like its present form, one can see Hemingway rereading the first three chapters and realizing at some point that he could never publish it if it developed along the lines he had laid out there. It would have deflated his self-image of the he-man and confirmed him as a "bloody sodomite." Again, this is not to suggest that Hemingway was a latent or repressed homosexual, but rather, in the host of modes in which humans elect to love each other physically, he chose from among those that defy or transcend traditional male and female roles. In the composition of the first part of *The Garden of Eden*, Hemingway gives full rein to his submissive and masochistic sensibility, a part of his character totally absent is his public persona.

Hemingway often spoke of the need to write from experience. "You need an awful lot of past performances," he writes in *Green Hills of Africa*, adding: "It's very hard to get anything true on anything you haven't seen yourself" (193). The scenes in Book One of *The Garden of Eden*, and the deleted sections involving Barbara and Nick Sheldon, ring too true to have been totally manufactured by the imagination. Consider Catherine's remark to David: "Truly you don't have to worry darling until night. We won't let the night things come in the day" (22). Later, when she tells him more explicitly, "I will only be a boy at night and I won't embarrass you" (56), she is reassuring him that he can trust her with the secret of their forbidden sexuality. She is entering into a verbal agreement with David that can be read as a version of the masochistic contract discussed earlier. Hemingway no doubt demanded and received similar assurances in his private life. If, as is likely, he and his wives engaged in transgendered activities including female-on-male sodomy, Hemingway would have insisted upon such assurances of discretion. Catherine's remark to David consists of a promise not to compromise him, not to reveal him as a "bottom," though she does put him on display in public, showing off his new haircut and offering him to Marita in another reversal of traditional gender roles. Typically, the man wants a "showpiece" as his wife or girlfriend. But in the early parts of the novel, Catherine, in her general care in dealing with David's masculine psyche, shows a quality that must have greatly appealed to Hemingway and he would have demanded this kind of discretion in his own relationships.

Catherine begins with the qualities of both loyalty and sexual domination. However, in her determination to "write" in competition with David, she attempts to usurp the phallus, the symbol of social domination, as distinct from sexual domination. She experiences frustration in her attempts to write, anticipating the theories of Hélène Cixous, for as Willingham points out, Catherine writes with her body, her sexuality.[45] In Catherine's effort to impose her carnality on David's artistic production, she competes with her husband in her wish to help create the narrative of their lives. Such a narrative would represent a form of symbiosis between the two, a theme so attractive to Hemingway. However, this attempt ultimately threatens David's masculine self-identification. The threat comes, not so much through Catherine's sexuality, but through her efforts to control David's artistic production, a male prerogative. She has broken her promise and allowed "the night things to come into the day" (22). To David, as to Hemingway, masochistic sexuality remains attractive but art belongs exclusively in the realm of the masculine. This further explains Hemingway's need to destroy Catherine.

Early in the novel, David realizes that Catherine's sexuality has begun to undermine his work when he muses, "I used to be a writer. Never mind that. This is much more interesting."[46] Much later, Catherine dismisses the importance of David's fiction and wants him to continue the narrative of their own sexual explorations instead. By this time David, back at work on his own stories, shows his irritation at Catherine's project when he refers to "the god damned narrative" (238). Catherine often expresses regrets at her lack of artistic ability. She laments that, "I know wonderful things to write and I can't even write a letter" (53). She tells her husband repeatedly, "I can't write things, David" (222, 223). But she wants to be directly involved in the project and tells David "we have to start seeing about getting the book out" (188). Finally, frustrated in her attempt to involve herself in David's artistic creation, she burns the manuscripts of his short stories, which she sees as rivals to their autobiographical narrative. She tells David his stories were "worthless and I hated them" (219). A stunned David inspects the ashes. Catherine tells him "I really thought I ought to make a clean sweep. . . . Now you can go right on with the narrative and there will be nothing to interrupt you. You can start in the morning" (222). Actions such as these have the effect of driving David into the arms of the submissive Marita. Bitterly, he tells Marita, "She burned every fucking thing except the narrative. The stuff about her" (230). With Marita's unqualified support, David ends the published version of the novel with his artistic talents restored. Hemingway (through Jenks) resolves the conflict with Catherine by destroying her sanity. Her destruction indicates Hemingway's extreme ambivalence in surrendering to female domination and his subsequent rejection of it. Catherine's transformation from the alternately comforting and demanding sexual adventurer into an active competitor with her husband in the realm of art represents a violation of the "contract." According to Deleuze: "In the cold-hearted alliance between man and woman, it is this cruelty and sentimentality in woman that compel man to thought and properly constitute the masochistic ideal" (54). Catherine violates this "masochistic ideal" by becoming a rival in thought. At this point the masochist, already in control, exercises his authority and terminates the contract.

CHAPTER 6

HEMINGWAY, RACE, AND
COLONIALISM

To the discussion of theories of reactionary masochism in chapter 1, another nonprogressive element must be added—the suggested engagement of masochism with colonialism. Spilka has demonstrated that Hemingway, in his youth, absorbed the fiction of Kipling and Marryat and this can account in part for his easy acceptance of colonial projects. Both Silverman and Siegel comment on the incongruous conjunction of masochism and colonialism. Siegel maintains that "male masochism, forbidden direct expression in the modern world, collaborates with colonialism" (25). In this connection, she discusses the work of Mary Webb, Thomas Hardy, and others. A more perfect union of colonialism and masochism finds expression in the life and work of T.E. Lawrence to whom Silverman devotes a long and incisive chapter (299–338). Despite the masochism and homoeroticism of his written work and his visceral attachment to the Arab cause, Lawrence never seriously deviated from British policy in the Middle East, even when he knew the Foreign Office was lying through its teeth to the Arabs during World War I.[1] In Lawrence, a case could be made for his empathy with an oppressed race, that as an official of a decadent ruling race, he recognized and sought to identify with the Arab Revolt. In a different context, Frantz Fanon comments on African American folktales (i.e., Br'er Rabbit stories) in which the characters identified as blacks outsmart and ultimately defeat their supposedly more sophisticated opponents. Fanon writes that "the Negro makes stories in which it is possible for him to work off his aggression; the white man's unconscious justifies this aggression and gives it worth by turning it on himself, thus reproducing the classic schema of masochism."[2] A similar process may be at work in Lawrence's embrace of the Arab Revolt. However, the analogy contains important distinctions. The Arab uprising was not, of course, directed against the empire that Lawrence represented but rather against the Ottoman Turks. If Lawrence's espousal of the Arab cause demonstrates masochism, and even this remains questionable, it was essentially risk-free and without a binding commitment. It seems more likely that Lawrence would have given rein to his homosexual and masochistic impulses in whatever milieu he found himself. Yet, part of his motive can be seen as a submissive form of sexual imperialism.

Lawrence's motives, like those of Hemingway, are exceedingly complex. Lawrence demonstrated incredible physical endurance and in Chapter LXXX of *Seven Pillars of Wisdom*, he presents a vivid example of this in an account of his capture by the Turks at Deraa. Lawrence describes at length his punishment, humiliation, and near sodomization by his captors.[3] In this chapter, Lawrence masochistically idealizes his punishment in almost rapturous terms (450–455). Lawrence's description of the evening at Deraa, rife with the breathless excitement of sexual danger and violation during which his very life is on the line, exhibits a sensuality that characterizes his entire career among the Arabs. With all its beauty, mingled with a guilty melancholy, *Seven Pillars of Wisdom* represents Lawrence's abiding sense of joy among his Arab colleagues, pleasures he would never again experience.

Hemingway's journeys to Africa, especially his 1953 safari—during which he told his wife, "This has been the happiest week of my life."[4]—can be compared to Lawrence's quest in Arabia, although on a much less grandiose scale. Both men, while in exotic locales, adopted native dress. Lawrence, of course, wore the entire outfit of the bedouin and essentially "Arabized" himself to the degree to which it was possible. Hemingway's adoption of native dress was much less complete but his wife Mary reports that upon her return to Kimana Swamp from Nairobi, she "found Papa with his head shaved and shiney and showing all its scars" and "a portion of Papa's wardrobe [dyed] into various shades of the Masai rusty pink ocre."[5] Writing of Lawrence, Dennis Porter refers to such makeovers as "cultural transvestism" that "enhanced the ambiguities of a self already subject to doubt in the sexual sphere."[6] Hemingway's own cultural cross-dressing in Africa allowed him to "go native" and invent his own version of "tribal law."[7]

In a deleted chapter of *The Garden of Eden*, Andy Murray, who acts as narrator for this section, has written a story about his friends Nick and Barbara Sheldon. In his narrative, he describes their dark suntans and their matching hair and clothing styles that flaunt conventional mores and that he finds "very primitive."[8] Hemingway's own experiments with gender transformation were inextricably tied to a perceived primitiveness that he identified with in Africa especially in 1953.

Hemingway, like so many other Western travelers, ostensibly sought a simpler, more primitive life among third world people. But Hemingway brought an unusual store of first world sexual complexities with him and tried to use a perceived primitive setting as an arena in which to act out his own forbidden desires. Hemingway could attempt to act out his fantasies in Africa because he had no macho image to uphold among the native people he mingled with. He was simply the rich, eccentric foreigner. Hemingway went so far in an effort to Africanize himself after his own fashion that after shaving his head and dyeing his clothes he was prepared to have his ear pierced to conform to Wakamba tribal ritual when Mary intervened to stop him. Eby quotes from her note reminding her husband that he is "a wise, thoughtful, realistic, adult white American male," the very patriarchal entity he so often alternated between exaggerating and escaping.[9]

Like Lawrence, Hemingway was born in the late and increasingly imperialist Victorian era and he similarly took a great interest in military matters. Discussing *Seven Pillars of Wisdom*, Porter comments on the "pursuit of adventure and intense sensation at the limit," which

> conflicts with the Victorian code of chivalry and service to country. . . . The modern epic of battles and preparation for battle, of bedouin camps at night, of councils of war and the clash of wills and purposes, of strategy and tactics, is joined to the romance theme of personal quest, self-testing and discovery. (232–233)

Porter sees in Lawrence, "the split between public and private, between the man of action and the guilt-ridden, self-castigating man of desire" (233). Hemingway's behavior in Africa reveals a similar split. Although the official duties of Papa as a game warden in *True at First Light* are inconsequential compared to those of Lawrence in Arabia, he nevertheless takes them seriously, and while there is no real reason for him to engage in "councils of war" or "strategy and tactics," he does so on a modest scale when the Mau-Mau uprising seems to threaten his area (TAFL 85). But for both Lawrence and Hemingway, the sexual allure of the third world formed perhaps as much a cornerstone of their travels as any military or sportsman's motive. Lawrence writes in openly homoerotic terms of the sensual pleasures afforded by his mission among the Arabs: "We got off our camels and stretched ourselves, sat down or walked before supper to the sea and bathed by hundreds, a splashing, screaming, mob of fish-like naked men of all earth's colors" (158–159). Elsewhere he comments: "It was pretty to look at the neat, brown men in the sunlit sandy valley" (168). Hemingway's descriptions are more circumspect but his enjoyment of the sensual pleasures of Africa and its people are evident, especially in the relationship of Papa and the young African woman Debba in *True at First Light*, and in his own transgendered experiments with his wife. Mary Hemingway reports in her journal of a party at Kimana Swamp:

> [S]omebody had brought the local Wakamba girls to help the celebration. Papa took them to Laitokitok and brought them dresses for Christmas, brought the girls back to camp and invited them to dinner but no dinner was served. He took the girls to our tent and the celebration there was so energetic that they broke the bed.[10]

The descriptions of both Lawrence and Mary Hemingway relate revels with local people—Lawrence and his male comrades splashing naked in sea, and Hemingway with local African girls partying in a tent in the bush. Each episode indicates the different erotic object choice of each man.

Siegel writes that "the urge to possess a daughter of nature seems almost interchangeable with the urge to enter a country perceived as primitive" (38). Papa's sexual interest in Debba is emblematic of Hemingway's interest in Africa. But Hemingway's sexuality in Africa was anything but heteronormative. The new names that he, writing in his wife's journal, devised for himself and Mary include "Mary Peter Hemingway" and "Kathrin Ernest Hemingway."[11] Clearly, Hemingway did not wish to engage in a traditional man–woman relationship and the freedom from constraints offered by Africa allowed him to indulge his transgendered fantasies.

After the betrayal of the Arabs, Lawrence turned his back on a promising career in the British establishment to become an airman in the RAF, then a regular soldier in the army as if to atone for his complicity with Britain's colonial project in the Middle East. A Hemingway character comments briefly but apparently approvingly on Lawrence's self-demotion from imperialist hero to common soldier in the short story, "Homage to Switzerland." Hemingway, like Lawrence, mixed easily with military brass but identified with the common soldier. Like Lawrence, Hemingway maintained a comfortable relationship with imperialism on his African journeys in 1934 and 1953. He traveled in the company and felt himself part of the British colonial establishment in Africa. As we have seen, the character of Papa in *True at First Light* holds the official, though minor, position of game warden in the military apparatus of the occupying power in Kenya. Hemingway's narrator, whose job (which includes some enforcement duties) is of some importance to him, expresses apprehension at the thought of fighting the Mau Mau if they conducted a "full-scale raid" on his camp (85). "I had no police authority and was only the acting Game Ranger and I was quite sure, perhaps wrongly, that I would have very little backing if I got into trouble" (85). Hemingway, through Papa, does not blame the Mau Mau for their uprising: "And now their game had been killed off by the white men . . . Their own Reserve was overcrowded and overfarmed and when the rains failed there was no pasture for the cattle and the crops were lost" (67). Clearly, he sympathizes with the predicament of the colonized but there is little doubt whose side he would be on if fighting broke out. Despite a few mild remarks acknowledging the contradiction of his position concerning colonialism, such as "[w]e are the intruders" (GHOA 285), and confessing that he wants "to know more about this country than I had any right to know" (TAFL 39), Hemingway accepts the imperial patronage and never seriously questions the legitimacy of British colonialism. Susan Gubar notes that in *The Garden of Eden*, "presenting a portrait of the artist as colonizer, Hemingway admits with some guilt his reliance on an Otherness with which he cannot abide," which she identifies as "African wildness/sexual wildness."[12] This comment highlights Hemingway's deep ambivalence about the conflicts between the colonial and sexual projects that place him in the company of other artists like Lawrence.

Hemingway, like Lawrence, apparently engages in sexual imperialism as he relates Papa's affair with Debba in *True at First Light*. In that novel, Papa conducts his courtship of Debba virtually before the eyes of Miss Mary who is based on Hemingway's wife. In a letter, Hemingway wrote of this relationship that "Miss Mary stays the hell away from it and is understanding and wonderful" (SL 826). Papa sees Debba as superior to most Western women (Miss Mary excepted) as he recalls some female companions of the past.

> [H]ow lucky I had been to have known fine women that loved Africa. I had known some really terrible ones who had only gone there to have been there and I had known some true bitches and several alcoholics to whom Africa had been just another place for more ample bitchery or fuller drunkenness. . . . Africa took them and changed them all in some ways. If they could not change they hated it. (TAFL 138)

In these comments, Hemingway remarks on Africa's effects on Westerners. He remains largely silent on the West's effects on Africa. Hemingway engaged actively in the plunder of Africa although he

directed his violence at the continent's animal life with his prodigious
big game hunting. His daily contact with the Masai and other Kenyan
people appears to have had little effect on his basically apolitical position regarding Africa, a position that tacitly endorses colonialism. In
his role as Great White Hunter, Hemingway viewed Africa as a play-
ground to which he had a perfect right. The empathy he so often
displays deserts him here. As Gubar, writing of *The Garden of Eden*,
remarks: "African wildness/ sexual wildness furnish the aphrodisiac to
fuel the writing that sentences them to extermination" (194). Her
point is that Hemingway fed off Africa without any intention of
nurturing it, much as Western imperialism did, as Walter Rodney so elo-
quently explains in *How Europe Underdeveloped Africa*. Hemingway's
attitude toward colonialism bears a resemblance to that of the major
Victorian writers before him. Edward Said writes of the Victorians:

> What Ruskin, Tennyson, Meredith, Dickens, Arnold, Thackeray,
> George Eliot, Carlyle, Mill—in short, the full roster of significant
> Victorian writers—saw was a tremendous international display of British
> power virtually unchecked over the entire world. It was both logical
> and easy to identify themselves in one way or another with this power,
> having through various means already identified themselves with
> Britain domestically.[13] (C&I 105)

Hemingway's attitude has much in common with this Victorian identification with the power and privilege of the West *vis-á-vis* colonized
peoples. As Moddelmog points out, "Africa serves Hemingway as an
imaginative space onto which he can project white characters and
conflicts without considering the ethics of their occupation of Africa
or the humanity of the black people who stand before them" (113).
Hemingway's engagement with British colonialism seems casual, lacking any deep commitment. Lawrence, on the other hand, maintained
deep ties with British imperialism and necessarily had to consider the
ethics of his position as a colonial agent, a position that cost him
greatly in guilt. Lawrence reports that "hardly one day in Arabia
passed without a physical ache to increase the corroding sense of my
deceitfulness toward the Arabs" (450). Hemingway does not appear
to suffer such guilt, nor has he nearly as great a reason to do so. And
like Lawrence, Hemingway's colonial association seems to have no
causal relationship with masochism.

The alleged conjunction of colonialism and masochism suggests
that the latter does not necessarily imply a progressive position and
this bears on Hemingway's depiction of race both in his fiction and his
nonfiction. Racial stereotypes, which find expression in his work, also

appear in Sacher-Masoch's *Venus in Furs*. After Wanda assumes control of Severin and he performs as her slave, she introduces "[t]hree slender young Negresses, like ebony carvings, all dressed in red satin and each with a rope in her hand" (222). Only one of the three, Haydée, is named. All three, at Wanda's command, bind Severin to a pillar and one of them hands Wanda the whip with which she beats him. After the whipping they unbind Severin and serve as witnesses as Wanda commands him: "Kneel and kiss my foot" (224). Later, Wanda instructs her servants (they are not slaves) to lead Severin into the vineyard. Severin relates: "The blackamoors tied me to a stake and amused themselves by pricking me with golden hairpins" (232). Wanda rejoins them and orders that Severin be yoked and attached to a plough. "The black demons pushed me through the field; one drove the plough, the other led me by a leash, and the third goaded me with the whip, while Venus in Furs stood by, watching the scene" (232). Despite the racial stereotypes, this scene presents the aesthetic, almost painterly, sensibility of Sacher-Masoch's prose with the central tortured victim, a chorus of exotic and punishing women, and the goddess serenely viewing the spectacle. Although the three "Negresses" perform the role of assistants to Wanda, thereby increasing the masochistic desire for exhibitionistic display, they remain subordinate to the despotic woman, the supreme object of Severin's desire. They function as mere works of art, adornments in the masochistic scenario. Although Haydée at least is given a name, she has no words of dialogue, nor have the other two. They have no independent function apart from executing Wanda's will which of course, is Sacher-Masoch's will. The author lacks a frame of reference, and perhaps a true interest, from which to depict them as human beings with independent agency.

In Hemingway's work, a similar depersonalization occurs, especially in *To Have and Have Not* as Toni Morrison has pointed out. Harry, in his role as narrator, never refers to Wesley, his ship's mate, by name. Wesley is referred to as "the nigger" throughout all of Harry's narrative. When he addresses Wesley in dialogue, Harry calls him by name. When Marie Morgan, in bed with Harry enjoying pillow talk, asks him if he's ever been with a "nigger wench" and, if so, what she was like, Harry answers, "Sure," but not with the name of a woman or any contextualizing comment, but startlingly likens the woman to "nurse shark" (113). While it may be impossible to know what Hemingway had in mind here, Morrison has treated on the bizarreness of this simile, suggesting that Harry places the "black female as the furthest thing from human, so far away as to be not even mammal but fish. The figure evokes a predatory, devouring eroticism and signals

the antithesis to femininity, to nurturing, to nursing, to replenishment"
(85). While careful not to attribute Harry's racism to Hemingway,
Morrison finds the words an "extraordinary" example of the author's
dread. Yet, on his 1953 trip to Kenya, Hemingway apparently fell in
love with, or perhaps fetishized, the African woman Debba, who he
refers to in a letter as "my Wakamba Fiancée" (SL 825). Was it the
imagined predatory sexuality of the Other that appealed to
Hemingway? Insofar as the Other represents a female-centered and
"Edenic" liberation from bourgeois taboos and proprieties, and
promises dangerous yet erotic adventure, Hemingway is eager to
engage with it but on his own terms. In *The Garden of Eden*, both
Catherine and Marita attempt to assume a racial otherness when they
refer to themselves respectively as "Kanaka girl"[14] and "Mbuli girl."[15]
Hemingway's view of Africa shares, perhaps, the two governing ideas
that Marianna Torgovnick finds at the root of Western ideas of the
primitive—"a rhetoric of control, in which demeaning colonialist
tropes get modified only slightly over time; and a rhetoric of desire."[16]

Morrison discusses how the consciousness of race has influenced
the development of American literature since its inception. In her
valuable study, *Playing in the Dark*, Morrison demonstrates how
white authors use racial motifs in literary renderings of the American
experience. She provides cogent discussions of Edgar Allan Poe, Willa
Cather, and others. Morrison points out that in Poe's "The Gold
Bug," the black slave, Jupiter, feels free to threaten to whip his white
master, just as Haydée and the other "Negresses" in *Venus in Furs* are
given leave to punish Severin. Morrison also discusses Hemingway's
story, "The Battler," in which an African American man liberally pun-
ishes a white man. Morrison's remarks recall Fanon's comments on
white masochism. A collective white guilt, according to Fanon,
informs this masochism.

> There is first of all a sadistic aggression toward the black man, followed
> by guilt complex because of the sanction against such behavior by the
> democratic culture of the country in question. The aggression is then
> tolerated by the Negro: whence masochism. . . . Perhaps this situation
> is not classic. In any event, it is the only way to explain the masochistic
> behavior of the white man. (177–178)

Fanon cites as examples of this masochism, "men who go to 'houses'
to be beaten by Negroes; passive homosexuals who insist on black
partners" (177). Morrison's remarks place Hemingway uncertainly
within this context. There does not seem to be evidence, however,
that Hemingway suffered greatly from white guilt. Yet, at least twice

Hemingway portrays black men capable of violent aggression. In "The Battler," the African American Bugs blackjacks the white Ad Francis when he steps out of line by threatening Nick Adams. Ad, a former boxing star, is now punch-drunk and washed-up. He had fallen on hard times after his wife, who may have been his sister ("Looked enough like him to be twins," says Bugs), leaves him and he "just went crazy" and is sent to prison.[17] In jail Ad meets Bugs, serving a sentence "for cuttin' a man" (103), who becomes his friend, protector, and, when necessary, disciplinarian. The first chapter of *To Have and Have Not* features a sensationally violent gun battle on the streets of Havana, the most memorable participant in which is an unnamed black man with a ferocious Tommy Gun who possesses a kind of awful grace under pressure. But despite these two portrayals of powerful, if dangerous, black men, Hemingway usually portrays Africans and African Americans as cringing or docile as Morrison points out. However, her comments, while so often perceptive, seem to overlook some elements of Hemingway's consciousness of race and how it relates to his sexuality. A discussion of Hemingway's racial attitudes and Morrison's interpretation of his work seems appropriate here, especially in light of the presumed relation between masochism and colonialism, which always involves racism.

Hemingway's attitude toward African Americans and black people in general, whether North American, Cuban, or African (the areas of his experience), is one of general disinterest. To be sure, Hemingway interacted with blacks often. He boxed with black fighters in Key West. He lived among the Masai people on his two journeys to Africa. At the Floridita bar in Havana, Hemingway mixed easily with Afrocuban musicians and told Kenneth Tynan, "I'm an honorary Negro."[18] But in all these cases, the social dynamics were characterized by an essential inequality. The blacks—often athletes, entertainers, or service personnel—were always in positions of social inferiority.

We have seen how Hemingway identified with British colonialism during his African safaris and how he portrays blacks impersonally at best. Even in a powerful story set in Africa, "The Snows of Kilimanjaro," the African characters remain almost invisible. In a penetrating analysis of the colonial implications of this story, Moddelmog writes, "Hemingway is complicit with the reasoning that allows Harry to stage his life drama on the backs of African Others without realizing that he is doing so or having to contemplate what that means for his moral stocktaking" (102). As Chinua Achebe remarks, writing of Conrad, such distancing characterizes, "Africa as setting and backdrop which eliminates the African as human factor."[19] (12). Of "The Snows of Kilimanjaro," Moddelmog writes that "the true setting of the story is the plains of East Africa with capitalist-imperialism so permeating the stage as to be invisible, as is any ideology for those whose behavior is structured by it" (102). She sees in this story a narrative of "American individualism . . . written over a story of capitalist-imperialism" (102). Hemingway adhered to the idea of American individualism and also enjoyed a cordial relationship with British colonialism in Africa. Even in *True at First Light*, which takes place in the early 1950s, when the days of British colonialism in Kenya were numbered and when Jomo Kenyatta was becoming a postcolonial hero, Hemingway does not display enough curiosity about his environment to note such events as these with any sustained interest.

In the earlier *Green Hills of Africa*, Hemingway describes the Masai people of southern Kenya in romantic and rapturous terms: "They were the tallest, best-built, and handsomest people I had ever seen and the first truly light-hearted happy people I had seen in Africa" (219). The full description is detailed and beautifully written. But he contrasts them with the northern Masai who he finds "sullen" and "contemptuous" (219). It seems never to have occurred to him that perhaps they and many people throughout Africa at that time lived under the control of white settlers and the arbitrary rule of colonial authorities, and had little reason to appear "light-hearted." The point is not so much that he was unaware of this possibility, but that he did not care enough about the indigenous people in his host country to get to know them better. In the same book, he writes, somewhat wistfully: "A continent ages quickly once we come. The natives live in harmony with it. But the foreigner destroys" (284–285). Yet, Hemingway does not take his own words seriously. In a 1954 dispatch for *Look*, Hemingway writes of his temporary employment as a game warden (later developed fictionally in *True at First Light)*. He writes with some humor of the inconveniences and "minor forms of emergency" he faces: "This type of emergency could consist in the arrival of one Masai who had been slightly speared about the head and face and chest by another Masai, who must then be detained. We might be in bed when this incident arose" (BL 425). It seems almost callous that Hemingway, so often empathic, can write with such detachment of a person gravely injured as a disturbance to his night's rest. Here, he exhibits the unmistakable mark of the colonialist. The irony of his position seems to escape him.

Such lack of empathy with those in his immediate environment in colonial settings, coupled with stereotyping, extends to other Hemingway racial characterizations, including Asians like Mr. Sing, "the chink" in *To Have and Have Not*, Jews like Robert Cohn in *The Sun Also Rises*, and many Native Americans in the short stories. Hemingway also shows little positive interest in Mexicans, as depicted in "The Mother of a Queen," in which a homosexual bullfighter refuses to pay for the upkeep on his dead mother's grave. Lynn regards this as a Hemingway jab at his own mother (408) while Comley and Scholes point to another, more racist, interpretation: "Since no red-blooded, American boy would treat his Mummy this way, the job is given to a Mexican 'queen,' who fights bulls badly . . . [and] combines cowardice with stinginess" (32). Surprisingly, Hemingway generally endows Cubans with more humanity, as in *The Old Man and the Sea*. On the whole, however, Hemingway concerns himself with non-Jewish white Americans and Europeans, perhaps finding enough diversity there to suit his interests.

Hemingway seems to take a modified Jungian approach to race. In a 1935 article in *Esquire*, he mentions creativity and imagination as enigmas but suggests that "racial experience" (BL 215) may account for them. In a 1958 interview with George Plimpton, he refers to "inherited racial experience" and "forgotten racial or family experience."[20] In all these instances, he speaks about himself and his race. Yet, in the same interview, he directly condemns segregation. Asked what he thinks of Ezra Pound's influence on the "segregationalist Kaspar," Hemingway defends Pound as a poet despite his fascism, his imprisonment, and commitment to a mental institution, but adds that "I would be happy to see Kaspar jailed as soon as possible."[21] And he adds, correctly, "I am sure it will take a footnote to this paragraph in ten years to explain who Kaspar was."[22]

In light of such comments it would be too extreme to call Hemingway a racist despite his easy use of epithets but a disturbing depersonalization of African Americans and other minorities characterizes much of his work. The usual Hemingway empathy is conspicuously absent in his consideration of oppressed racial minorities. In 1938, in his "Foreword" to *The First Forty-Nine*, Hemingway lists seven of his stories that are his personal favorites. Among them is "The Light of the World," which he writes, "nobody else ever liked."[23] This story of two drifters stopping in at a bar contains little conventional action but a lot of unusual dialogue. Comley and Scholes suggest that homosexuality provides the overriding theme here although much of the dialogue involves the two prostitutes who Hemingway portrays with gentleness. Each disputes the claim of the other to the love of a boxer, now dead. One of them talks about the fighter's career and how he lost to Jack Johnson. "It was a trick," she claims and then goes on to insult Johnson calling him, "that big dinge," "the big black bastard," and "that black son of a bitch from hell" (CSS 295–296). Such characterizations recall Severin's references to the "black demons" in *Venus in Furs*. They anticipate some of the racist comments of Marie Morgan in *To Have and Have Not*. The question of where this hostility comes from and why it is often articulated in Hemingway's fiction by marginal (ignorant, poor, or generally trashy) white women is an intriguing one. One answer could be that Hemingway may be attempting to distance himself from his own prejudices.

Occasionally Hemingway seems to go out of his way to provide a gratuitous epithet as in *A Farewell to Arms*. When Catherine learns of Frederic's desertion she says, "Othello with his occupation gone," to which he answers, "Othello was a nigger" (257). Any number of other allusions, not even necessarily prejudiced, would have served just as well here. Catherine could have said something like, "Samson without his hair," and Frederic could have answered, "Samson was a Jew." Or "Grant without his army," followed by "Grant was a drunk." The point is that Hemingway probably felt safer, and personally more comfortable, offending blacks than any other group. This highlights one of Hemingway's least appealing traits. One could see his willingness to use this epithet here—seemingly out of the blue—as bullying and therefore cowardly, contradicting the Hemingway myth of sportsmanship and fair play. By the 1950s, as a new era began to emerge, the racist remarks of Hemingway's characters diminish accordingly. In *Across the River*, the colonel and his driver compare tough towns in America. The driver suggests that Memphis is a tough town, to which the colonel responds, "Memphis is only tough if you are a Negro" (41). It is hard to imagine any Hemingway character written even a decade earlier, whatever his or her social class, saying "Negro" instead of using the racist epithet.

While calling attention to Hemingway's use of insulting remarks, Morrison places perhaps too much emphasis on his occasional use of what she calls "Africanist" characters that represent an author's envy or dread. Hemingway seems to have been immune from such envy and ridiculed it in others as his attack on Sherwood Anderson in *The Torrents of Spring* demonstrates. Hemingway also exchanged congratulatory words with Wyndham Lewis, later an enemy (see *A Moveable Feast* 108–109), upon the publication of Lewis's allegedly racist *Paleface*, which praises Hemingway's *The Torrents of Spring*, and likewise condemns the supposed glorification of African culture in jazz and other art forms (SL 264).[24] Hemingway, according to Meyers, "rejected the fashionable assumption that the emotional and sensual life of the dark races was superior to that of the white."[25] He scorned those who he felt indulged in what Gubar calls "racechange," that is, "the traversing of race boundaries, racial imitation or impersonation, cross-racial mimicry or mutability, white posing as black or black passing as white, pan-racial mutuality" (5)[26]. Yet Hemingway conforms to at least one of Gubar's criteria when in what seems a major slippage in *True at First Light*, Papa reflects on "wishing again that I had a black skin like any other Kamba"[27] There are other slippages as well, as when Catherine in *The Garden of Eden* says, "I don't want to be a white girl anymore,"[28] and other characters make similar comments.

Morrison notes that the white Harry Morgan, in *To Have and Have Not*, acts as an authorial model of stoicism compared to the black Wesley after they are both wounded escaping from Cuban customs officials. And she points out that Hemingway places racist words in the mouth of Harry's wife, Marie. But the remarks here have the ring of an easy indifference, deplorable in itself, rather than either a pronounced and virulent racism, or a subconscious envy or dread. Envy and dread may be present in Hemingway's view of African Americans but Morrison does not shed enough light on these in her analysis. If there is more to Hemingway's racial views than indifference, it remains unilluminated. In the main body of his work, we are more likely to encounter simple racial slurs, naive and romanticized descriptions of Africans, and undeveloped African American characters. Morrison chooses *To Have and Have Not* and the short story, "The Battler," to illustrate her points and generally succeeds in doing so. However, her analysis of *The Garden of Eden*, in which no black characters appear except in David Bourne's fiction, misses some of the thrust of Hemingway's art and sees an "Africanization" at work that may in fact be more of a nonspecific racialization or an attempt at self-Othering.

Hemingway was the product of an era that had recently witnessed the successful white Southern propaganda that began with the counterrevolution known as the Redemption, which ended Reconstruction and institutionalized racial discrimination in the South. This effort became so effective that it gained acceptance in the nation at large as history was rewritten by (mainly white Southern) academics whose influence was so broad that it extended to the White House of Woodrow Wilson, a president who praised D.W. Griffith's racist masterpiece, *Birth of a Nation*. Many of the sensitive writers of the post–World War I era saw through this injustice but to Hemingway it was of small concern. Fitzgerald, Faulkner, and many others had at least a passing interest and when in New York, made the almost mandatory trip uptown with Carl Van Vechten during the Harlem

Renaissance even if some of these visitors were little more than cultural tourists. There seems to be no evidence that Hemingway had the slightest interest in any aspect of African American culture[29]. Nor does his work contain many elements of the social realism of Steinbeck, Farrell, and others, though a partial exploration can be found in *To Have and Have Not* in the allusions to "relief" and the scenes of neglected veterans of World War I. Hemingway generally accepted the prevailing ethos of a divided America on the issue of race with all the prejudices that accompanied it. Morrison states that, "he has no need, desire, or awareness of them [African Americans] either as readers of his work or as people existing anywhere other than in his imaginative (and imaginatively lived) world" (69). While Hemingway may not have considered African Americans as potential readers, several black modernists expressed admiration for his work. Living in Paris when Hemingway first burst upon the scene, Claude McKay was initially put off by "the white hope of the ultra-sophisticates."[30] After reading *In Our Time*, McKay changed his opinion and writes: "I cannot imagine any ambitious young writer of the time who was not fascinated in the beginning. . . . Many of them felt they could never go on writing as before after Hemingway" (251). A young Ralph Ellison also felt the influence of Hemingway as he recalled in an interview: "At night I practiced writing and studied Joyce, Dostoievsky, Stein and Hemingway. Especially Hemingway; I read him to learn his sentence structure and how to organize a story. I guess many young writers were doing this."[31] But Ellison did not read Hemingway uncritically and faults him for his blindness on racial issues.

In *Green Hills of Africa*, Hemingway instructs a curious Austrian on American literature: "All modern American literature comes from one book by Mark Twain called *Huckleberry Finn*. If you read it you must stop where the Nigger Jim is stolen from the boys. That is the real end" (22). While many agree that Twain's novel becomes chaotic toward the end, few would concur with Hemingway's appraisal today. Morrison calls the closing chapters of *Huckleberry Finn*, "the hell it puts its readers through" and sees Twain commenting on "the parasitical nature of white freedom" (57). She sees Huck as personifying "a critique of slavery and the pretensions of the would-be middle class" (55) with Jim as "enabler." Hemingway's remark seems callous and highlights his failure of empathy with the plight of African Americans. Of *Huckleberry Finn* and Hemingway's comments on it, Ellison writes:

> So thoroughly had the Negro, both as a man and as a symbol of man, been pushed into the underground of the American conscience that

Hemingway missed the structural, symbolic and moral necessity for that part of the plot in which the boys rescue Jim. Yet it is precisely this part which gives the novel its significance. Without it, except as a boy's tale, the novel is meaningless.[32]

Despite his debt to Hemingway, Ellison faults him for "seeking a technical perfection rather than moral insight" (38). Ellison vigorously criticizes Hemingway's blindness on racial issues and finds his position artistically unethical because he admired Twain's innovative skills while ignoring his moral imperative. "What for Twain was a means to a moral end," he writes, "became for Hemingway an end in itself" (35). Ellison seems to capture much of Hemingway's view of race when he writes:

> It is instructive that Hemingway, born into a civilization characterized by violence, should seize upon the ritualized violence of the culturally distant Spanish bullfight as a laboratory for developing his style. For it was, for Americans, an amoral violence (though not for Spaniards) which he was seeking. Otherwise he might have studied that ritual of violence closer to home, the ritual in which the sacrifice is that of a human scapegoat, the lynching bee. (37)

Ellison views Hemingway's portrayal of African Americans as stereotypes and when he remarks, "the object of the stereotype is not so much to crush the Negro as to console the white man" (41), he comes close to agreement with Morrison's statement on the "parasitical nature of white freedom" (57). Indeed, in a 1964 essay, "The World and the Jug," Ellison anticipates Morrison's thesis in *Playing in the Dark* when he writes: "Southern whites cannot walk, talk, sing, conceive of laws or justice, think of sex, love, the family or freedom without responding to the presence of Negroes."[33] Morrison would expand that argument to include all, not just Southern, whites. It is for reasons such as these, as well as his lack of curiosity about African Americans and his acceptance of the post-Reconstruction view of race, that Hemingway's attitude can be considered one of indifference at best.

In her discussion of *The Garden of Eden*, Morrison sees Hemingway as vacillating between women who she sees are nurturers or destroyers and who she calls "nurses" and "sharks," from Harry Morgan's comment in *To Have and Have Not* (113). Morrison adds that such nurses can be male and, indeed, one of her examples from Hemingway is Bugs in "The Battler." Bugs's blackness marginalizes him in a similar manner to the way women are marginalized and his assumption of the role of punisher places him in a similar position to the punishing woman celebrated in masochism and conforms him to Fanon's comment on whites who wish "to be beaten by Negroes" (177). Morrison points to the incongruous images of blacks assuming power over whites in personal relationships. Morrison's discussion of nurses and sharks focuses on race but it can be used more broadly in a discussion of masochism. The dominant woman in masochistic fantasy exhibits both the nurturing quality of the nurse and the destructive capacity of the shark as Morrison defines them. Morrison sees Catherine in the early stages of *The Garden of Eden* as a nurse but maintains that her character metamorphoses into a shark with Marita assuming the role of nurse. Morrison correctly calls attention to hair-cutting and suntanning in *The Garden of Eden* but her feeling that Catherine represents an Africanization, or merely that, remains problematic because the race is less important than the Otherness.

Morrison's categories of nurses and sharks form part of her broader discussion of how many white writers use "Africanization" as a kind of literary shorthand to help define unorthodox or daring characteristics in their fiction. In the case of Hemingway's ambiguous sexuality, she uses her category of "fetishization" as a means of interpretation. Morrison sees such fetishization as "useful in evoking erotic fears or desires" (68). However, there seems both more and less than a racial fetishization at work in this novel. The significance Morrison finds in the obsessive suntanning leads her to consider Catherine an "Africanized" character (88). But it is more the sense of her own self-achieved difference that concerns Catherine as she says, "It's the changing that is as important as the dark."[34] The haircuts and the sun-tans and the nude sunbathing constitute sensual pleasures, almost autoerotic, for both Catherine and David. The darkening of the skin by the sun implies more than an Africanization as Morrison uses that term. While Catherine does indeed tell David, "I'll be your African girl" (29), she also tells him, "I wish I had some Indian blood. I'm going to be so dark you won't be able to stand it" (31). This, too, might be considered Africanization by extension but it stretches the use of the term. As David muses, "we are going to be a special dark race of our own," implying an entirely new category of Otherness.[35] Catherine's determination to darken her skin and lighten her hair appears to be more of an effort to alter herself physically as well as mentally, to move herself "further away from other people" (30), than a conscious or unconscious attempt by the author to impose an Africanized presence. Morrison also quotes these lines (86) but interprets them as examples of Africanization. When David muses that he looks like "a white headed Cherokee," he clearly imagines that he and

Catherine have transcended racial categories through their body modifications. As Eby notes: "Catherine's dark skin, like that of all the other characters, signifies her alienation from 'proper' (read *white*) society and her transgression of social taboos" (160–161).[36] While Morrison presents powerful arguments in *Playing in the Dark* about American literature in general, including some of Hemingway's other work, she underestimates the complexity of Hemingway's eroticism in her analysis of *The Garden of Eden*. Sensuality is indeed the issue but sensuality, even a forbidden one, need not imply Africanization, even if it involves obsessive suntanning. The significance indeed lies in Hemingway's ambiguous attitudes toward women and sexuality but the Africanist element remains superficial at best. The sad fact is that Hemingway did not take Africa or Africans seriously enough to indulge in any true "Africanization" as defined by Morrison.

According to Morrison

> At the heart of *The Garden of Eden* is "Eden": the story of David writing about his adventures in Africa. It is a tale replete with male bonding, a father–son relationship, and even the elephant they track is loyal to his male companion. This fictional, Africanized Eden is sullied by the surrounding events of the larger Catherine-David Africanist Eden. Africa imagined as innocent and under white control, is the inner story; Africanism, imagined as evil, chaotic, impenetrable, is the outer story. (89)

The significance of the inner story in *The Garden of Eden* is not solely of a romanticized Africa, but also David's identification with the elephant rather than with the hunters in his short story. Hemingway, through David, demonstrates an empathy with the victim of aggression, just as David himself has become the willing recipient of Catherine's aggressive sexuality. Beegel notes that while Catherine and David become as siblings, "David comes to understand that the elephant also is his 'brother.' "[37] Hemingway probably observed and realized that in much of Africa, animals are considered part of the same great family as humans. In any case, the empathy comes through clearly and not only in this novel. In a dispatch to *True* magazine in 1954, Hemingway, referring to himself in the third person, writes: "The author of this article, after taking a long time to make up his mind, and admitting his guilt on all counts, believes it is a sin to kill any non-dangerous game animal except for meat"[38] (BL 419). Hemingway comes very late in life to such a sentiment and in *The Garden of Eden*, he gives voice to David's feeling of empathy with the elephant as another sentient being. Yet while David can portray his empathy with the elephant, Hemingway himself remains woefully indifferent to what Fanon calls the "sadistic aggression toward the black man" (177). Hemingway fails to employ one of his most appealing qualities—empathy—in his portrayal of Africans and other blacks.

Morrison pinpoints Hemingway's view of Africa as a romantic state of mind that functions as a regained Eden. His fantasy life appears exceptionally rich on his 1953 safari with his wife Mary. As Eby remarks, it was on this trip that Hemingway indulged some of his most significant fetishes, shaving his own head and washing and dyeing his wife's hair. This is where he placed the entry in Mary's diary, "She loves me to be her girl, which I love to be."[39] Mary records in *How It Was* that Hemingway wrote that "Mary has never had one lesbian impulse but has always wanted to be a boy" (467). He goes on to expressions of disdain for all "tactile contact" with men, saying, in effect, that like Mary he has never had one homosexual impulse but has always wanted to be a girl. In the same entry, Hemingway apparently alludes to a sexual experience with Mary, which was "outside all tribal law": "On the night of December 19th we worked out these things and I have never been happier" (467). Hemingway and Mary seem to have brought their sexual relationship to a new level through unspecified acts involving reversals of traditional sexual roles. Sodomy is a logical conjecture since it is discussed on the previous page of Mary Hemingway's memoir (466).

As Eby notes of *The Garden of Eden*, "the radically edited version of the novel published by Scribners in 1986 mutes Hemingway's concern with race considerably, but the concern is hardly subtle in the original" (158). Eby also discusses how in 1953 Hemingway's fetishistic "and transvestic behavior in Africa links his cross-racial and cross-gender identifications directly to the games of Catherine and David Bourne in *The Garden of Eden*" (179). These behaviors, as we have seen, included shaving his head and expressing a desire to have an ear pierced, and also an eagerness to receive tribal marks. So, while David in that novel expresses the wish to become a "special dark race of our own,"[40] this may include some degree of "Africanization," even if not to the extent that Morrison suggests, and even if it merely represents a stage on the way to a new sexual Otherness. Hemingway himself acknowledges this in a handwritten entry in 1953: "After a while Miss Mary came in to the bed and I put the other Africa away somewhere and we made our own Africa."[41] Here, Africa represents the forbidden, but it is mutable to Hemingway as he and his wife make "our own Africa." Naturally existing Others, whether Africanist, Orientalist, or Native American, are the frames of reference for

Catherine and David in *The Garden of Eden* but they clearly hope to move beyond these and "get further away from other people" (30).

It is in the novel of this Kenya trip, *True at First Light*, that Papa falls in love, despite the presence of his wife, with the Wakamba girl Debba. In a letter, Hemingway describes his own adoption of African rites: "Have my head shaved because that is how my fiancée likes it" (SL 827), to match her shaved head. He continues describing how "she likes to feel all the holes in my head and the wealts [sic]" (SL 827). This recalls the colonel in *Across the River* examining his welts after an encounter with Renata, and David in *The Garden of Eden* examining his scars ("red welts")[42] in the mirror. In the letter, Hemingway adds: "My girl is completely impudent, her face is impudent in repose, but absolutely loving and delicate rough" and continues, "I better quit writing about it . . . it gives me too bad a hardon" (SL 827). Clearly, on his 1953 African journey, Hemingway allowed his fantasies to emerge more forcefully than he might have in a more "civilized" setting. The 1953 safari, more than his journey of 1934, places Hemingway in the company of other artists who indulged in "colonial fantasy" or "sexual imperialism." The adventures of Andre Gide and Paul Bowles in North Africa, and Jean Genet in Palestine, although homosexual, correspond to the search for the sexually exotic that Hemingway also indulged in on his last trip to Africa.

Hemingway's relationship with the real-life counterpart of Debba appears to have been chaste, which, as we have seen, is characteristic of some masochistic encounters. In this, and other regards, he is similar to Michel Leiris, the eccentric French anthropologist and author of *L'Afrique fantôme*, who "fell in love while in Gondar with an Ethiopian woman."[43] While he "never made love with her," Leiris admits to "chance encounters with Somali girls [which recalls David's 'Somali girl' in *The Garden of Eden*] in the native quarter of Djibout" (140). Leiris, who is rather direct regarding his own masochism, found these affairs "absurd and unfortunate, but [they] have left me with an impression of Paradise" (140). Torgovnik writes that for "Leiris (and he claims for his generation, the generation that made Josephine Baker a star) Africa is 'Edenic,' a place of 'ritual intoxication' " (110). And with the title of *The Garden of Eden* and its explorations of gender-crossing, Hemingway would seem to agree. Torgovnik suggests that "the crossing between male and female was, for some moderns and postmoderns, a significant lure of African art," even if there is "no reason to believe that primitive cultures have any cure for sexual difference or any magical formula for sexual harmony" (117). The perception of Africa as a land where difference can be confronted and overcome may have been one of its greatest attractions for Hemingway.

Leiris and Hemingway both have a well-developed sense of the tragic that seems directly related to their sexuality. While Leiris fully admits his empathy with "wounded men" (64) and "wounded women" (43), Hemingway, with a similar empathy, is less direct. He delivers the countless images of brutal death in his work with his trademark hard-boiled style that gives an initial impression of insensitivity yet on reflection his words have an arresting power with a visceral effect that a more sympathetic description might lack, and beneath them lies Hemingway's empathy for the wounded and the dead.

Both Hemingway and Leiris were aficionados of bullfighting. Hemingway nearly defined it for an American audience both fictionally in *The Sun Also Rises* and factually, if impressionistically, in *Death in the Afternoon*. We have seen earlier that Ralph Ellison faults Hemingway for seeking "an amoral violence" in the *corrida* (37), yet Leiris may touch on some of the elements that appealed to Hemingway. To Leiris, bullfighting is almost synonymous with the act of love. He refers to love as "the terrain of truth," the same phrase used for the bullfighting arena (37). Moddelmog notes "images of sexual foreplay and consummation" in the "meeting of bull and bullfighter" (96) in Hemingway's work and other scholars have recognized the sexual content as well. Commenting on the elaborate and androgynous costumes and rituals involved, Willingham writes that in his enthusiasm for the bullfight, Hemingway's "particular sexual interests from transsexuality and androgyny to hair fetishism is overtly evident."[44] Willingham further comments on Hemingway's appreciation for Spanish culture and his familiarity with the work of Havelock Ellis, whose book, *The Soul of Spain*, reports on the "masculine boldness" of Spanish women who "wish to choose their partners . . . they play the man's part, and it is for him to yield and sacrifice himself."[45] This aspect of Spanish culture appeals to masochistic artists as diverse as Leiris and Hemingway.

Leiris, who had a publicly gentle nature that was totally opposed to Hemingway's image, admits, "I am a fervent admirer of bullfights . . . I have the impression of watching something real: a ritual death" (37–38). Leiris sees a similarity to lovemaking and writes that this "gives the *corrida* an emotional value insofar as the presence of something sacred causes a disturbance that involves the sexual emotion" (38). The descriptions of bullfighting by Hemingway are almost didactic. He plays the role of the American expert to a largely American audience and while his enthusiasm is apparent, he retains a somewhat detached persona. He attempts to treat the deaths—of the bulls, the horses, and the occasional matador—glibly, thereby seeking to demonstrate to his readers his manliness and stoicism in the face of what he recognizes as tragedy (BL 90). (Demonstrations of manliness never concern Leiris.) Yet, beneath the surface, Hemingway continues to display an empathy with matador, bull, and spectators. Leiris unabashedly remarks on the tragic, erotic, and almost sacred quality of bullfighting. He writes, "there is a union along with the combat—as there is in love and in sacrificial ceremonies, in which there is close contact with the victim" (39). Hemingway shares this empathy, which is similar to the imaginings of masochistic pleasure. Both Leiris and Hemingway display, throughout their work, empathy with the victims of violence. In addition, Leiris compares the writer's craft, unfavorably perhaps, to the bullfight and asks, "if there is nothing in the art of writing a work that is equivalent . . . to the bull's keen horn, which alone . . . affords the *torero*'s art a human reality, prevents it from being no more than the vain grace of a ballerina?" (154). Although Hemingway would undoubtedly have written these sentiments differently, there is much in them that conforms to his own thinking.

To return to *The Garden of Eden*, Gubar sees David's empathy as a childlike expression of sympathy and identification with the dark forces, suggesting a pre-Oedipal innocence. This darkness, forbidden to David as a man, reappears nonetheless in the person of Catherine with her darkened body and her transgressive sexuality. According to Gubar, "Catherine merits her own destruction because she represents the male author's dependency upon dangerously unmanning sources of inspiration," specifically herself and her sexuality (194). Like Morrison, Gubar attributes to Catherine an "Africanization" but she goes much further, writing that

> David is Catherine and so is Hemingway himself, who uses Catherine's female gender to camouflage the ways she encodes his own fascination with sexual transgression. The African queen of *The Garden of Eden* is queer, Hemingway's drag persona. (Paradoxically, such a lesbian self-image can be understood as oddly bracing Hemingway's view of his heterosexuality as if he were exclaiming "even if I were a woman, I'd still desire women—not men, never men.") (194)

Gubar continues by asserting Hemingway's "contradictory version of himself as imperialist and as lesbian" (194) as a way of accounting for the ambivalence of both his psychological investment in Africa and his identification with Catherine. Gubar identifies what she refers to as "Hemingway's tendency to imagine homosexuality in heterosexual terms" (192). Yet, as we have seen, the desire to submit to passive sodomy cannot be so readily conflated with homosexuality. There can be little doubt that Hemingway's desire was anything but straight, but it was decidedly heterosexual. Some critiques continue to insist that a man's desire to be sodomized by a woman necessarily indicates homosexuality, a position that replicates the discourse of Victorian psychiatry and early psychoanalysis that stigmatized all nonnormative forms of sexuality as perversions.

While others have remarked on Hemingway's self-identification as a lesbian pointing to the fact that he refers to himself as "her girl" in the journal of his wife Mary,[46] and to biographical details of his early life, this remains an issue that, if not beside the point, skirts it. Hemingway identifies himself as adamantly, almost fanatically, heterosexual throughout his career, but this alone cannot substantiate claims that he was anything other than that. The setting of Africa undoubtedly had a liberating effect on Hemingway's libido, allowing him to indulge his masochistic and transgendered fantasies. *The Garden of Eden* was still very much a work-in-progress at the time of the 1953 safari, and the African setting obviously informed that work as Eby points out (179). But while Hemingway clearly identified himself with British colonialism, Gubar overstates it when she writes: "Dramatizing Hemingway's contradictory version of himself as imperialist and as lesbian, *The Garden of Eden* remains surprisingly fair-minded in its analysis of the sexual antagonism of its protagonists" (194–195). While it remains too extreme to call Hemingway an outright imperialist and to insist on his lesbian self-identification, Gubar correctly notes the author's balance in the portrayals of David and Catherine. David represents the passive side of Hemingway's sexuality as he is willing, though with "remorse," to be led into forbidden areas of desire. Catherine represents the author's urge to break through patriarchal taboos and barriers. Ultimately however, Hemingway felt that it was Catherine who represents the threat and warrants destruction.

Hemingway remains notoriously difficult to pigeonhole. Catherine is not simply an Africanist character as Morrison contends, nor is she a representation of Hemingway's repressed homosexual desire as Gubar asserts. Morrison is entirely correct when she says *The Garden of Eden* "*is* about her" (emphasis in original 89) but her interpretation of this character misses Catherine's function as the dominant woman of masochism and general sexual iconoclast, and attributes her transgression almost exclusively to an Africanization. The Africanization is apparent but it only accounts for part of the story. Hemingway's racial allusions in *The Garden of Eden* are almost as polymorphous as his sexual allusions, with references to Kanaka, Mbuli, Indian, Arab, Somali, Octoroon, platinum blondes, and others. Any race at all (other than his own whiteness with which he had to maintain a Eurocentric machismo) would have provided him with a way of escape from the patriarchal mandate. One cannot argue with Morrison's analysis of Willa Cather, or Poe, or even *To Have and Have Not*. Morrison effectively identifies Hemingway's casual racism as well as suggesting how white American authors in general have engaged, while trying to avoid, the question of race. But since *The Garden of Eden* is such an individual and eccentric artistic statement, it remains difficult to fit it neatly into Morrison's overall theoretical discussion.

In closing this discussion of Hemingway, colonialism, and race, it may be appropriate to draw attention to the first racial Others (and colonial victims) of his experience—Native Americans. Meyers suggests that Hemingway had "a profound understanding" of Native Americans' "behavior, customs, and religion."[47] Hemingway celebrates the sexuality of Trudy Gilroy in "Fathers and Sons" who "did first what no one has ever done better" (CSS 376). And in "Ten Indians," Prudence captures the heart of young Nick. Both Trudy and Prudence are based on Prudy Bolton, a young woman Hemingway knew in Michigan. Hemingway's readiness to place Nick Adams in sexual relationships with young Native American women may reveal an early example of his personal ease among people with whom he had no image to uphold. Of Hemingway's relationship with Prudy, Lynn remarks: "Somehow, he didn't feel threatened by her—possibly because she was of a lower class, possibly because she belonged to a conquered race" (53). "Indian Camp," one of Hemingway's most discussed stories, which as the opening tale of the original *in our time* (previously published in the *transatlantic review*) may have been the first of his work that many early critics read. This story has led to a great deal of speculation—"from the obvious to the absurd," writes Meyers—over the cause of the Indian man's suicide after Nick's father has successfully delivered his wife's child through Caesarian section.[48] Meyers briefly surveys some of the critical interpretations offered over the years. Brenner recounts some of these as well in a footnote but he himself claims with certainty that the character of Uncle George is the father of the child and that the Indian man's knowledge that he has been cuckolded drives him to take his own life (239). Hemingway, apparently, never provided the "key" to this story so the debate will go on. But while Meyers admits "Hemingway's ambiguous attitude to primitivism," he sees a "notable success in portraying the primitive." Meyer's own interpretation suggests that white medicine has caused the Indian man to witness "the defilement of his wife's purity" and to counteract this he "focuses the evil spirits on himself,"[49] a theory that has, perhaps, as much or as little credibility as many earlier ones.

The Native Americans portrayed in Hemingway's stories are Ojibwa. Another view of "Indian Camp" suggests itself by a comparison of that story with the 1988 novel *Tracks* by Louise Erdrich, an Ojibwa author, which deals with her people around the same time that Hemingway's story takes place. *Tracks* centers around the life of the Ojibwa woman Fleur Pillager, a powerful, imposing, and haunting female character. Part of the novel deals with Fleur's relationship with the Ojibwa man, Eli Kashpaw (note the similarity of his name to Eddie Tabeshaw in Hemingway's "The Doctor and the Doctor's Wife"). At one point, Eli nervously awaits the commencement of labor in the pregnant Fleur who has been stoically silent for days. Nanapush, the narrator, relates that finally, "the stillness broke and then it was as if the Manitous all through the woods spoke through Fleur."[50] He describes a cacophony of sounds from the forest—"the Eagle's high shriek, Loon's crazy bitterness, Otter, the howl of the Wolf, Bear's low rasp" (59)—answering Fleur's screams, which recall the woman's cries in "Indian Camp." At this point, Nanapush relates that "Eli had broken when the silence shattered, slashed his arm with his hunting knife, and run out of the clearing, straight north" (59). This type of self-mutilation may bear some resemblance to the violent suicide of the husband in "Indian Camp."

Both stories depict Native American men in the early decades of the twentieth century, who react with self-destructive anxiety before the natural power of women and who may have shared with Hemingway a sense of "something frightening in the trauma of childbirth" (Lynn 228). The impulse is not so much a wish to die but a manifestation of an unbearable empathy with the power of woman, especially in childbirth, which must be shared and released even if in self-mutilation. Hemingway may have internalized some of this awe of the female from his early observations of the interactions of Ojibwa men and women. These youthful memories, filtered through a deteriorating Western value system, may have reinforced his sense of awe before the feminine and later informed his masochism.

CHAPTER 7

REAFFIRMING THE CODE

HOMOPHOBIA, MISOGYNY, REVISIONISM

None of the speculations in these pages concerning Hemingway's sexual preoccupations are meant to detract from his genius as an author and they are irrelevant to his overall morality as a man. If Hemingway and his wives indulged in similar activities to those depicted in his fiction, fewer today would cast moral aspersions on them. Such sexual behavior contains elements of psychodrama involving perhaps mild consensual pain along with domination and submission, and in most masochistic relationships, of course, no one is actually injured. Haircutting games followed by women sexually dominating their lovers hardly seems as perverse today as in the past, even if such scenes involve "unnatural acts" such as sodomy performed on the man by the woman. But if, as seems likely, this was the pattern of Hemingway's love life, he felt he had good reason to conceal it considering the almost universal opinion in his time of male masochism as repulsive and deviant. Indeed, it still has this reputation in some quarters today. So, while it remains difficult to fault him for concealing his sexuality, in his insistent support for the idea of traditional masculinity to the point of homophobia and misogyny, Hemingway crosses an ethical boundary. A man with such an unorthodox sexuality might have been expected to demonstrate some tolerance but Hemingway generally proved incapable of this. It would be gratifying to assert that Hemingway resisted the coercion of the new regime of "compulsory heterosexuality," but unfortunately we cannot make that claim for him.

Hemingway's homophobia reveals itself in perhaps its most startling form in *Death in the Afternoon*, arguably his most self-consciously macho book in which he refers to homosexuals as "unfortunate" and "abnormal" (179–180). A few pages later, he unleashes an astonishing and unexpected attack on homosexuality and El Greco who, he writes, believed

> in life after death and death after life and in fairies. If he was one
> he should redeem, for the tribe, the prissy exhibitionistic, aunt-like,
> withered old maid moral arrogance of a Gide; the lazy, conceited
> debauchery of a Wilde who betrayed a generation; the nasty, sentimental
> pawing of humanity of a Whitman and all the mincing gentry. Viva El
> Greco El Rey de los Maricones. (205)

Hemingway singles out these artists because of their real or alleged
homosexuality, even though elsewhere he expresses admiration for El
Greco's work.[1] Comley and Scholes suggest that "to distance himself
from his own views with mockery is one of Hemingway's strong qualities as a writer" (129) but this judgment can hardly be extended to
the comments in *Death in The Afternoon*. For if Hemingway mocks
himself he does everything he can to obscure it, which represents not
a virtue but an ethical lapse. In *Death in the Afternoon*, by employing the
character of the Old Lady as a sympathetic supporter of bullfighting, he
implies that this frail creature has more gumption and is more "manly"
than those—who must be either delicate women or *maricones*—who do
not enjoy this blood sport. This sometimes aggravating character
goads the narrator on to his numerous attacks on homosexuals, literary rivals, and others until Hemingway finally (and mercifully to the
reader) dismisses her from the text.

So ingrained was Hemingway's homophobia that he is even said to
have resorted to physical "queer-bashing" on occasion. Brian reports
that Hemingway's friend, the Brooklyn-born bullfighter Sidney
Franklin, claims that in Spain Hemingway once "crossed the road
to knock an obvious homosexual to the ground with a punch."[2]
McLendon reports that Hemingway assaulted a gay man at Sloppy
Joe's in Key West (153). Yet, Hemingway could also show kindness
and support to individual gay men. Spender recalls an incident during
the Spanish Civil War in which Hemingway defended him against a
gay-baiting communist and he marvels at "the curious fact of receiving Hemingway's support in a situation where I should never have
expected it" (231). In his impulses, Hemingway seems to adhere to
his code of fair play but when he is "on" for an audience he feels he
must revert to the social code he had long since adopted.

Hemingway clearly recognizes the subversive quality of Lesbianism
and relishes it vicariously. Yet, he denies this same quality to male
homosexuality. And Hemingway occasionally manifests homophobia
even with respect to lesbianism. In the posthumous *A Moveable Feast*,
his account of the expatriate literary life of Paris in the 1920s, the

narrator attempts to convince his readers that he is an innocent abroad in the midst of decadence. In the chapter, "A Strange Enough Ending," he describes with thinly veiled and certainly insincere revulsion, overhearing a lovers' quarrel between Gertrude Stein and Alice B. Toklas that caused him to flee their home in moral horror (118). In the homophobic description of Stein and Toklas, Hemingway adopts a tone of naïvete:

> I heard someone speaking to Miss Stein as I had never heard one person speak to another: never, anywhere, ever. Then Miss Stein's voice came pleading and begging, saying "Don't pussy. Don't. Don't, please don't. I'll do anything, pussy, but please don't do it. Please don't. Please don't, pussy." I swallowed the drink and put the glass down on the table and started for the door. (118)

One wonders who he thought, writing in the twilight of his career, would be fooled by this account. Could Hemingway have truly been scandalized by the relationship of Stein and Toklas? Could he not have known about it before this after having spent many evenings in their company? Tavernier-Courbin writes that "only through incredible naïvete could Hemingway have avoided knowing how things were" (80). Hemingway even contradicts his earlier remarks on Stein in the same book in which he reveals that they frankly discussed homosexuality. He admits an interest in the lifestyle of Stein and Toklas, who had "her hair cut like Joan of Arc" (MF 14), a style he must have appreciated given his fascination with hair. Hemingway felt that he was slandering Stein and Toklas in *A Moveable Feast* and, as Brenner points out, he did not name Toklas in the memoir because she was still living at the time and he wanted to avoid a possible lawsuit.[3] Hemingway states explicitly that overhearing a lovers' quarrel between Stein and Toklas was reason enough for him to end the friendship, which strikes those who knew him in those days as absurd.[4] Perhaps he thought somehow that his account of the conversation with Stein about male and female homosexuality earlier in *A Moveable Feast* and the many other references to lesbianism in his work would be forgotten or summed up by what he had to say in "A Strange Enough Ending." The passage is homophobic and misogynistic as well as disingenuous when we consider Hemingway's long fascination with lesbianism. Hemingway and Stein had been friends, and he is even said to have had an "impossible" crush on her and he admitted that, "I always wanted to fuck her and she knew it."[5] Very early in their friendship, he became quite aware of her sexual orientation.

Hemingway's treatment of women has come under revision in recent years. Instead of a misogynist, some critics now view him as a misunderstood feminist. Willingham writes of *The Garden of Eden*:

> The novel . . . prefigures many contemporary theories concerning *l'écriture féminine*, as articulated by Hélène Cixous. Viewed from this perspective, *Garden* not only contributes to our understanding of important gender-related issues, but moreover demands a revaluation of Hemingway's literary treatment of women, for *Garden* vividly calls into question previous critical charges of misogyny. (46)

While the novel certainly dwells on "gender-related issues," and while Catherine presents its most vibrant character, Hemingway's misogyny, insincere though it may have been, remains a problem for readers. Just because Hemingway demonstrated an uncertainty of, or an unwillingness to face, the irregularities of his sexuality does not mean he was not both explicitly homophobic and misogynistic in many of his writings. Moddelmog answers some of the criticism that seeks to make Hemingway into a proto-feminist when she writes: "Simply put, although these revisionist critics claim to be doing feminist service to Hemingway's history and fiction, their efforts actually reinstate both within a sexist, heterosexist, and homophobic matrix" (29). The marked homophobia most clearly spelled out in *Death in the Afternoon* but always present simply cannot be ignored or glossed over.

Some critics see "The Short Happy Life of Francis Macomber" as Hemingway's most explicit statement of misogyny. It remains difficult to answer this charge. In a revisionist essay, Nina Baym makes the purely logical case that Margot Macomber shoots her husband to death accidentally and a close reading of the text can substantiate this view.[6] And Kert cites an earlier review by Warren Beck that supports the position that Margot is portrayed sympathetically as she is modeled on Jane Mason with whom Hemingway may have had an affair, and who had his sympathy because she felt personally thwarted in her marriage (275–276). But despite these views, at least part of Hemingway's intention in this story is to demonstrate the destructive power of women. The portrayal of Margot throughout the story emphasizes her frustration and resentment at her essentially failed life and her loveless marriage. Her frustration leads her to flaunt what little power she can command, as she remains "enameled in that American female cruelty."[7] While on safari in Africa, Margot shoots, in cold blood, her hapless husband Francis, after she has cuckolded him with Wilson, the British hunting guide. Accident or not, the story portrays Margot as a black widow. Wilson, in disgust, asks her, "Why

didn't you poison him? That's what they do in England" (28). The
construction of this story, regarded by many as one of Hemingway's
finest, relies heavily on what here seem caricatures of Hemingway
concerns. Francis Macomber has shown cowardice in the face of danger, a charging lion. His rescue by Wilson leaves him shamed and
unmanned, and he must redeem himself on the next day's hunt.
Margot gloats over his cowardice, sleeps with Wilson, and kills her
husband before he can enjoy his newly discovered courage. "The
Short Happy Life of Francis Macomber" represents Hemingway's
most aggravatingly simplistic moralizing. Everything is set up by the
author to force Macomber into a test of courage, which he must first
fail, then finding reserves of moral strength, pass. The loveless and
resentful woman hijacks the man's victory. Maddeningly, the story
succeeds on its premises. While the misogyny is unmistakable, perhaps
Hemingway had more in mind than the portrait of a simply vicious
woman. His masochistic sensibility may have sought to create a woman
capable of such enormity of power over a man. Hemingway gives
Margot the power of life and death over her husband. The delegation
of such absolute power to the dominant woman may serve, in part, as
a demonstration of Hemingway's masochism. However, the misogy-
nous aspect of woman as destroyer cannot be ignored.

Like Willingham, Spilka sees Hemingway's "androgynous" literary
expressions as admirable, perhaps even approaching the heroic:

> Hemingway's childhood twinning with his older sister Marcelline may
> have made him more sensitive to such [androgynous] desires and more
> strongly liable first to suppress and then ultimately to express them; but
> he was in fact expressing something common, difficult, and quite pos-
> sibly crucial to coming of age as a man in this century's white bourgeois
> circles. His admiration for the liberated ladies of the 1920s was widely
> shared, and his ultimate enslavement by their androgynous powers may
> tell us more about ourselves and our times than we care to know. (204)

Spilka tacitly acknowledges masochism with the word "enslavement"
but gives Hemingway more credit perhaps than he deserves. In his
more honest moments, Hemingway certainly confronted his own
"androgynous" desires in his work, but we have no evidence that he
ever demonstrated a tolerance for these same desires in others or for
any man who did not fit into his public vision of masculinity. He never
seems to have revised his homophobia, developed so thoroughly in
Death in the Afternoon and other writings. And he never seems to have
been able to cope with a woman (at least one who was a potential
partner) who was not compliant to his will, as his stormy relationship

with Martha Gellhorn attests. As Leonard J. Leff notes: "He may have been smitten with the Brett Ashleys of the world, yet he would not have condoned their behavior (or called them 'ladies') had they been under his protection."[8]

Hemingway's public myth of machismo was so strong and he sought to be identified with it so completely that he dared not do anything publicly to undermine it. Burwell notes that Hemingway "did not feel comfortable about disclosing" the theme of *The Garden of Eden* even in his personal letters (97). What he merely hinted at in earlier works regarding his submissive sexuality becomes overt in the early chapters of *The Garden of Eden*. Realizing how he had revealed himself in these pages, he tries to tinker with the character of Catherine as he makes her manipulative, vindictive, jealous, and then drives her insane. But he could not have explained away those first three chapters either to his friends or to his public. Even as he was destroying Catherine, he was dismantling another part of his myth by having David write about experiences in Africa and identifying with the hunted elephant rather than with the hunters. It was as if the two sides of Ernest Hemingway, so long separate, were finally coming together in a way no one had ever seen or imagined, perhaps least of all himself. It is as if he realized he had sprung a leak in the vessel of his image with the creation of Catherine. He then set about trying to stop that leak with the development of the lifeless Marita and the subplot of David's African hunting story only to realize with shock that he had created another breach in the masculine façade he had chosen to embrace. If we look beneath the surface, it is not difficult to imagine the two sides of Hemingway wrestling each other in the writing of *The Garden of Eden*. More than any of his other work, this novel tries to have it both ways and presents the conflict within Hemingway's conception of masculinity. Hemingway must have known this, which is part of the reason why he kept reworking the novel and trying to balance what he wanted to say about sexuality with the exigencies of maintaining his image. He had become a captive of this image and *The Garden of Eden* represents his personal attempt to come to grips with his self-imposed confinement within a narrow, inherited worldview.

Hemingway became a prisoner of his own myth. He lived in this rigid world for a number of reasons. His conception of masculinity, inherited from the Victorians, was perhaps arrested at the adolescent stage. But *Tom Brown's Schooldays* were long gone by the time Hemingway was born, despite the fact that his parents tried after their fashion to uphold such values. Hemingway came to reject most of the personal values of his parents but could never shake himself entirely free of the social code he was born into. Beegel writes of his parents' expressions of shock and outrage at their son's early writings as "the reaction of an older generation whose most deeply held assumptions were being challenged . . . It was the reaction of the last Victorians to the Lost Generation."[9] Success came early to Hemingway and his confidence was reinforced through recognition by others than his despised parents. The more he dwelt on the "masculine" virtue of courage in the face of death, the more he was roundly praised, the few dissenters drowned out in the chorus of applause. Whitlow suggests that Hemingway "the man never really grew up, whereas the writer did" (107). It seems more accurate to say that Hemingway, the man, hid behind a veneer while the writer often addressed his themes honestly.

As Meyers writes: "A man is essentially what he hides. The real and most important of the many Hemingways was the reflective man who wrote books and concealed his innate sensitivity under the mask of a man of action" (241). Unfortunately, it was most often the more sensitive side of his character that Hemingway chose to suppress. *Islands in the Stream*, as published, presents perhaps Hemingway at his weakest. In this semi-autobiographical novel the author attempts to reinforce his macho image by including many incidents from his own life, often embellished, designed to showcase his manliness. Here, more than in most of his fiction, Hemingway tries to portray Thomas Hudson as a version of himself as the ultra-masculine hero his image had already made him but the effort seems both forced and half-hearted. He hardly needed to bother at this stage of his career, in the 1950s. Thomas Hudson is a painter, a departure from the many author-heroes. Feeling, as Burwell puts it, the "feminine aspect of his own creative imagination" (4), Hemingway tries to masculinize the arts with his portrayal of Hudson. In *For Whom the Bell Tolls*, Hemingway presents an American professor of Spanish as his hero, an odd choice considering his general disdain for academics. But he carefully portrays Robert Jordan as a man of action in spite of his occupation. Despite the choice of such heroes, much of Hemingway's work demonstrates a discomfort with the artist, an impression that art perhaps represents a feminine nature and projects unmanly qualities as Burwell suggests (32). Hemingway gives these characters a hard-boiled edge to balance the soft, artistic, or intellectual vocation.

Spender recalls meeting Hemingway in Valencia and encountering, "a black-haired, bushy-moustached, hairy-handed giant" (229) who was surprisingly forthcoming on the subject of Stendhal's *The Charterhouse of Parma*. When Spender tried to continue the literary discussion by mentioning Shakespeare, Hemingway, perhaps remembering his

image, snapped, "Don't you realize I don't read books?" (230). Yet
he left behind a library of some 9,000 volumes. Hemingway comes off
at his most loutish, perhaps, in the infamous profile by Lillian Ross in
The New Yorker, in which, admitting his status as an author but using
the language of the prizefight, he says: "I beat Mr. Turgenev. Then
I trained hard and I beat Mr. de Maupassant. I've fought two draws
with Mr. Stendhal, and I think I had the edge in the last one. But
nobody's going to get me in any ring with Mr. Tolstoy."[10] As Meyers
points out, Hemingway often "refused to speak and act like an
intellectual—even though he thought and felt like one" (464), and
that the popular perception of both the author and his heroes was of
characters "more at home with a gun than a pen" (428). Thomas
Hudson in *Islands in the Stream* conforms to this model and handles
his weapons as readily as his paintbrushes.

CONCLUSION

If as some critics believe, Hemingway's "androgyny" represents a
transgressive agency undermining traditional gender concepts, they
must also address Hemingway's numerous expressions of misogyny
and homophobia. These critics are entirely correct in recognizing that
the alternative sexuality presented in Hemingway's work represents a
clear threat to the future of patriarchal institutions. Many of the critics who have discerned homosexual desire in Hemingway's work offer
intriguing hypotheses on possible psychological motivations and suppressed impulses. But clearly, Hemingway was homophobic for his
entire adult life. Even David in *The Garden of Eden*, who experiences
prolonged alternative heterosexuality and receptive sodomy with two
women, has the following exchange with Marita, after the departure
of Catherine. They are speaking of the brief lesbian affair of Catherine
and Marita and David remarks:

> "I'm glad you went through that nonsense and know it's worthless."
>
> "It's only for those people," Marita said. "It's not for us. Anymore than
> queers would be for you."
>
> "We've always had them and I'm never rude unless I have to be. But
> they give me the creeps."[11]

Hemingway himself made many such comments both privately and
publicly and we should take him at his word. If Hemingway had gay
desires, he may never have allowed them to enter fully into his
consciousness. Or he may have clearly recognized these desires and

determined through an effort of will to repress them and if that was his choice we as readers must accept and respect his position as a conscious heterosexual even while we condemn his homophobia. But it seems more likely that Hemingway did not, in fact, have homoerotic desires. He seems to have simply preferred to perform certain sexual acts with women, acts such as submitting to sodomy, that are erroneously associated in the popular mind strictly with male homosexuality. He may have enjoyed anal sex but truly recoiled at the idea of submitting to it from a man. He would not be alone in this.

In this age of the Internet, there are hundreds of websites devoted to men who enjoy being the passive partner in sodomy imposed by a dominant woman. There are hundreds, if not thousands more, devoted to other forms of female domination. And if most of these sites are depressing and degrading, this is likely because they are oriented toward commerce rather than communion. Although because of the Internet it is more visible now, it is simply impossible that this type of sexuality sprang up suddenly in the very late twentieth century for as Nacht remarks, masochism "is as old as the world" (32). Hemingway's misfortune may have been to be born into the late Victorian era when the new science of psychiatry was busy trying to do yeoman's service to uphold an archaic idea of masculinity while diagnosing homosexuality, masochism, and many other sexualities as deviant perversions. Certainly a case can be made for the subversive gendering in the work of artists like Forster, Wilde, Genet, and others because they generally embodied what Foucault calls an "interior androgyny, a hermaphroditism of the soul" (43) and often expressed progressive social opinions in both their art and their public statements. The same cannot be said for Hemingway. His masochistic sexuality, though undeniable, exists almost as an anomaly amidst more traditional standards of masculinity. But that it exists at all is more than enough reason to celebrate Hemingway's work even more than we already have.

Is masochism inherently progressive or conservative? There are compelling reasons to view masochism as an alternative sexuality embodying a subversive threat to prevailing phallocentric norms of masculinity. Hemingway's work incorporates much of masochism's subversive potential. Yet his simultaneous championship of so much that upholds and even exaggerates traditional masculinity considerably weakens any effort to locate his work as an unambiguous model of transgression. While Hemingway almost certainly practiced an alternative heterosexuality in his personal life, in his written work he most often chooses to conceal or obscure his desires because they do not conform to the prevailing ideal of masculinity. Hemingway accepted this ideal for the most part and when he avows his masochism directly, as in *The Garden of Eden*, he does so almost defiantly, seeking to incorporate it into his own personal code of manhood. The masochistic aesthetic displayed in his novels and stories can be seen as inevitable glimpses of truth that reveal themselves in any great art and no serious student can doubt Hemingway's monumental achievements. Hemingway, the man as opposed to the artist, may not have been nearly so interested in truth. Hemingway's masochism cannot be interpreted as an example to either promote a progressive social agenda or to retard one. Hemingway's work remains the expression of a singularly complex and gifted artist and consistently resists easy classification. How an individual behaves in the bedroom does not always conform to a logical expectation of what he or she may profess on social issues. This does not refer only to those who find it necessary to remain in a closet. Many figures in history have led sexually "transgressive" lifestyles, proudly proclaimed their "otherness," and still held extremely nonprogressive social views. The homosexual General Ernst Roehm and other members of the Nazi SA provide an extreme example. The homoerotic masochism of T.E. Lawrence did not prevent him, despite a guilty conscience, from serving as a loyal agent of British imperialism. As Dollimore notes, "we know only too well the political blindness of sexual desire" (334).

This does not mean to imply that Hemingway represents a modernist Caligula. But neither does it mean that Hemingway's interest in and practice of alternative sexualities led him to enlightened views of gender relations. Often a private sexual practice remains just that. In Hemingway's case, compensation for the submissive sexuality he recognized in himself, and acted upon in personal relationships, likely played a role in his façade of masculinity. However, it seems an injustice to see him merely as a sensitive man who found it difficult to grapple with his sexual identity, as Spilka portrays him. This conception depicts him as a helpless author groping his way toward the truth. There may be some justice in this idea, but on the whole, Hemingway felt he knew exactly what to do about his situation. He turned himself into an icon of traditional masculinity.

One can argue that we must separate the art from the man, that the man may have been a failure but the art may yet serve as a didactic and a corrective. But even here, the instances of "androgyny" and masochism in Hemingway's art coexist with exceedingly phallocentric notions of society. Spilka portrays Hemingway as a liberated male, far ahead of his time, and a suffering hero—just the type of characterization

Hemingway would have appreciated—but it hardly seems an accurate judgment. But Spilka's work, and the work of so many others discussed in these pages, have enabled many to see another side of Hemingway and for this alone we can be thankful. Willingham calls for a revision of Hemingway's reputation as a misogynist. Yet, certainly he often displayed misogyny and an extreme homophobia as well. These were his conscious, everyday opinions. These were views he wanted others to share. If in his writings Hemingway's passive and masochistic sexual nature emerges, this does not outweigh his voluminous portrayals of traditional masculinity outside of his bedroom. Hemingway certainly did *not* hate women or even gay men. But he felt it necessary to act with hostility toward them at times to support the image that he wore like a leaden jacket, which is almost as bad as true contempt. But in the last resort, we can be grateful to Hemingway for his radical subversion of some twentieth-century manifestations of patriarchy, even if we can hardly pretend that this was his project.

Notes

Introduction

1. Debra A. Moddelmog, *Reading Desire, In Pursuit of Ernest Hemingway* (Ithaca: University of Cornell Press, 1999), 84. All references to this work are cited by page in the text.

2. Gerry Brenner, *Concealments in Hemingway's Works* (Columbus: Ohio State University Press, 1983), 20. Unless otherwise noted all references to Brenner are to this work and are cited by page in the text.

3. Mark Spilka, *Hemingway's Quarrel with Androgyny* (Lincoln: University of Nebraska Press, 1990), 204. Unless otherwise noted all references to Spilka are to this work and are cited by page in the text.

4. Carl P. Eby, *Hemingway's Fetishism: Psychoanalysis and the Mirror of Manhood* (New York: SUNY Press, 1998), 212. Unless otherwise noted all references to Eby are to this work and are cited by page in the text.

5. Gilles Deleuze, "Coldness and Cruelty," in *Masochism*, trans. Jean McNeill (New York: Zone Books, 1991). All references are to this edition and are cited by page in the text.

6. Sarah Boxer, "Masochism Finally Gets Even," *New York Times* (January 27, 2001), B11.

7. Anita Phillips, *A Defense of Masochism* (New York: St. Martins, 1998), 75. All references are cited by page in the text.

8. Sigmund Freud, *Three Essays on the Theory of Sexuality*, trans. James Strachey (New York: Basic Books, 1962), 24.

9. Sigmund Freud, *A General Introduction to Psychoanalysis*, trans. Joan Riviere (New York: Permabooks, 1953), 314–315.

   See also Robert Stoller, *Observing the Erotic Imagination* (New Haven: Yale University Press, 1985). In this work, Stoller comments: "If you are as I was, you are so struck by the absurdity or monstrousness of the behavior that you stop thinking, comfortable with perversion in its accusatory sense" (10). Stoller, however, softens this view by asserting that: "Erotic choice, really, is a matter of opinions, taste, aesthetics" (15).

10. Robert Stoller, *Perversion: The Erotic Form of Hatred* (New York: Pantheon, 1975), ix. Unless otherwise noted, all further references to Stoller are to this work and are cited by page in the text.

Stoller's concept of "perversion" is broad and may represent one reason why many have abandoned the term. Stoller repeatedly states that the pervert "is motivated by a desire to harm the object, and [the act] is sensed as an act of revenge" (6–7) and always involves "a dehumanized object" (9). He includes among the perversions: "necrophilia, fetishism, rape, sex murder, sadism, masochism, voyeurism, pedophilia—and many more" (9). Later he refers to "such obvious perversions as rape, exhibitionism, sadism, or homosexuality" (109). Oddly, Stoller does not include bestiality in his perversions, considering it only an "abberation" (51). And while he qualifies his remarks, especially on homosexuality (195–206), and he expresses tolerance for all the perversions, his work remains a prime example of what some critics of psychoanalysis have long objected to.

11. Jonathan Dollimore, *Sexual Dissidence: Augustine to Wilde, Freud to Foucault* (London: Clarendon Press, Oxford University Press, 1991), 170. All references are cited by page in the text.

12. Laura Frost, " 'With This Ring, I Thee Own': Masochism and Social Reform in *Ulysses*," in *Sex Positives: The Cultural Politics of Sexual Diversity, Genders 25*, ed. Thomas Foster, Carol Siegel, Ellen E. Berry (New York and London: New York University Press, 1997), 227. All references are cited by page in the text.

13. Richard von Krafft-Ebing, *Psychopathia Sexualis* (New York: G.P. Putnam & Sons, 1965), 237. All references are to this edition and are cited by page in the text.

14. Sigmund Freud, "The Economic Problem of Masochism," in *The Standard Edition of the Complete Psychological Works of Sigmund Freud, Vol. XIX*, trans. James Strachey (London: The Hogarth Press, 1961), 277. All references are to this edition and are cited by page in the text.

15. Sigmund Freud, "A Child is Being Beaten," from *The Standard Edition of the Complete Psychological Works of Sigmund Freud, Vol. XVII*, trans. James Strachey (London: The Hogarth Press, 1955), 199. All references are to this edition and are cited by page in the text.

16. Carol Siegel, *Male Masochism, Modern Revisions of the Story of Love* (Bloomington and Indianapolis: Indiana University Press, 1995), 136. All references are cited by page in the text.

17. Michael Foucault, *The History of Sexuality, An Introduction, Volume I*, trans. Robert Hurley (New York: Pantheon, 1978), 105. All references are cited by page in the text.

18. Sacha Nacht, "*Le Masochisme* An Introduction," in *Essential Papers on Masochism*, ed. Margaret Ann Fitzpatrick Hanly (New York: New York University Press, 1995), 32. All references are to this edition and are cited by page in the text.

19. American Psychiatric Association, *Diagnostic and Statistical Manual of Mental Disorders*, third edition, revised (Washington: Author, 1987). "Self-defeating personality disorder" was the term used to

pathologize "self-sacrificing" people, especially women (and which could classify battered women as neurotic). Feminists both inside and outside of the psychiatry profession were naturally outraged and finally succeeded in excising "self-defeating personality disorder" from the DSM.

20. Stoller writes: "I doubt if masochists, in the strict sense of sexual perversion, often choose sadists, in the strict sense of sexual perversion, for their sexual partners. I would think that each intuitively knows, when observing the other's excitement, that the partner's fantasies do not fit his" (*Perversion* 58). And Deleuze states: "a genuine sadist would never tolerate a masochistic victim . . . Neither would the masochist tolerate a truly sadistic torturer" (40).

21. There are exceptions to this, of course, such as Jean-Jacques Rousseau, Charles Baudelaire, Algernon Charles Swineburne, and Leopold von Sacher-Masoch. Others like Kenneth Tynan confined their feelings on the subject to private journals, which were published posthumously.

22. See *Hemingway and Women: Female Critics and the Female Voice*, ed. Lawrence R. Broer and Gloria Holland (Tuscaloosa and London: University of Alabama Press, 2002).

23. Angela Carter, *The Sadeian Woman: An Exercise in Cultural History* (London: Virago, 1979), 21. All references are to this edition and are cited by page in the text.

24. Charles Hatten, "The Crisis of Masculinity, Reified Desire, and Catherine Barkley in *A Farewell to Arms*," in *Journal of the History of Sexuality*, 4(1) (1993), 86. All references are cited by page in the text.

25. Bernice Kert, in *The Hemingway Women* (New York: Norton, 1983), comments on all of Hemingway's marriages. All references are cited by page in the text.

    Gellhorn worked as a correspondent for Colliers and went to Europe to cover World War II in advance of her husband who vacillated in Havana. While Hemingway engaged in his somewhat ludicrous submarine-hunting patrols in the Caribbean—that Gellhorn considered "rot and rubbish" (qtd. in Kert 385)—his wife was already reporting from Europe. Hemingway belatedly traveled to Europe to cover the war and both he and Gellhorn, separately, attempted to land with the D-Day invasion forces. Only she succeeded, "an achievement" that Hemingway "never forgave her for." See Carlos Baker, *Hemingway: A Life Story* (New York: Bantam, 1970), 395. All references are cited by page in the text.

26. See Spilka's 1958 essay, "The Death of Love in *The Sun Also Rises*," in *Hemingway and His Critics*, ed. Carlos Baker (New York: Hill and Wang, 1961), 80–92.

27. Donald Junkins, "Mythmaking, Androgyny, and the Creative Process, Answering Mark Spilka," in *Hemingway Repossessed*, ed. Kenneth Rosen (Westport, CT: Praeger, 1994), 60.

28. Kenneth Lynn, *Hemingway* (New York: Fawcett-Columbine, 1987), 402. All references are cited by page in the text.

29. Ernest Hemingway, *Death in the Afternoon* (New York: Charles Scribner's Sons, 1932), 204. All references are to this edition and are cited by page in the text. Where necessary for clarification, this title will be abbreviated to DIA.

30. Adrienne Rich, "Compulsory Heterosexuality and the Lesbian Experience," *Signs* 5, 1980: 632–660 <www.mercurycenter.com/ archives/womenhistory/perspective/ ideas4.htm> (August 11, 2004).

31. Jeffrey Meyers, *Hemingway: A Biography* (New York: Harper & Row, 1983), 247–248, 494. Unless otherwise noted, all references to Meyers are to this work and are cited by page in the text.

32. Nancy Comley and Robert Scholes, *Hemingway's Genders: Rereading the Hemingway Text* (New Haven and London: Yale University Press 1994), 60. All references are cited by page in the text.

33. Barbara Probst Solomon, "Where's Papa?" in *The New Republic* (March 9, 1987), 31.

34. In the following pages, all references to the published version of *The Garden of Eden* (New York: Macmillan, 1987) are cited by page in the text. Where necessary for clarification, the title will be abbreviated to GOE. All references to the unpublished manuscript versions of *The Garden of Eden* at the Kennedy Library (Manuscripts, Hemingway Collection, Kennedy Library, Boston) and the Princeton library (Manuscripts, Charles Scribner's Archives, Firestone Library, Princeton University) are cited in endnotes by item, folder, and page numbers. The Kennedy Library are abbreviated to JFK and the Princeton library to PUL.

Chapter 1   Hemingway and Theories of Masochism

1. Sigmund Freud, *Five Introductory Lectures on Psycho-Analysis*, trans. James Strachey (New York: Norton, 1977), 44.

2. Ibid.

3. Thomas Strychacz, *Hemingway's Theaters of Masculinity* (Baton Rouge: University of Louisiana Press, 2003), 77–86. Unless otherwise noted, all references to Strychacz are to this work and cited by page in the text.

4. Freud, *Five Introductory Lectures*, 44.

5. Leo Bersani, *Homos* (Cambridge: Harvard University Press, 1995), 101.

6. Leo Bersani, *The Freudian Body: Psychoanalysis and Art* (New York: Columbia University Press, 1986), 134. Unless otherwise noted all references to Bersani are to this work and are cited by page in the text.

7. Gaylyn Studlar, *In the Realm of Pleasure: von Sternberg, Dietrich, and the Masochistic Aesthetic* (New York: Columbia University Press, 1988), 14. All references are cited by page in the text.

8. Theodor Reik, *Masochism in Sex and Society* (New York: Grove Press, 1962), 136.

9. Thomas Strychacz, "Dramatizations of Manhood in Hemingway's *In Our Time* and *The Sun Also Rises*," *American Literature*, 61(2) (1989), 245.

10. Ibid., 247.

11. Robert E. Gajdusek, "The Mad Sad Bad Misreading of Hemingway's Gender Politics/Aesthetics," *The North Dakota Quarterly*, 64(3) (1997), 37.

12. Jacqueline Tavernier-Courbin, *Ernest Hemingway's A Moveable Feast: The Making of a Myth* (Boston: Northeastern University Press, 1991), 65. All references are cited by page in the text.

13. Victor N. Smirnoff, "The Masochistic Contract," in *Essential Papers on Masochism*, ed. Margaret Ann Fitzpatrick Hanly (New York: New York University Press, 1995). All references are to this edition and are cited by page in the text.

14. Rudolph M. Lowenstein, "The Psychoanalytic Theory of Masochism," in *Essential Papers on Masochism*, ed. Margaret Ann Fitzpatrick Hanly, 36. All references are to this edition and are cited by page in the text.

15. Wyndham Lewis, "Ernest Hemingway: The Dumb Ox," in *Men Without Art* (1934) (Santa Barbara: Black Sparrow Press, 1987), emphasis in original, 26.

16. The suicide of Hemingway's father played no small part in his later psychology. Though father and son were never close after Ernest's childhood, a case can be made that Hemingway's subsequent construction of a personal and exaggerated masculinity, which was only in part sincerely felt as we can see in his often remarkable portraits of women and his masochism, can be attributed to feelings of both restitution and rejection of his dead and pitied father.

17. Susan F. Beegel, "Santiago and the Eternal Feminine: Gendering *La Mar* in *The Old Man and the Sea*," in *Hemingway and Women*, ed. Lawrence R. Broer and Gloria Holland, 144–145.

18. Kaja Silverman, *Male Subjectivity at the Margins* (New York and London: Routledge, 1992), 2. All references are cited by page in the text.

19. Greg Forter, "Melancholy Modernism: Gender and the Politics of Mourning in *The Sun Also Rises*," *The Hemingway Review*, 21(1) (Fall 2001), 25. All references are cited by page in the text.

20. James Joyce, in *Ulysses* (1922) (New York: Vintage, 1986), presents a veritable catalog of masochistic activities. Specialized masochistic fantasies performed or referred to include spanking, queening or smothering, coprophilia, urolagnia, and forced feminization. Bella/Bello dominates Bloom by: calling him a "dungdevourer" (433); passing gas on Bloom's "buttocksmothered" face (436); riding him like a horse as Bello "squeezes his mount's testicles roughly" (436); and dressing him like a prostitute and offering him for hire (436–437). All

references to this work are to this edition and are cited by page in the text.

21. Ernest Hemingway, *A Farewell to Arms* (1929) (New York: Macmillan, 1986), 257. All references to this work are to this edition and are cited by page in the text. Where necessary for clarification, this title is abbreviated to AFTA.

22. The idea of female castration has of course been contested by many for decades. Angela Carter writes of "the social fiction of the female wound, the bleeding scar left by her castration, which is a psychic fiction as deeply at the heart of Western Civilization as the myth of Oedipus. . . . Female castration is an imaginary fact that pervades the whole of men's attitudes towards women and our attitude to ourselves, that transforms women from human beings into wounded creatures who were born to bleed" (23).

23. Leslie Fiedler, *Love and Death in the American Novel*, revised edition (New York: Stein and Day, 1975), 316.

24. Ernest Hemingway, *For Whom the Bell Tolls* (New York: Charles Scribner's Sons, 1940), 175, 410–411. All references to this work are to this edition and are cited by page in the text. Where necessary for clarification, this title is abbreviated to FWTBT.

25. Ernest Hemingway, *The Sun Also Rises* (New York: Charles Scribner's Sons, 1926), 55. All references to this work are to this edition and are cited by page in the text. Where necessary for clarification, this title is abbreviated to SAR.

26. Ernest Hemingway, *Islands in the Stream* (1970) (New York: Charles Scribner's Sons, 1997), 296. Unless otherwise noted, all references to this work are to this edition and are cited by page in the text. Where necessary for clarification, this title is abbreviated to ITTS.

27. Lawrence, of course, celebrates the "phallic consciousness." In a perceptive reading of *Lady Chatterley's Lover*, Dollimore asks, "was Lawrence a heterosexual sodomite or a 'repressed homosexual'?" And he answers: "Neither: let us say rather that what is most significant . . . is the way so much is fantasized from the position of the woman (including anal ecstasy and, elsewhere, Lawrence's almost as notorious worship of the phallus), and in a voice that is at once *blindingly heterosexist and desperately homoerotic*" (emphasis in original 274–275).

28. Ernest Hemingway, *Across the River and Into the Trees* (New York: Charles Scribner's Sons, 1950), 24. All references are to this edition and are cited by page in the text. Where necessary for clarification, this title is abbreviated to ARIT.

29. Linda Wagner-Martin, "The Romance of Desire in Hemingway's Fiction," in *Hemingway and Women*, ed. Lawrence R. Broer and Gloria Holland, 68. All references are cited by page in the text.

30. Hemingway did everything in his power to please Adriana, a struggling artist, and even convinced his publisher to allow her to illustrate two of his novels although her work was considered substandard

(see Meyers, 1983, 443–445). Adriana provided both the model for the heroine in *Across the River* and the inspiration for one of Hemingway's greatest works, *The Old Man and the Sea*, much of which he wrote during her visit to Cuba. Although biographers conclude that Hemingway and Adriana did not have a sexual relationship, Hemingway nevertheless played the adoring submissive to her mistress. If their relationship had any physical element at all it may have taken a form similar to what Reynolds (216), Russo (166), and Brenner (161) suggest of the sexual relations between Colonel Cantwell and Renata in *Across the River*—that is: Hemingway, though remaining chaste himself, may have nevertheless willingly pleasured Adriana. See the remarks of Deleuze and Studlar on the elements of denial and suspense in male masochism.

31. See Brenner, 1983, 161; Michael Reynolds, *Hemingway: The Final Years* (New York: W.W. Norton & Co., 1999), 216; John Paul Russo, "To Die is Not Enough: Hemingway's Venetian Novel," in *Hemingway in Italy and Other Essays*, ed. Robert W. Lewis (New York: Praeger, 1990), 166–167. All references to these works are cited by page in the text. *Across the River* is discussed further in chapter 2.

32. Hemingway, "Mr. and Mrs. Elliot," in *In Our Time* (New York: Charles Scribner's Sons, 1930), 111. All references to this work are to this edition and are cited by page in the text.

33. Ernest Hemingway, *A Moveable Feast* (New York: Charles Scribner's Sons, 1961), 190. All references to this work are to this edition and are cited by page in the text. Where necessary for clarification, this title will be abbreviated to MF.

34. Ernest Hemingway, *Selected Letters, 1917–1961*, ed. Carlos Baker (New York: Charles Scribner's Sons, 1981), 835. Where necessary for clarification, this title will be abbreviated to SL.

35. Quoted in Denis Brian, ed., *The True Gen: An Intimate Portrait of Hemingway by Those Who Knew Him* (New York: Grove Press, 1988), 64–65.

36. Ibid., 64.

37. Quoted in Siegel, 151.

38. Quoted in Sarah Boxer, "Masochism Finally Gets Even," *New York Times* (January 20, 2001), B11.

39. Suzanne R. Stewart, *Sublime Surrender: Male Masochism at the Fin-de-Siècle* (Ithaca: Cornell University Press, 1998), 5. All references are cited by page in the text.

40. Nick Mansfield, *Masochism: The Art of Power* (Westport, CT and London: Praeger, 1997), 50. All references are cited by page in the text.

41. Freud, quoted in David Savran, *Taking It Like a Man: White Masculinity, Masochism and Contemporary American Culture* (Princeton: Princeton University Press, 1998), 31. All references are cited by page in the text.

Chapter 2   Elements of Masochism in Hemingway's Work

1. Jacques Lacan, *The Four Fundamental Concepts of Psychoanalysis*, ed. Jacques-Alain Miller, trans. Alan Sheridan (New York: Norton, 1998). All references are to this edition and are cited by page in the text.

    According to Lacan, every human being retains part of the "egg" which represents the pre-birth (or nonliving) state and thus resembles death. This becomes the myth of the lamella, which Lacan puns as *l'hommelette* (197). The lamella, according to Lacan, is almost a synonym for libido. He describes both as having characteristics of an organ. This lamella, he says, "survives any division" (197) such as that described by Aristophanes.

2. Plato, *The Symposium, Part One*, trans. Benjamin Jowett <http://evans-experientialism.freewebspace.com/plato_symposium01.htm> (August 11, 2004).

3. Hemingway, "Soldier's Home" in *In Our Time* (New York: Charles Scribner's Sons, 1930), 97.

4. Hemingway, "The Last Good Country" in *The Complete Short Stories: Finca Vigia Edition* (New York: Charles Scribner's Sons, 1987), 532. All references to this work are to this edition and are cited by page in the text. Where necessary for clarification, this collection will be abbreviated CSS.

5. Robert E. Fleming, "The Endings of Hemingway's *Garden of Eden*," *American Literature*, 61 (2) (1989), 268–269.

6. *The Garden of Eden*, JFK 442.6, p. 7; PUL 29 "Provisional Ending," pp. 4–5. Quoted in Fleming, ibid., 269.

7. Ibid., PUL, 29 "Provisional Ending," p. 6.

8. Quoted in Fleming, 268–269; ibid., PUL, 29 "Provisional Ending," p. 6.

9. Leopold von Sacher-Masoch, "Lola" in *The Master Masochist: Tales of a Sadistic Mistress*, ed. Vyuyan Howarth, trans. Eric Lemuel Randall (London: Senate, 1996), 49.

10. Quoted in Camile Paglia, *Sexual Personnae, Art and Decadence from Nefertiti to Emily Dickinson* (New York: Vintage, 1991), 436.

11. See Studlar (39–45), in which she discusses the work of Freud, Gregory Zilboorg, Charles Socarides, Eva Feder-Kittay, Robert Dickes, P.J. Van der Leeuw, John Ellis, M. Wulff, and others.

12. Ernest Hemingway, *To Have and Have Not* (New York: Charles Scribner's Sons, 1937), 116. All references to this work are to this edition and are cited by page in the text. Where necessary for clarification, this title will be abbreviated to THHN.

13. Rose Marie Burwell, *Hemingway: The Postwar Years and The Posthumous Novels* (Cambridge: Cambridge University Press, 1996), 102. All further references are cited by page in the text.

14. Quoted in Spilka, 286; *The Garden of Eden*, 422.9, 2, pp. 48–49.

15. Quoted in Eby, 203.

16. "Forced feminization" is a common theme in the pornography of masochism and female domination. See also the cross-dressing in the "Nighttown" passages of *Ulysses* (436–437).

17. Toni Morrison, *Playing in the Dark: Whiteness and the Literary Imagination* (New York: Vintage, 1992), 80.

18. Lisa S. Starks, " 'Like the lover's pinch, which hurts and is desired' ": the narrative of male masochism and Shakespeare's *Antony and Cleopatra*," *Literature and Psychology*, 45 (4) (1999), 58–73.

19. Compare this with Frederic's comments in *A Farewell to Arms*: "I watched her brushing her hair, holding her head so the weight of her hair all came on one side" (258).

20. Leopold von Sacher-Masoch, "Venus in Furs" in *Masochism*, trans. Jean McNeill (New York: Zone Books, 1991), 247. All references will be to this edition and are cited by page in the text.

21. Mark Spilka, "The Death of Love in *The Sun Also Rises*," in *Hemingway and His Critics*, ed. Carlos Baker (New York: Hill and Wang, 1961), 90.

22. Aaron Lathan, "A Farewell to Machismo," *New York Times Magazine* (October 16, 1977), 97.

23. Brenner also notes that in *Across the River*, "the ecstasy is a 'great bird' " (161). Hemingway used the metaphor of a great flying bird for female orgasm earlier in "Fathers and Sons," when he describes Nick Adams and Trudy Gilroy making love: "[S]he did first what no one has ever done better . . . plump brown legs, flat belly, hard little breasts, well holding arms, quick searching tongue, the flat eyes, the good taste of mouth, then uncomfortably, tightly, sweetly, moistly, lovely, tightly, achingly, fully, finally, unendingly, never-endingly, never-to-endingly, suddenly, ended, the *great bird* flown like an owl in the twilight" (emphasis added, "Fathers and Sons" in CSS 376). A little further on in this story, the narrator relates: "When you have shot one bird flying you have shot all birds flying. They are all different and they fly in different ways but the sensation is the same and the last one is as good as the first" (376). Though these comments can be read as sexist, by 1950 in *Across the River*, Hemingway's use of the metaphor of the "great bird" seems to be less so in that it relates to the Colonel unselfishly providing Renata with an orgasm without an expected payback.

24. Eby suggests that this line indicates sodomy performed on the colonel by Renata. " 'He Felt the Change So that It Hurt Him All Through': Sodomy and Transvestic Hallucination in Late Hemingway," 25 (1) (Fall 2005).

25. Jeffrey Jerome Cohen, "Masoch/Lancelotism," Department of English and Program in the Human Sciences, The George Washington University, 1995 <http://www.georgetown.edu/labyrinth/conf/cs95/ papers/cohen.html> (August 11, 2004).

26. Tania Modelski, *Feminism Without Women, Culture and Criticism in a "Post-Feminist" Age* (New York: Routledge, 1991), 73.

27. Cohen, "Masoch/Lancelotism," 1995 <http://www.georgetown.edu/labyrinth/conf/cs95/ papers/cohen.html> (August 11, 2004).

28. Edward Said, *Reflections on Exile and Other Essays* (Cambridge: Harvard University Press, 2000), 233.

29. Dorothy C. Hayden, CSW, CAC, "Psychological Dimensions of Masochistic Surrender" 2000 <http://www.sextreatment.com/psych.htm> (August 11, 2004).

30. Edmund Wilson, "Introduction" to *In Our Time*, by Ernest Hemingway (New York: Charles Scribner's Sons, 1925), xi. All references are cited by page in the text.

31. Lisa S. Starks, " 'Batter My [Flaming] Heart': Male Masochism in the Religious Lyrics of Donne and Crashaw," *Enculturation*, 1 (2) (Fall 1997) <http://www.uta.edu/huma/enculturation/1_2/starks. html> (August 11, 2004).

32. H.R. Stoneback, "In the Nominal Country of the Bogus: Hemingway's Catholicism and the Biographies," in *Hemingway: Essays of Reassessment*, ed. Frank Scafella (New York: Oxford University Press, 1991), 105–140. Stoneback makes a compelling case that Hemingway was a Catholic believer throughout much of his adult life and seems correct in his assertion of "the facile assumption made by most Hemingway biographers that Hemingway was a 'nominal' Catholic [or] a 'bogus' Catholic" (106–107).

33. Hemingway opens a 1949 letter to the conservative Cardinal of New York, Francis Spellman, with the words: "In every picture that I see of you there is more mealy mouthed arrogance, fatness, and over-confidence." Hemingway proceeds to call the cardinal a liar and a "strike breaker" (SL 661). In this letter, Hemingway refers to his Catholicism in the past tense: "I was a dues-paying member" (661). According to editor Carlos Baker, this letter may not have been sent. After the Spanish Civil War, Hemingway is said to have ceased praying because: "It seemed somehow crooked to have anything to do with a religious institution so closely allied to Fascism" (qtd. in *Hemingway in Cuba*, Hilary Hemingway and Carlene Brennen, New York: Ruggedland, 2003), 108.

34. Christopher Newfield, "The Politics of Male Suffering: Masochism and Hegemony in the American Renaissance," *Differences,* 1 (3) (Fall 1989), 55–87.

35. William E. Coté, "Correspondent or Warrior?: Hemingway's Murky World War II 'Combat' Experience," in *The Hemingway Review*, 22 (1) (Fall 2002), 88–104. All references are cited by page in the text.

Chapter 3   Desire and Denial

1. Leo Bersani, "Is the Rectum a Grave?" in *AIDS, Cultural Analysis, Cultural Activism*, ed. Douglas Crimp (Cambridge: MIT Press, 1988), 220.

2. Bersani, *Homos*, 78.

3. The Boston Women's Health Collective, *The New Our Bodies, Ourselves: A Book By and For Women* (New York: Simon and Shuster, 1984, 1992), 218.

4. Susie Bright, interview, in *Angry Women*, ed. Andrea Juno and V. Vale (San Francisco: Re/Search Publications, 1991), 216.

5. Jonathan Goldberg, *Reclaiming Sodom* (New York and London: Routledge, 1994), 3. All references are cited by page in the text.

6. Tristan Taormino, "Bend Over Boys," in "Pucker Up" column in *The Village Voice* (March 1–7, 2000) <http://www.villagevoice.com/issues/0009/taormino.php> (August 4, 2004).

7. The fisting in *Ulysses* occurs when Bella/Bello forces his arm up to the elbow into Bloom's "vulva" (440).

8. Patrick Paul Garlinger, " 'Homo-Ness' and the Fear of Femininity," in *Diacritics*, 29(1) (1999), 63–64.

9. Bersani, "Is the Rectum a Grave?" 217.

10. Jacques Laplanche, "Aggressiveness and Sadomasochism," in *Essential Papers on Masochism*, ed. Margaret Ann Fitzpatrick Hanly, 122.

11. Bersani, "Is the Rectum a Grave?" 220.

12. Bersani, *Homos*, 60.

13. Feinberg Leslie, *Transgender Warriors: Making History from Joan of Arc to RuPaul* (Boston: Beacon Press, 1996), X.

14. Ramon Johnson, "Trannie 101: The Meaning of the Words Transsexual, Transgender and Transvestite" *Gaylife* with Ramon Johnson, October 15, 2003 <http://gaylife.about.com/library/weekly/aa042303a.htm> (July 18, 2004).

15. Tristan Taormino, "The Queer Heterosexual," "Pucker Up" column in *The Village Voice*, April 30, 2003 <http://www.villagevoice.com/issues/0319/taormino.php> (September 24, 2004). Taormino writes: "And who do you think is teaching straight women how to wield a strap-on dick like they own it and reassuring men that they can be macho and still take it up the ass? Queers, of course."

16. Clyde Smith, "How I Became a Queer Heterosexual," in *Straight With a Twist: Queer Theory and the Subject of Heterosexuality*, ed. Calvin Thomas (Urbana and Chicago: University of Illinois Press, 2000), 61.

17. Dollimore writes of Norman Mailer's view (commenting in *The Prisoner of Sex* on D.H. Lawrence) of men who deny same-sex desires and will themselves straight, that "anyone who has succeeded in repressing his homosexuality has earned the right not to be called homosexual" (46). Dollimore correctly labels Mailer's view "denigrating" (264). Whether or not Hemingway repressed homosexual desires is almost beside the point since he was a life-long heterosexual and always identified as such. However, what is at work in Hemingway does not seem to be a repression of homosexual desires but rather a reluctant embrace of a passively expressed heterosexuality, which may have seemed at times even worse for his macho image than homosexuality would have been. And despite Mailer's hero-worship of Hemingway, we should not equate the latter's views with the former's.

18. Bersani, *Homos*, 87.
19. All quotations in this paragraph from *The Garden of Eden*, JFK 422.5, 6, pp. 4–13.
20. Ibid., JFK 422.5, 7, pp. 3–4.
21. Ibid., JFK 422.5, 6, p. 16.
22. Ibid., JFK 422.5, 9, p. 29.
23. Quoted in Brian 188.
24. Mary Welsh Hemingway, *How It Was* (New York: Ballantine, 1976), 466. All references will be to this edition and are cited by page in the text.
25. Judith Fetterly, *The Resisting Reader: A Feminist Approach to American Fiction* (Bloomington, Indiana University Press, 1978), 71.
26. Rena Sanderson, "Hemingway's Literary Sisters: The Author though the Eyes of Women Writers," in *Hemingway and Women*, ed. Lawrence R. Broer and Gloria Holland, 286. All references are cited by page in the text.
27. Gerry Brenner, *A Comprehensive Companion to Hemingway's A Moveable Feast: Annotation to Interpretation*, Studies in American Literature, Volumes 37a and 37b (Lewiston: The Edwin Mellon Press, 2000), 330.
28. Arnold Samuelson, *With Hemingway: A Year in Key West and Cuba* (New York: Holt, Rinehart and Winston, 1984), 64. All references are cited by page in the text.
29. Roger Whitlow, *Cassandra's Daughters: The Women in Hemingway* (Westport, CT and London: Greenwood Press, 1984), 113. All references are cited by page in the text.
30. Lawrence R. Broer and Gloria Holland, eds., "Introduction" *Hemingway and Women*, ix.
31. Kathy G. Willingham, "Hemingway's *The Garden of Eden*: Writing with the Body" in *The Hemingway Review*, 12(2) (1993), 46. Unless otherwise noted, all references to Willingham are to this work and are cited by page in the text.
32. Amy Lovell Strong, " 'Go to Sleep, Devil': The Awakening of Catherine's Feminism in *The Garden of Eden*," in *Hemingway and Women*, ed. Lawrence R. Broer and Gloria Holland, 192–193. All references are cited by page in the text.
33. Ibid., 198.
34. Nancy R. Comley, "The Light from Hemingway's Garden: Regendering Papa," in *Hemingway and Women*, ed. Lawrence R. Broer and Gloria Holland, 212.

CHAPTER 4   HEMINGWAY AND THE FEMININE COMPLEX

1. See Spilka, *Hemingway's Quarrel with Androgyny*, Part I, 17–174.
2. Peter Griffin, *Less Than a Treason: Hemingway in Paris* (New York: Oxford University Press, 1990), 49. All references are cited by page in the text.

3. Stephen Spender, *World Within World* (1951) (New York: St. Martin's Press, 1994), 230. All references will be to this edition and are cited by page in the text.

4. Freud, *Three Essays*, 39.

5. See Lynn, 100–101, 322; Gadjusek, 47; See also Marie J. Kuda, "Was Hemingway's Mother a Lesbian?" in *Outlines*, 13(14), September 8, 1999 <http://astro.ocis.temple.edu/~ruby/opp/grace.html> (September 30, 2004).

6. Quoted in Lathan 94–96.

   Paul Hendrickson reports a domestic incident in the adult Hemingway's home that recalls his mother's comments in his baby book: "Once, when the eldest son was visiting his father and a stepmother in Key West, he did something horrible. He no longer remembers what it was. . . . Anyway he had to have a whipping. Papa took him into the bathroom and sat him on the hopper and then proceeded to pull down his own pants and whack himself with a hairbrush. 'When I come out,' he whispered to his son, 'Mother will know you were punished.' " Paul Hendrickson, "Papa's Boys: The Random Legacy of the Hemingways" *The Washington Post* (July 29, 1987).

7. See James R. Mellow, *Hemingway: A Life Without Consequences* (New York: Houghton Mifflin Co., 1992), 11. See also Meyers 9; Lynn 37–38.

8. Emily Brontë, *Wuthering Heights* (1847) (New York: Barnes & Noble 1993), 70.

9. Kerry Kelly Novick and Jack Novick, "The Essence of Masochism," in *Essential Papers on Masochism*, ed. Margaret Ann Fitzpatrick Hanly (New York: New York University Press, 1995), 250–251.

10. Eby quotes these lines on page 179 of his book. In a footnote, he indicates that Mary Hemingway's version is "a little altered" from the original notebooks, specifically where Hemingway wrote "She loves me to be her girl." In Mary Hemingway's transcription, this appears as "She loves me to be her girls" in the plural.

11. See Sanderson on Hemingway and Parker, 276–294.

12. Quoted in Bernice Kert, *The Hemingway Women* (New York: Norton, 1983), 63. All references will be to this edition and are cited by page in the text.

13. Quoted in Brian, 25–26.

14. J. Gerald Kennedy, *Imagining Paris: Exile, Writing, and American Identity* (New Haven: Yale University Press, 1993), 135–137. All references will be to this edition and cited by page in the text.

15. See Kert, 364; Baker, 353.

16. According to Meyers, "there is no evidence that he [Hemingway] ever participated, as Greene did, in the low life of the city" (327). In Greene's novel, *Travels with My Aunt*, the following dialogue takes place: " 'Are you really a Roman Catholic?' I asked my aunt with interest. She replied promptly and seriously, 'Yes, my dear, only I just

don't believe in all the things they believe in' " (New York: Viking, 1969), 135. Hemingway's Catholicism may have been just as serious and just as selective.

17. Barlow, Jamie, "Re-Reading Women II: The Example of Brett, Hadley, Duff, and Women's Scholarship," in *Hemingway and Women*, ed. Lawrence R. Broer and Gloria Holland, 30.

18. Ernest Hemingway, *Green Hills of Africa* (New York: Charles Scribner's Sons, 1935), 66. All references will be to this edition and are cited by page in the text. Where clarification is necessary, the title will be abbreviated to GHOA.

19. Samuelson, 16.

20. Brian, 188; Lynn, 301; Meyers, 346.

21. Kert quotes Hemingway's son Patrick: "Aunt Jinny was lesbian and she was quite keen on getting my mother to be homosexual as well" (374). Another son, Gregory, disputes the friendship of his father and Jinny when he writes in *Papa, A Personal Memoir*, "My aunt hated my father's guts" (6). This memory probably postdates his father's divorce from Pauline.

22. Bersani, *Homos,* 28.

23. Also cited by Tavernier-Courbin (77), who relates that Hemingway claims to have carried out this act after a conversation on lesbianism with Gertrude Stein.

24. Ernest Hemingway, "Up in Michigan," in *The Complete Short Stories*, 62. All references will be to this edition and are cited by page in the text. Where clarification is necessary this collection will be abbreviated to CSS.

25. Alice Hall Petry, "Coming of Age in Hortons Bay: Hemingway's 'Up in Michigan,' " in *New Critical Approaches to the Short Stories of Ernest Hemingway*, ed. Jackson J. Benson (Durham & London: Duke University Press, 1990), 353.

26. Griffin, 50–51.

27. For an account of Hemingway's perception of his need for financial independence, see Robert W. Trogden, "Money and Marriage: Hemingway's Self-Censorship in *For Whom the Bell Tolls*," in *The Hemingway Review* 22(2) (Spring 2003), 6–18.

28. Quoted in Brian, 30.

29. To enhance his reputation after his initial literary successes, Hemingway permitted the fabrication to be reported that he had also served in Italy's elite forces, the Arditi.

30. See James McLendon, *Papa: Hemingway in Key West* (Key West: Langley Press, Inc., 1990), 163. All references will be to this edition and are cited by page in the text.

31. Ernest Hemingway, "The Snows of Kilimanjaro," in *The Complete Short Stories*, 45. All references will be to this edition and are cited by page in the text. Where clarification is necessary this collection will be abbreviated to CSS.

32. Quoted in Samuelson, 42.
33. Kennedy, 123.
34. *The Garden of Eden*, JFK 422.1, 8, p. 16.
35. Philip Young, *Ernest Hemingway*, University of Minnesota Pamphlets on American Writers, Vol. 1 (Minneapolis: University of Minnesota Press, 1959), 15.
36. H.R. Stoneback, "In the Nominal Country of the Bogus: Hemingway's Catholicism and the Biographies," in *Hemingway: Essays of Reassessment*, ed. Frank Scafella (New York: Oxford University Press, 1991), 109.
37. Gregory Hemingway, *Papa: A Personal Memoir* (Boston: Houghton Mifflin Co. 1976), 7–12. Hemingway and his son Gregory blamed each other for Pauline's death. In 1951, Gregory was arrested on a drug charge. Shortly after this, Pauline called Hemingway to discuss the situation and the conversation ended in a "brutal" shouting match. A few hours later, Pauline died. Hemingway told his son that his trouble with the law had "killed Mother" (8). Gregory later wrote to his father, as he writes in his memoir, "that it was not my minor troubles that had upset Mother but his brutal conversation with her eight hours before she died" (12).

CHAPTER 5   DEFYING THE CODE

1. Quoted in George Plimpton, "An Interview with Ernest Hemingway," in *Hemingway and His Critics*, ed. Carlos Baker (New York: Hill and Wang, 1961), 29.
2. J.F. Buckley, "Echoes of Closeted Desires: The Narrator and Character Voices of Jake Barnes," in *The Hemingway Review*, 19(2) (Spring 2000), 79.
3. Wolfgang E.H. Rudat, "Hemingway's Sexual Otherness: What's Really Funny in *The Sun Also Rises*," in *Hemingway Repossessed*, ed. Kenneth Rosen (Westport, CT: Praeger, 1994), 176.
4. Ira Elliott, "Performance Art: Jake Barnes and 'Masculine' Signification in *The Sun Also Rises*." *American Literature*, 67(1) (1995), 86. All references are cited by page in the text.
5. It is unfortunate that one of the few recorded interactions between Hemingway and Dietrich is the exchange reported by Lillian Ross in the *New Yorker* profile that amounts to little more than inane prattle. See Lillian Ross's 1950, *Portrait of Hemingway* (New York: Avon Library, 1961, 52–58). Dietrich's daughter recently donated 30 letters to her mother from Hemingway to the JFK Library but these are unavailable to the public until 2007. See James Roth, "News From the Hemingway Collection," *Hemingway Review*, 23 (1) (Fall 2003), 137.
   It seems possible that two such sexually ambiguous figures as Hemingway and Dietrich would have shared more than what Ross presents. Hemingway's friendship with Dietrich, who he met on a

transatlantic crossing in 1934, offers several intriguing possibilities. Both of course were antifascists and strong supporters of the Allies in World War II: Hemingway as journalist and unofficial combatant, and Dietrich as a USO entertainer, as is Thomas Hudson's ex-wife in *Islands in the Stream*. But Hemingway may have also been attracted to Dietrich's renowned and audacious sexual ambiguity. Studlar writes of Dietrich's importance in von Sternberg's films, which personify the masochistic aesthetic. Of the film, *Morocco*, Studlar writes: "when Private Brown [Gary Cooper, another Hemingway friend] first sees Amy Jolly [Dietrich] in a rowdy Moroccan nightclub, he attempts to quiet the audience. Attired in tails and top hat, she gazes from her position above him on the stage. Brown is placed in the passive, feminine position and becomes a fetishized object glamorized in two-dimensional close-ups." Studlar then quotes Andrew Sarris on the scene's "perverse interchange of masculine and feminine characteristics." Studlar continues: "This 'perverse interchange' might be regarded as a liberation from the masculine/feminine polarities dominating notions of sexual identity in a patriarchal structure" (64). It is unclear whether Hemingway ever felt this "perverse interchange" while in the gaze of Dietrich but there is every indication that he would have enjoyed it if he had. And Lynn asserts that Hemingway felt "a profound attraction to her sexual ambivalence" (418).

6. All quotations in this and the following paragraph are from Ernest Hemingway, *Islands in the Stream*, Manuscripts (Hemingway Collection, Kennedy Library, Boston), JFK 112, pp. 94–99.

7. Ibid., IITS, JFK 113, p. 84.

8. Ibid., IITS, JFK 113, p. 88.

9. Ernest Hemingway, *True at First Light* (New York: Charles Scribner's Sons, 1999), 281. All references are to this edition and cited by page in the text. Where clarification is necessary, the title is abbreviated to TAFL.

10. Taormino, "Bend Over, Boys."

11. Pat Califia, "Introduction," *Sex Changes* (San Francisco: Cleis Press, 1997) <http://www.sexuality.org/l/transgen/scpc.html> (August 11, 2004).

12. Allen Josephs, "Reality and Invention in *For Whom the Bell Tolls*, or Reflections on the Nature of the Historical Novel," in *Hemingway Repossessed*, ed. Kenneth Rosen (Westport, CT: Praeger, 1994), 94.

13. Ernest Hemingway, "The Light of the World," in *The Complete Short Stories*, 293. All references are to this edition and cited by page in the text. Where clarification is necessary, this collection is abbreviated to CSS.

14. Sandra Whipple Spanier, "Catherine Barkley and the Hemingway Code," Paper presented at NEMLA, Hartford, CT (March 19, 1985). Ernest Hemingway Collection (Kennedy Library, Boston), 13.

15. *The Garden of Eden*, JFK 422.1, 1, p. 18.

16. Quoted in Moddelmog, 69; JFK 422.1, 1, p. 20.
17. Similarly, in *True at First Light*, Miss Mary tells Papa, "I am a warrior. I'm your wife and your lover and your small brother. . . . Kiss your warrior brother." Papa responds, "Get in your own bed and stay there" (40). Even when play-acting, Hemingway wants no part of anything that even suggests male homosexuality.
18. *The Garden of Eden*, JFK 422.1, 8, p. 16.
19. Ibid., JFK 422.5, 1, p. 1.
20. Ibid., JFK 422.5, 1, p. 2.
21. *Islands in the Stream*, JFK 112, p. 99.
22. *The Garden of Eden*, JFK 422.5, p. 3.
23. Ibid.
24. Ibid.
25. Carl P. Eby, " 'He Felt the Change So that It Hurt Him All Through': Sodomy and Transvestic Hallucination in Late Hemingway," 25(1) (Fall 2005).
26. Frederic describes how Catherine Barkley's hair "would all come down and she would drop her head and we would both be inside of it" (AFTA 114).
27. *The Garden of Eden*, JFK 422.5, 1, p. 19.
28. Ibid., JFK 422.5, 1, p. 29.
29. All references in this paragraph are to *The Garden of Eden*, JFK 422.5, 2, pp. 3, 11–12.
30. *The Garden of Eden*, Manuscripts, Charles Scribner's Archives (Firestone Library, Princeton University) Hemingway IV, *Garden of Eden*, 14, p. 11.
31. Ibid., 21–22.
32. Ibid., 22.
33. Ibid.
34. *The Garden of Eden*, qtd. in Moddelmog 76; JFK 422.1 3, p. 6.
35. *The Garden of Eden*, PUL 14, pp. 1, 14.
36. *The Garden of Eden*, JFK 422.2, pp. 5, 39.
37. *The Garden of Eden*, PUL 14, p. 24.
38. Ibid., 36, 43.
39. Ibid., 28.
40. Ernest Hemingway, "The Sea Change," in *The Complete Short Stories*, 302. All references will be to this edition and are cited by page in the text. Where necessary for clarification this collection will be abbreviated to CSS.
41. *The Garden of Eden*, qtd. in Eby, 158; JFK 422.1, 2, p. 4.
42. Ibid.
43. *The Garden of Eden*, JFK 422.5, 16, p. 38.
44. Quoted in Samuelson, 43.
45. Kathy G. Willingham, "Hemingway's *The Garden of Eden*: Writing with the Body" in *The Hemingway Review* 12(2) (1993), 46–61. More recently, Marc Hewson applies Cixous's theories to *A Farewell*

to Arms, in " 'The Real Story of Ernest Hemingway': Cixous, Gender and *A Farewell to Arms*," *Hemingway Review* 22(2) (Spring 2003), 51–62.

46. *The Garden of Eden*, JFK 422.1 2, p. 3.

CHAPTER 6   HEMINGWAY, RACE, AND COLONIALISM

1. It should be remembered that the betrayal of the Arabs at Versailles led to the British occupation of Iraq after World War I, a disturbing prelude to the Anglo-American occupation of 2003 and thereafter.

2. Frantz Fanon, *Black Skin, White Masks* (New York: Grove Press, 1967), 176.

3. T.E. Lawrence, *Seven Pillars of Wisdom*, 1926 (Harmondsworth, England: Penguin, 1973). All references are to this edition and are cited by page in the text.

   Lawrence, on a spying mission, is taken captive at Deraa in Syria and brought before the Bey. The Turks, according to Lawrence's account, were unaware of the identity and importance of their prisoner. Here, writes Lawrence, "[they] made me wash myself carefully" to prepare for his encounter with the official, as he muses: "Tomorrow, perhaps, leave would be permitted if I fulfilled the Bey's pleasure this evening" (451). Lawrence relates in rather explicit detail, what passes in this encounter. "Then he [the Bey] began to faun on me, saying how white and fresh I was. . . . I was obdurate, so he changed his tone, and sharply ordered me to take off my drawers" (452). Lawrence withstands the advances of the Bey and is severely beaten for his resistance: "The Bey cursed me with horrible threats and made the man holding me tear my clothes away, bit by bit" (452). The Bey then "began to paw me over. . . . He leaned forward, fixed his teeth into my neck and bit till the blood came. Then he kissed me" (452). Lawrence, while homosexual, was not willing to be taken forcefully by the Bey, who perhaps sensing a sexual kinship in his captive, says, "You must understand that I know: and it will be easier for you if you do as I wish" (453). When the Bey speaks these words, Lawrence becomes frightened that the Bey knows of his role in the Arab Revolt. However, the Bey may be suggesting a sexual recognition, that what he knows is that Lawrence is homosexual. Lawrence still refuses the Bey and is beaten again more severely, this time with "a whip of the Circassian sort, a thong of supple black hide" (453). During the beating, Lawrence reveals an aesthetic awareness, typical of masochism, as he writes, "[s]omewhere a cheap clock ticked loudly and it distressed me that the beating was not in its time" (453). At intervals, Lawrence reports that his captors would "play unspeakably with me" (453). After the beating, Lawrence is brought again to the Bey who "now rejected me in haste, as a thing too torn and bloody for his bed" (454).

The historical veracity of Lawrence's account has been questioned and if it is indeed a product of fantasy, it reveals even more about his masochism.

By saying, "You must understand that I know," the Bey seems to acknowledge Lawrence's homosexuality, and tries to convince him to cease resisting his advances. This recalls the coded language used by Brett in *The Sun Also Rises* when, after Count Mippipopolous displays his wounds, referred to as "welts," when she tells Jake that the count is "one of us" (61)—which could be a inclusive reference to a forbidden sexuality (61) and an identification of a "sexual outlaw."

4. Quoted in Mary Hemingway, *Mary's African Journal*, Manuscripts (Hemingway Collection, Kennedy Library, Boston), JFK 355A, p. 210.
5. Ibid., 202.
6. Dennis Porter, *Haunted Journeys: Desire and Transgression in European Travel Writing* (Princeton: Princeton University Press, 1991), 230. All references are cited by page in the text.
7. Quoted in Mary Hemingway, *How It Was*, 467.
8. *The Garden of Eden*, PUL 4 14, 1.
9. Quoted in Eby, 179.
10. Mary Hemingway, *Mary's African Journal*, JFK 355A, p. 202.
11. Ibid., p. 204; quoted in Eby, 179.
12. Susan Gubar, *Racechanges: White Skin, Black Face in American Culture* (New York and Oxford: Oxford University Press, 1997), 194. All references are cited by page in the text.
13. Edward Said, *Culture and Imperialism* (New York: Vintage, 1993), 105.
14. *The Garden of Eden*, JFK 422.1, 2, p. 3.
15. Ibid., JFK 422.5, 15, p. 24.
16. Marianna Torgovnick, *Gone Primitive: Savage Intellects, Modern Lives* (Chicago and London: University of Chicago Press 1990), 245. All references are cited by page in the text.
17. Ernest Hemingway, "The Battler," in *The Complete Short Stories*, 103. All references will be to this edition and are cited by page in the text.
18. Kenneth Tynan, "A Visit to Havana," in *Conversations with Ernest Hemingway*, ed. Matthew Bruccoli (Jackson and London: University of Mississippi Press, 1986), 152.
19. Chinua Achebe, "An Image of Africa: Racism in Conrad's *Heart of Darkness*," in *Hopes and Impediments* (New York: Doubleday, 1989), 12.
20. Quoted in George Plimpton, "An Interview with Ernest Hemingway," in *Hemingway and His Critics*, ed. Carlos Baker, 26, 36.
21. Ibid., 37.
22. Ibid., 37–38. John Kaspar was a racist rabble-rouser active in the South and an unsavory associate of Ezra Pound in the late 1950s.

23. Ernest Hemingway, "Foreword" to *The Complete Short Stories: Finca Vigía Edition* (New York: Charles Scribner's Sons, 1987), 3.

24. Jeffrey Meyers, biographer of both Lewis and Hemingway (and others), maintains that Lewis's *Paleface* "gave him the undeserved reputation of a racist" (*Enemy*, London: Routledge & Kegan Paul, 1980, 146). Lewis reproduces Hemingway's letter of support in his 1951 autobiography *Rude Assignment* (Santa Barbara: Black Sparrow Press, 1984): "I am very glad you liked *The Torrents of Spring*," Hemingway wrote to Lewis, "and I thought you destroyed the Red and Black enthusiasm very finely in *Paleface*" (qtd. 218). Commenting on this 25 years after the facts, Lewis writes: "In fact, *The Torrents of Spring* was, in fiction form, performing the same purgative function as *Paleface*" (219). Hemingway, in what Meyers calls "the most vicious portrait in *A Moveable Feast*," (86) claims never to have liked Lewis, saying, "I had never seen a nastier-looking man" (MF 109) but this was, of course, after Lewis wrote his 1934 essay, "Ernest Hemingway, The Dumb Ox" included in his collection *Men Without Art*, a play on Hemingway's *Men Without Women*. Hemingway happened upon this review in Sylvia Beach's bookstore, Shakespeare and Co., and was so angered that he mildly trashed the place (and paid for the damages). Hemingway got his revenge with *A Moveable Feast*, published after both authors were dead.

25. Jeffrey Meyers, "Hemingway's Primitivism and 'Indian Camp,' " in *New Critical Approaches to the Short Stories of Ernest Hemingway*, ed. Jackson J. Benson (Durham & London: Duke University Press, 1990), 303.

26. One of the personalities profiled by Gubar in *Racechanges* in Nancy Cunard, who she identifies as a sexual outlaw, victimized by "racist and sexist resentment at her revolutionary values and lifestyle," but who nevertheless was "a vamp who used her social status, her money, and her promiscuity to work her willful ways" (152), perhaps a too-harsh judgment of a strong-willed and iconoclastic woman who sincerely worked for social improvement. Cunard, heir to the shipping fortune, is perhaps remembered more for her interracial love affairs that for her important contributions as an author, editor, poet, and political activist. In 1933, she produced the massive volume, *Negro: An Anthology*, the most ambitious collection of African and African diaspora prose and poetry at the time. Cunard knew Hemingway in Paris in the 1920s and some believed, erroneously, that she was the model for Brett Ashley in *The Sun Also Rises.* (Anne Chisholm, *Nancy Cunard*, New York: Penguin, 1979, 119.) All references to this work are cited by page in the text.

Lynn implies that Cunard and Hemingway were well-acquainted and refers to "slim, bisexual Nancy Cunard [. . .] whose Ile St-Louis apartment made a convenient stopping-place for Hemingway on his way from the *transatlantic review*" in the 1920s (238). Cunard and

Hemingway met again briefly in Madrid during the Spanish Civil War where they both served as journalists. Cunard's biographer, Anne Chisholm, identifies what might be some common ground shared with Hemingway when she recounts descriptions of Cunard's sexuality "as if she were a martyr or an ascetic who undertook sex as a kind of ordeal or torture, finding a voluptuous pleasure in degrading herself" and that "a kind of purity, almost self-sacrifice, seemed to lie behind her wild behavior" (234–235). Though Hemingway's public behavior cannot be considered sexually "wild" and while he did not share Cunard's celebration of blackness in his public pronouncements, he shares with her both a commitment to the Loyalist cause in Spain as well as a masochistic sexuality.

Cunard, who was working for the Loyalist cause with painter John Banting, recalls her meeting with Hemingway in Madrid in the following terms: "[S]uddenly, we thought of Hemingway. I can't remember if he had sent a message or no, but we knew he was in Madrid. Sure enough, there he was—massively—in a warm room in the Hotel Florida. There were about six others—mostly Spanish, I seem to remember. He and I had not seen each other since the twenties. A fine, strong drink was given to both of us—and I remember Hem taking off my boots and warming the cold feet" (quoted in Chisholm, 322), a position that suggests submission to a beautiful woman, which Cunard was. Chisholm reports that Banting recalls the meeting differently. Hemingway, Banting remembers, told the couple that "we were too late to be put in a play he had just written about the 'war tourists.' [*The Fifth Column*] . . . I thought that the mental 'hair on the chest' seemed rather artificial and so did Nancy" (quoted in Chisholm, 322–323). Pablo Neruda recalls how Cunard, in Santiago after the fall of Spain, became involved with a Chilean-Basque lover who "gave her nightly beatings that forced her to appear in public wearing enormous dark glasses" (quoted in Chisolm, 341).

27. Ernest Hemingway, *African Book*, Manuscripts (Hemingway Collection, Kennedy Library, Boston), JFK, 34, p. 579.
28. *The Garden of Eden*, JFK, 422.1, 2, p. 2.
29. Hemingway did have some interest in Afrocuban culture. Hilary Hemingway and Charlene Benson report that the Cuban government has identified "almost two dozen religious relics from Africa and the Afro-Cuban religion of Santeria" in Hemingway's home on the outskirts of Havana, *Hemingway in Cuba* (New York: Ruggedland, 2003), 106.
30. Claude McKay, *A Long Way from Home* (1937) (London: Pluto Press 1985), 249. All references are cited by page in the text.
31. Ralph Ellison, "The Art of Fiction: An Interview," *Shadow and Act* (New York: Quality Paperback Book Club, 1994), 168.
32. "Twentieth Century Fiction and the Black Mask of Humanity," in *Shadow and Act* (New York: Quality Paperback Book Club, 1994), 34.

Unless otherwise noted, all references to Ellison are to this work and are cited by page in the text.

33. "The World and the Jug," in *Shadow and Act* (New York: Quality Paperback Book Club, 1994), 116.

34. *The Garden of Eden*, JFK 422.1, 2, p. 3.

35. *The Garden of Eden*, qtd. in Burwell 105; qtd. in Eby, 158; JFK 422.1, 2, p. 3.

36. JFK, 422.1, 23, p. 18.

37. Susan Beegel, "Santiago," 139.

38. Ernest Hemingway, *By-Line Ernest Hemingway* (New York: Charles Scribner's Sons, 1967), 419. All references are to this edition and are cited by page in the text.

39. Mary Hemingway, *How It Was*, 467; qtd. in Eby, 176.

40. *The Garden of Eden*, qtd. in Burwell, 105; qtd. in Eby, 158; JFK 422.1 2, p. 3.

41. *African Book*, JFK, 223a, 29, pp. 748–749.

42. *The Garden of Eden*, JFK 422.1, 23, p. 18 insert.

43. Michel Leiris, *Manhood: A Journey from Childhood into the Fierce Order of Virility* (Chicago: University of Chicago Press, 1992), 140. All references are to this edition and are cited by page in the text.

44. Kathy Willingham, "The Sun Hasn't Set Yet: Brett Ashley and the Code Hero Debate," in *Hemingway and Women*, ed. Lawrence R. Broer and Gloria Holland, 39.

45. Quoted, ibid., 42.

46. Mary Hemingway, *How It Was*, 467; qtd. in Eby, 176.

47. Meyers, "Hemingway's Primitivism," 308.

48. Ibid., 300.

49 Ibid., 308.

50. Louise Erdrich, *Tracks* (New York: Perennial, 1988), 59. All references are cited by page in the text.

CHAPTER 7   REAFFIRMING THE CODE

1. See for example, Lillian Ross, *Portrait of Hemingway*, 85.

2. Quoted in Brian, 217.

3. Brenner, *A Comprehensive Companion to Hemingway's A Moveable Feast*, 347; See also *Selected Letters*, in which as early as 1952, Hemingway writes: "About Gertrude: I have decided not to let any letters I wrote her be published as long as that Toklas—is still alive" (781). Toklas was still living as Hemingway prepared *A Moveable Feast* for publication.

4. See Brian, 66–67.

5. See Griffin, 15; *Selected Letters*, 650.

6. Nina Baym " 'Actually, I Felt Sorry for the Lion,' " in *New Critical Approaches to the Short Stories of Ernest Hemingway*, ed. Jackson J. Benson, 114.

7. Ernest Hemingway, "The Short Happy Life of Francis Macomber," in *The Complete Short Stories*, 9. All references are to this edition and cited by page in the text. Where clarification is necessary, this collection will be abbreviated to CSS.

8. Leonard J. Leff, *Hemingway and His Conspirators* (Lanham, MD: Rowman and Littlefield, 1999), 100.

9. Susan Beegel, " 'That Always Absent Something Else': 'A Natural History of the Dead' and Its Discarded Coda," in *New Critical Approaches to the Short Stories*, ed. Jackson J. Benson, 78.

10. Quoted in Ross, 48–49.

11. *The Garden of Eden*, JFK 422.5, 16, p. 40. Quoted in Moddelmog, 82.

WORKS CITED

Achebe, Chinua (1989). "An Image of Africa: Racism in Conrad's *Heart of Darkness*," in *Hopes and Impediments*. New York: Doubleday.

American Psychiatric Association (1987). *Diagnostic and Statistical Manual of Mental Disorders*. Third Edition, Revised. Washington: Author.

Baker, Carlos (ed., 1961). *Hemingway and His Critics*. New York: Hill and Wang.

——— (1970). *Ernest Hemingway: A Life Story*. New York: Bantam.

Barlow, Jamie (2002). "Re-Reading Women II: The Example of Brett, Hadley, Duff, and Women's Scholarship," in *Hemingway and Women: Female Critics and the Female Voice*. Edited by Lawrence R. Broer and Gloria Holland. Tuscaloosa and London: University of Alabama Press, 23–32.

Baym, Nina (1990). " 'Actually, I Felt Sorry for the Lion,' " in *New Critical Approaches to the Short Stories of Ernest Hemingway*. Edited by Jackson J. Benson. Durham & London: Duke University Press, 112–120.

Beegel, Susan F. (1990). " 'That Always Absent Something Else': 'A Natural History of the Dead' and Its Discarded Coda," in *New Critical Approaches to the Short Stories of Ernest Hemingway*. Edited by Jackson J. Benson. Durham & London: Duke University Press, 73–95.

——— (2002). "Santiago and the Eternal Feminine: Gendering *La Mar* in *The Old Man and the Sea*," in *Hemingway and Women: Female Critics and the Female Voice*. Edited by Lawrence R. Broer and Gloria Holland. Tuscaloosa and London: University of Alabama Press, 131–156.

Bersani, Leo (1986). *The Freudian Body: Psychoanalysis and Art*. New York: Columbia University Press.

——— (1988). "Is the Rectum a Grave?," in *AIDS, Cultural Analysis, Cultural Activism*. Edited by Douglas Crimp, Cambridge: MIT Press.

——— (1995). *Homos*. Cambridge: Harvard University Press.

Boxer, Sarah (January 27, 2001). "Masochism Finally Gets Even," *New York Times*, reprinted on <http://www.nytimes.com/2001/01/27/arts/27MASO.html> (August 4, 2004).

Brenner, Gerry (1983). *Concealments in Hemingway's Works*. Columbus: Ohio State University Press.

——— (2000). *A Comprehensive Companion to Hemingway's A Moveable Feast: Annotation to Interpretation*. Studies in American Literature, Volumes 37a and 37b, Lewiston: The Edwin Mellon Press.

Brian, Denis (ed., 1988). *The True Gen: An Intimate Portrait of Hemingway by Those Who Knew Him*. New York: Grove Press.

Broer, Lawrence R. and Gloria Holland (2002). Introduction to *Hemingway and Women: Female Critics and the Female Voice*. Edited by Lawrence R. Broer and Gloria Holland. Tuscaloosa and London: University of Alabama Press, ix–xiv.

Brontë, Emily (1993). *Wuthering Heights*. New York: Barnes & Noble.

Brown, Norman O. (1959). *Life Against Death: The Psychoanalytical Meaning of History*. Middletown, CT: Wesleyan University Press.

Bruccoli, Matthew J. (ed., 1986). *Conversations with Ernest Hemingway*. Jackson and London: University of Mississippi Press, 152.

Buckley, J.F. (Spring 2000). "Echoes of Closeted Desires: The Narrator and Character Voices of Jake Barnes." *The Hemingway Review*, 19(2): 74–87.

Burwell, Rose Marie (1996). *Hemingway: The Postwar Years and The Posthumous Novels*. Cambridge: Cambridge University Press.

Califia, Pat (1997). *Sex Changes*. San Francisco: Cleis Press, "Introduction," <http://www.sexuality.org/l/transgen/scpc.html> (August 11, 2004).

Carter, Angela (1979). *The Sadeian Woman: An Exercise in Cultural History*. London: Virago.

Chisholm, Anne (1979). *Nancy Cunard*. New York: Penguin.

Cohen, Jeffrey Jerome (1995). "Masoch/Lancelotism," Department of English and Program in the Human Sciences, The George Washington University, <http://www.georgetown.edu/labyrinth/conf/cs95/papers/cohen. html> (August 11, 2004).

Comley, Nancy R. (2002). "The Light from Hemingway's Garden: Regendering Papa," in *Hemingway and Women: Female Critics and the Female Voice*. Edited by Lawrence R. Broer and Gloria Holland. Tuscaloosa and London: University of Alabama Press, 204–217.

Comley, Nancy R. and Robert Scholes (1994). *Hemingway's Genders: Rereading the Hemingway Text*. New Haven and London: Yale University Press.

Coté, William, E. (Fall 2002). "Correspondent or Warrior?: Hemingway's Murky World War II 'Combat' Experience," in *The Hemingway Review*, 22(1): 88–104.

Deleuze, Gilles (1991). *Coldness and Cruelty* (1969), in *Masochism*. Translated by Jean McNeill, New York: Zone Books.

Dollimore, Jonathan (1991). *Sexual Dissidence: Augustine to Wilde, Freud to Foucault*. London: Clarendon Press, Oxford University Press.

Eby, Carl P. (1998). *Hemingway's Fetishism: Psychoanalysis and the Mirror of Manhood*. New York: SUNY Press.

——— (Fall 2005). " 'He Felt the Change So that It Hurt Him All Through': Sodomy and Transvestic Hallucination in Late Hemingway," in *The Hemingway Review*, 25(1).

Elliott, Ira (1995). "Performance Art: Jake Barnes and 'Masculine' Signification in *The Sun Also Rises*." *American Literature*, 67(1): 77–94.

Ellison, Ralph (1994). "Twentieth Century Fiction and the Black Mask of Humanity," in *Shadow and Act*. New York: Quality Paperback Book Club, 24–44.

———— (1994). "The World and the Jug," in *Shadow and Act*. New York: Quality Paperback Book Club, 107–143.

———— (1994). "The Art of Fiction: An Interview," in *Shadow and Act*. New York: Quality Paperback Book Club, 167–183.

Erdrich, Louise (1988). *Tracks*. New York: Perennial.

Fanon, Frantz (1967). *Black Skin, White Masks*. New York: Grove Press.

Feinberg, Leslie (1996). *Transgender Warriors: Making History from Joan of Arc to RuPaul*. Boston: Beacon Press.

Fetterly, Judith (1978). *The Resisting Reader: A Feminist Approach to American Fiction*. Bloomington: Indiana University Press.

Fiedler, Leslie (1975). *Love and Death in the American Novel*. Revised edition. New York: Stein and Day.

Fleming, Robert E. (1989). "The Endings of Hemingway's *Garden of Eden*," *American Literature*, 61(2): 261–270.

Forter, Greg (Fall 2001). "Melancholy Modernism: Gender and the Politics of Mourning in *The Sun Also Rises*," *The Hemingway Review*, 21(1): 22–37.

Foucault, Michel (1978). *The History of Sexuality*. Translated by Robert Hurley. New York: Pantheon.

Freud, Sigmund (1953). *A General Introduction to Psychoanalysis*. Translated by Joan Riviere. New York: Permabooks.

———— (1955). "A Child is Being Beaten," from *The Standard Edition of the Complete Psychological Works of Sigmund Freud, Vol. XVII*. Translated by James Strachey. London: The Hogarth Press.

———— (1961). "The Economic Problem of Masochism," from *The Standard Edition of the Complete Psychological Works of Sigmund Freud, Vol. XIX*. Translated by James Strachey. London: The Hogarth Press.

———— (1962). *Three Essays on the Theory of Sexuality*. Translated by James Strachey. New York: Basic Books.

———— (1977). *Five Introductory Lectures on Psycho-Analysis*. Translated by James Strachey. New York: Norton.

Frost, Laura (1997). " 'With This Ring, I Thee Own': Masochism and Social Reform in *Ulysses*," in *Sex Positives: The Cultural Politics of Sexual Diversity, Genders 25*. Edited by Thomas Foster, Carol Siegel, Ellen E. Berry, New York and London: New York University Press, 225–264.

Gajdusek, Robert E. (1997). "The Mad Sad Bad Misreading of Hemingway's Gender Politics/Aesthetics," *The North Dakota Quarterly*, 64(3): 36–47.

Garlinger, Patrick Paul (1999). " 'Homo-Ness' and the Fear of Femininity," in *Diacritics*, 29 (1): 57–71.

Goldberg, Jonathan (ed., 1994). *Reclaiming Sodom*. New York and London: Routledge.

Griffin, Peter (1990). *Less Than a Treason: Hemingway in Paris*. New York: Oxford University Press.

Gubar, Susan (1997). *Racechanges: White Skin, Black Face in American Culture*. New York and Oxford: Oxford University Press.

Hatten, Charles (1993). "The Crisis of Masculinity, Reified Desire, and Catherine Barkley in *A Farewell to Arms*," in *Journal of the History of Sexuality*, 4(1): 76–98.

Hayden, Dorothy C. (2000). CSW, CAC, "Psychological Dimensions of Masochistic Surrender," <http://www.sextreatment.com/psych.htm> (August 11, 2004).

Hemingway, Ernest. *African Book*. Manuscripts, Kennedy Library, Boston.

———. *The Garden of Eden*. Manuscripts, Hemingway Collection, Kennedy Library, Boston.

———. *The Garden of Eden*. Manuscripts, Charles Scribner's Archives, Firestone Library, Princeton University.

———. *Islands in the Stream*. Manuscripts, Hemingway Collection, Kennedy Library, Boston.

——— (1926). *The Sun Also Rises*. New York: Charles Scribner's Sons.

——— (1930). *In Our Time*. New York: Charles Scribner's Sons.

——— (1932). *Death in the Afternoon*. New York: Charles Scribner's Sons.

——— (1935). *Green Hills of Africa*. New York: Charles Scribner's Sons.

——— (1937). *To Have and Have Not*. New York: Charles Scribner's Sons.

——— (1940). *For Whom the Bell Tolls*. New York: Charles Scribner's Sons.

——— (1950). *Across the River and Into the Trees*. New York: Charles Scribner's Sons.

——— (1953). *The Old Man and the Sea*. New York: Charles Scribner's Sons.

——— (1958). *In Our Time*. New York: Charles Scribner's Sons.

——— (1961). *A Moveable Feast*. New York: Charles Scribner's Sons.

——— (1967). *By-Line Ernest Hemingway*. New York: Charles Scribner's Sons.

——— (1981). *Selected Letters, 1917–1961*. Edited by Carlos Baker. New York: Charles Scribner's Sons.

——— (1986). *A Farewell to Arms*. New York: Macmillan.

——— (1986). *The Garden of Eden*. New York: Collier Books, Macmillan.

——— (1987). *The Complete Short Stories: Finca Vigin Edition*. New York: Charles Scribner's Sons.

——— (1997). *Islands in the Stream*. New York: Charles Scribner's Sons.

——— (1999). *True at First Light*. New York: Charles Scribner's Sons.

Hemingway, Gregory (1976). *Papa: A Personal Memoir*. Boston: Houghton Mifflin.

Hemingway, Hilary, and Carlene, Brennen (2003). *Hemingway in Cuba*. New York: Ruggedland.

Hemingway, Mary Welsh (1976). *How It Was*. New York: Ballantine.

———. *Mary's African Journal*. Manuscripts, Hemingway Collection, Kennedy Library, Boston.

Hendrickson, Paul (July 29, 1987). "Papa's Boys: The Random Legacy of the Hemingways" in *The Washington Post*.

Hewson, Marc (Spring 2003). " 'The Real Story of Ernest Hemingway': Cixous, Gender and *A Farewell to Arms*, in *The Hemingway Review*, 22(2): 51–62.

Johnson, Ramon. "Trannie 101: The Meaning of the Words Transsexual, Transgender and Transvestite" *Gaylife* with Ramon Johnson, <http://gaylife.about.com/library/weekly/aa042303a.htm> (October 15, 2003).

Josephs, Allen (1994). "Reality and Invention in *For Whom the Bell Tolls*, or Reflections on the Nature of the Historical Novel," in *Hemingway Repossessed*. Edited by Kenneth Rosen, Westport, CT: Praeger, 87–95.

Joyce, James (1986). *Ulysses*. New York: Vintage.

Junkins, Donald (1994). "Mythmaking, Androgyny, and the Creative Process, Answering Mark Spilka," in *Hemingway Repossessed*. Edited by Kenneth Rosen, Westport, CT: Praeger, 57–67.

Juno, Andrea and V. Vale (eds., 1991). *Angry Women*. San Francisco: Re/Search Publications.

Kennedy, J. Gerald (1993). *Imagining Paris: Exile, Writing, and American Identity*. New Haven: Yale University Press.

Kert, Bernice (1983). *The Hemingway Women*. New York: Norton.

Krafft-Ebing, Richard von (1965). *Psychopathia Sexualis*. New York: G.P. Putnam & Sons.

Kuda, Marie J. (September 8, 1999). "Was Hemingway's Mother a Lesbian?," from *Outlines*, 13(14). <http://astro.ocis.temple.edu/~ruby/opp/grace.html> (March 9, 2005).

Lacan, Jacques (1998). *The Four Fundamental Concepts of Psychoanalysis*. Edited by Jacques-Alain Miller. Translated by Alan Sheridan. New York: Norton.

Laplanche, Jacques (1995). "Aggressiveness and Sadomasochism," in *Essential Papers on Masochism*. Edited by Margaret Ann Fitzpatrick Hanly. New York: New York University Press, 104–124.

Lathan, Aaron (October 16, 1977). "A Farewell to Machismo," *New York Times Magazine*: 52 ff.

Lawrence, T.E. (1973). *Seven Pillars of Wisdom*. Harmondswoth, England: Penguin.

Leff, Leonard J. (1999). *Hemingway and His Conspirators*. Lanham, MD: Rowman and Littlefield.

Leiris, Michel (1992). *Manhood: A Journey from Childhood into the Fierce Order of Virility*. Chicago: University of Chicago Press.

Leonard John (Spring 2003). "*The Garden of Eden*: A Question of Dates," in *The Hemingway Review*, 22(2): 63–81.

Lewis, Wyndham (1984). *Rude Assignment*. Edited by Toby Foshay. Santa Barbara: Black Sparrow Press.

——— (1987). "Ernest Hemingway: The Dumb Ox," in *Men Without Art* (1934). Edited by Seamus Cooney. Santa Barbara: Black Sparrow Press.

Lowenstein, Rudolph M. (1995). "The Pyschoanalytic Theory of Masochism," in *Essential Papers on Masochism*. Edited by Margaret Ann Fitzpatrick Hanly. New York: New York University Press, 35–61.

Lynn, Kenneth (1987). *Hemingway*. New York: Fawcett-Columbine.

Mailer, Norman (1971). *The Prisoner of Sex.* Boston: Little, Brown, and Co.

Mansfield, Nick (1997). *Masochism: The Art of Power.* Westport, CT and London: Praeger.

Marcuse, Herbert (1962). *Eros and Civilization: A Philosophical Inquiry into Freud.* New York: Vintage.

McKay, Claude (1985). *A Long Way from Home.* London: Pluto Press.

McLendon, James (1990). *Papa: Hemingway in Key West.* Key West: Langley Press, Inc.

Mellow, James R. (1992). *Hemingway: A Life Without Consequences.* New York: Houghton Mifflin Co.

Meyers, Jeffrey (1980). *The Enemy: A Biography of Wyndham Lewis.* London: Routledge & Kegan Paul.

——— (1983). *Hemingway: A Biography.* New York: Harper & Row.

——— (1983). *Hemingway: Life Into Art.* New York: Cooper Square Press.

——— (1990). "Hemingway's Primitivism and 'Indian Camp,' " in *New Critical Approaches to the Short Stories of Ernest Hemingway.* Edited by Jackson J. Benson, Durham and London: Duke University Press, 300–308.

Moddelmog, Debra A. (1999). *Reading Desire, In Pursuit of Ernest Hemingway.* Ithaca, NY: University of Cornell Press.

Modelski, Tania (1991). *Feminism Without Women, Culture and Criticism in a "Post-Feminist" Age.* New York: Routledge.

Morrison, Toni (1992). *Playing in the Dark: Whiteness and the Literary Imagination.* New York: Vintage.

Nacht, Sacha (1995). "*Le Masochisme* An Introduction," in *Essential Papers on Masochism.* Edited by Margaret Ann Fitzpatrick Hanly. New York: New York University Press, 18–34.

Newfield, Christopher (Fall 1989). "The Politics of Male Suffering: Masochism and Hegemony in the American Renaissance," *Differences,* 1 (3): 55–87.

Novick, Kerry Kelly and Jack Novick (1995). "The Essence of Masochism," in *Essential Papers on Masochism.* Edited by Margaret Ann Fitzpatrick Hanly. New York: New York University Press, 237–264.

Paglia, Camile (1991). *Sexual Personnae, Art and Decadence from Nefertiti to Emily Dickinson.* New York: Vintage.

Petry, Alice Hall (1990). "Coming of Age in Hortons Bay: Hemingway's 'Up in Michigan,' " in *New Critical Approaches to the Short Stories of Ernest Hemingway.* Edited by Jackson J. Benson. Durham & London: Duke University Press, 353–359.

Phillips, Anita (1998). *A Defense of Masochism.* New York: St. Martins.

Plato, *The Symposium, Part One.* Translated by Benjamin Jowett, <http://evans-experientialism.freewebspace.com/plato_symposium01.htm> (August 11, 2004).

Plimpton, George (1961). "An Interview with Ernest Hemingway," in *Hemingway and His Critics.* Edited by Carlos Baker. New York: Hill and Wang, 19–37.

Porter, Dennis (1991). *Haunted Journeys: Desire and Transgression in European Travel Writing*. Princeton: Princeton University Press.

Reik, Theodor (1962). *Masochism in Sex and Society*. New York: Grove Press.

Reynolds, Michael (1986). *The Young Hemingway*. New York: W.W. Norton & Co.

——— (1999). *Hemingway: The Final Years*. New York: W.W. Norton & Co.

Rich, Adrienne (1980). "Compulsory Heterosexuality and the Lesbian Experience," *Signs* 5, 1980: 632–660, <www.mercurycenter.com/archives/womenhistory/perspective/ ideas4. htm> (August 11, 2004).

Rodney, Walter (1984). *How Europe Underdeveloped Africa*. Washington, DC: Howard University Press.

Ross, Lillian (1961). *Portrait of Hemingway*. New York: Avon Library.

Roth, James (Fall 2003). "News From the Hemingway Collection," *Hemingway Review*, 23(1): 137–139.

Rudat, Wolfgang, E.H. (1994). "Hemingway's Sexual Otherness: What's Really Funny in *The Sun Also Rises*," in *Hemingway Repossessed*. Edited by Kenneth Rosen. Westport, CN: Praeger, 169–179.

Russo, John Paul (1990). "To Die is Not Enough: Hemingway's Venetian Novel," in *Hemingway in Italy and Other Essays*. Edited by Robert W. Lewis, New York: Praeger, 133–180.

Sacher-Masoch, Leopold von (1991). "Venus in Furs" in *Masochism*. Translated by Jean McNeill. New York: Zone Books, 1991.

——— (1996). "Lola," in *The Master Masochist: Tale of a Sadistic Mistress*. Edited by Vyvyan Howarth. Translated by Eric Lemuel Randall. London: Senate.

Said, Edward (1993). *Culture and Imperialism*. New York: Vintage.

——— (2000). *Reflections on Exile and Other Essays*. Cambridge: Harvard University Press.

Samuelson, Arnold (1984). *With Hemingway: A Year in Key West and Cuba*. New York: Holt, Rinehart and Winston.

Sanderson, Rena (2002). "Hemingway's Literary Sisters: The Author though the Eyes of Women Writers," in *Hemingway and Women: Female Critics and the Female Voice*. Edited by Lawrence R. Broer and Gloria Holland. Tuscaloosa and London: University of Alabama Press, 276–294.

Savran, David (1998). *Taking It Like a Man: White Masculinity, Masochism and Contemporary American Culture*. Princeton: Princeton University Press.

Siegel, Carol (1995). *Male Masochism, Modern Revisions of the Story of Love*. Bloomington and Indianapolis: Indiana University Press.

Silverman, Kaja (1992). *Male Subjectivity at the Margins*. New York and London: Routledge.

Smirnoff, Victor N. (1995). "The Masochistic Contract," in *Essential Papers on Masochism*. Edited by Margaret Ann Fitzpatrick Hanly. New York: New York University Press, 62–72.

Smith, Clyde (2000). "How I Became a Queer Heterosexual," in *Straight With a Twist: Queer Theory and the Subject of Heterosexuality*. Edited by Calvin Thomas. Urbana and Chicago: University of Illinois Press, 60–67.

Solomon, Barbara Probst (March 9, 1987). "Where's Papa?" in *The New Republic*.

Spanier, Sandra Whipple, "Catherine Barkley and the Hemingway Code," Paper presented at NEMLA, Hartford, CT, March 19, 1985, Ernest Hemingway Collection, Kennedy Library, Boston.

Spender, Stephen (1994). *World Within World*. New York: St. Martin's Press.

Spilka, Mark (1961). "The Death of Love in *The Sun Also Rises*," in *Hemingway and His Critics*. Edited by Carlos Baker. New York: Hill and Wang, 80–92.

——— (1990). *Hemingway's Quarrel with Androgyny*. Lincoln and London: University of Nebraska Press.

Starks, Lisa S. (Fall 1997). " 'Batter My [Flaming] Heart': Male Masochism in the Religious Lyrics of Donne and Crashaw," *Enculturation*, 1 (2) <http://www.uta.edu/huma/enculturation/1_2/starks.html> (October 5, 2004).

——— (1999). " 'Like the Lover's Pinch, which Hurts and is Desired': The Narrative of Male Masochism and Shakespeare's *Antony and Cleopatra*," *Literature and Psychology*, 45(4): 58–73.

Stewart, Suzanne R. (1998). *Sublime Surrender: Male Masochism at the Fin-de-Siècle*. Ithaca: Cornell University Press.

Stoller, Robert (1975). *Perversion: The Erotic Form of Hatred*. New York: Pantheon.

——— (1985). *Observing the Erotic Imagination*. New Haven: Yale University Press.

Stoneback, H.R. (1991). "In the Nominal Country of the Bogus: Hemingway's Catholicism and the Biographies," in *Hemingway: Essays of Reassessment*. Edited by Frank Scafella. New York: Oxford University Press, 105–140.

Strong, Amy Lovell (2002). " 'Go to Sleep, Devil': The Awakening of Catherine's Feminism in *The Garden of Eden*, in *Hemingway and Women: Female Critics and the Female Voice*. Edited by Lawrence R. Broer and Gloria Holland. Tuscaloosa and London: University of Alabama Press, 190–203.

Strychacz, Thomas (1989). "Dramatizations of Manhood in Hemingway's *In Our Time* and *The Sun Also Rises*," *American Literature*, 61(2): 245–260.

——— (2003). *Hemingway's Theaters of Masculinity*. Baton Rouge: Louisiana University Press.

Studlar, Gaylyn (1988). *In the Realm of Pleasure: von Sternberg, Dietrich, and the Masochistic Aesthetic*. New York: Columbia University Press.

Taormino, Tristan (March 1–7, 2000). "Bend Over, Boys!" in "Pucker Up" column in *The Village Voice* <http://www.villagevoice.com/issues/0009/taormino.php> (September 12, 2004).

——— (April 30, 2003). "The Queer Heterosexual," "Pucker Up" column in *The Village Voice* <http://www.villagevoice.com/issues/0319/taormino.php> (September 12, 2004).

Tavernier-Corbin, Jacqueline (1991). *Ernest Hemingway's A Moveable Feast: The Making of a Myth*. Boston: Northeastern University Press.

The Boston Women's Health Collective (1984, 1992). *The New Our Bodies, Ourselves: A Book By and For Women*. New York: Simon and Shuster.

Torgovnick, Marianna (1990). *Gone Primitive: Savage Intellects, Modern Lives*. Chicago and London: University of Chicago Press.

Trogdon, Robert W. (Spring 2003). "Money and Marriage: Hemingway's Self-Censorship in *For Whom the Bell Tolls*," in *The Hemingway Review*, 22 (2): 6–18.

Tynan, Kenneth (1986). "A Visit to Havana," in *Conversations with Ernest Hemingway*. Edited by Matthew J. Bruccoli. Jackson and London: University of Mississippi Press, 152.

Wagner-Martin, Linda (2002). "The Romance of Desire in Hemingway's Fiction," in *Hemingway and Women: Female Critics and the Female Voice*. Edited by Lawrence R. Broer and Gloria Holland. Tuscaloosa and London: University of Alabama Press, 54–69.

Whitlow, Roger (1984). *Cassandra's Daughters: The Women in Hemingway*. Westport, CN, London: Greenwood Press.

Willingham, Kathy G. (1993). "Hemingway's *The Garden of Eden*: Writing with the Body" in *The Hemingway Review*, 12 (2): 46–61.

——— (2002). "The Sun Hasn't Set Yet: Brett Ashley and the Code Hero Debate," in *Hemingway and Women: Female Critics and the Female Voice*. Edited by Lawrence R. Broer and Gloria Holland. Tuscaloosa and London: University of Alabama Press, 33–53.

Wilson, Edmund (1925). Introduction to *In Our Time* by Ernest Hemingway. New York: Charles Scribner's Sons.

Young, Phillip (1959). *Ernest Hemingway, University of Minnesota Pamphlets on American Writers, Vol. 1*. Minneapolis: University of Minnesota Press.

INDEX

Starks, Lisa S., 55, 65, 173 n18,
     174 n31
Stein, Gertrude, 80, 89, 91–2,
     111–12, 142, 155, 186 n3
Steinbeck, John, 142
Stendhal, 159, 160
Stewart, Suzanne R., 40–1, 44–5,
     63, 171 n39
Stoller, Robert, 3, 165–6 n9–10,
     167 n20
Stoneback, H.R., 65–6, 98, 174
     n32, 179 n36
Storrs, Anthony, 52
Strong, Amy Lovell, 90, 176 n32
Strychacz, Thomas, 17–21, 168 n3,
     169 n9
Studlar, Gaylyn, 18–21, 23–4, 44,
     48–53, 56, 59–60, 65, 103,
     114, 168 n7, 180 n5
   "masochistic aesthetic," 18–19,
     21, 60, 103, 168 n7
   "symbiosis/separation," 47–9
Swinburne, Algernon Charles, 12,
     44, 167 n21

Taormino, Tristan, 72, 76, 108,
     175 n15, 180 n10
Tavernier-Courbin, Jacqueline, 21,
     100, 155, 169 n12, 178 n23
Titian, 30
Toklas, Alice B., 112, 155, 186 n3
Tolstoy, Leo, 160
Tom Brown's Schooldays (Thomas
     Hughes), 11, 158
Torgovnick, Marianna, 136, 147,
     183 n16
transatlantic review, 151, 184 n26

transgender, 75–6, 127, 132, 150
transvestism, 54, 120, 146, 173 n16
Trogdon, Robert W., 178 n27
Turgenev, Ivan, 160
Twain, Mark, 85, 142–3
Twydsen, Duff, 80, 91, 93, 178 n17
Tynan, Kenneth, 137, 167 n21,
     183 n18

Vale, V., 175 n4
Van der Leeuw, P.J., 172 n11
Van Vechten, Carl, 140
Venus in Furs, 4, 7, 20, 24, 26, 30,
     43, 55–8, 61, 73, 78, 119,
     135, 136, 140; *see also*
     Sacher-Masoch
von Kurowsky, Agnes, 89, 94–6
von Sternberg, Josef, 19, 21, 103

Wagner, Richard, 63
Wagner-Martin, Linda, 30, 91,
     170 n29
Webb, Mary, 129
Whitlow, Roger, 82, 159, 176 n29
Whitman, Walt, 154
Wilde, Oscar, 11–12, 44, 154, 161
Wilke, Sabine, 40
Williams, Sherwood, 36
Willingham, Kathy G., 82, 127,
     148, 156, 157, 163,
     176 n31, 181 n45
Wilson, Edmund, 64–5
Wilson, Woodrow, 140
Wolfe, Thomas, 14
Wulff, M., 172 n11

Zilboorg, Gregory, 172 n11